D1643875

C016293249

DINOSAURS

HOW THEY LIVED AND EVOLVED

Darren Naish & Paul Barrett

Published by the Natural History Museum, London

First published by the Natural History Museum, Cromwell Road, London SW7 5BD
© The Trustees of the Natural History Museum, London, 2016

The Authors have asserted their right to be identified as the Authors of this work
under the Copyright, Designs and Patents Act 1988

ISBN 978 0 565 09311 2

A catalogue record for this book is available from the British Library

10 9 8 7 6 5 4 3 2 1

Copy-edited by Karin Fancett
Designed by Bobby Birchall, Bobby&Co.
Reproduction by Saxon Digital Services
Printed in China by C&C Offset Printing Co., Limited

Front cover: *Giganotosaurus* © The Trustees of the Natural History Museum, London
Back cover: top *Stegosaurus* © The Trustees of the Natural History Museum, London;
bottom *Archaeopteryx* © Bob Nichols/The Trustees of the Natural History Museum, London

CONTENTS

1

HISTORY, ORIGINS AND THEIR WORLD

DINOSAURS ARE ONE OF THE MOST spectacular and famous groups of animals that have ever existed. After appearing in the Triassic period about 230 million years ago, the group dominated life on land during the following Jurassic Period (between 201 and 145 million years ago) and Cretaceous Period (between 145 and 66 million years ago). Dinosaurs occupied every landmass during that vast span of time and evolved into hundreds of different species, over 1,000 of which have been discovered and named so far. Many of these are fantastic, bizarre animals that capture our imagination: the super-predator *Tyrannosaurus*, the plate-backed *Stegosaurus*, and the long-necked, long-tailed *Diplodocus* are among the most familiar and popular of animals, living or extinct. But dinosaurs are so much more than extinct giants destined for big-screen movie success or for use as centrepieces in museum displays. They were dynamic, complicated animals with amazing adaptations that evolved within the context of particular lifestyles, and they were a dominant and successful group of animals for more than 150 million years, a vast span of time. As we'll see later in this book, it's also correct to describe dinosaurs as one of the most successful groups of animals that *still* lives, because dinosaurs are not animals of the dim and distant past – they survive and thrive today as one of the most obvious and widespread of animal groups.

One of the most famous 'facts' about dinosaurs is that they were large. The biggest species were similar in size to modern whales though, unlike whales, the species concerned were adapted for life on land. Indeed, the evolution of giant size is an important part of the dinosaur story, and dinosaurs of several groups were extreme in terms of size. Numerous other evolutionary events and biological innovations occurred during dinosaur history and make them the focus of interest among scientists. The evolution and elaboration of body armour, horns, head crests, spines, plates and weaponized tails occurred several times during dinosaur history. Some of the most specialized teeth and tooth batteries that have ever evolved were present among dinosaurs, and one dinosaur group evolved the most incredible necks that ever existed among land-living animals.

Dinosaurs include both bipedal (or two-legged) and quadrupedal (or four-legged) groups and evolved from a group of ancestral reptiles that also included both bipeds and quadrupeds. An ability to evolve from a bipedal body shape to a quadrupedal one, and vice versa, makes dinosaurs unusual. Indeed, the apparent ease with which dinosaurs made these transitions may have contributed to their success.

A spectacular fossil record shows how small, feathered, predatory dinosaurs (called theropods) evolved into birds about 160 million years ago, and today we have an excellent body of evidence showing that

Dinosaurs excite and intrigue people of all ages, and many non-bird dinosaurs, like the *Allosaurus* and *Diplodocus* shown here, would have looked spectacular when alive.

Excellent fossils have shown that bird-like dinosaurs, like this *Sinornithosaurus millennii* from the Early Cretaceous of China, were fully feathered and more bird-like in appearance than was long realized.

birds are dinosaurs – not just relatives of dinosaurs, or descendants of dinosaurs, but members of the dinosaurian radiation. The evolution of feathers and flight are thus important components of the dinosaur story, and probably attract more current research interest than any other topic.

The fact that birds are dinosaurs is important. It means that we need to forget the idea that dinosaurs are extinct. They are not. Of the three main dinosaur groups – theropods, sauropodomorphs and ornithischians – members of a single sub-group within the theropods survived the extinction event that ended the Cretaceous Period, 66 million years ago, and exploded in diversity in the years that followed. The members of this theropod sub-group – the birds – exist today as approximately 10,000 species. Some experts estimate that as many as a million bird species have existed over geological time. The fact that most of bird evolution has occurred at small size – an 'average' bird is only about 40 g (less than 1½ oz) in weight and less than 20 cm (8 in) long – means that birds have been able to exploit lifestyles unavailable to other dinosaurs. We explore the story of bird origins, evolution and diversity more fully in Chapters 5 and 6.

Given how important birds are in terms of numbers of species, geographical distribution and anatomical innovation, it's important that the dinosaurian nature of birds is introduced early on in any discussion of dinosaur history and diversity. It also has to be said that the inclusion of birds within dinosaurs makes it difficult to make generalizations about dinosaurs as a whole. When talking about predatory dinosaurs, for example, are we discussing owls, hawks and falcons as well as *Allosaurus* and *Tyrannosaurus*? And when discussing dinosaur extinction, are we referring to the demise of dodos and passenger pigeons?

Palaeontologists get around this problem in several ways. A solution used in some books is to state up front that the term 'dinosaur' is being used as a synonym for 'non-bird dinosaur'. This might be convenient, but it's inaccurate – the fact that birds really are dinosaurs is so important that we should deliberately think of them, not ignore them, whenever we hear the word 'dinosaur'. Many scientists now use a number of technical terms that mean 'all dinosaurs excepting birds', most notably 'non-avian dinosaur' and 'non-avialan dinosaur'. In this book we use the term 'non-bird dinosaur' when needing to refer specifically to those dinosaurs that aren't birds, but also use 'non-bird dinosaurs and archaic birds' when talking of dinosaurs that do not include those birds that survived beyond the end of the Cretaceous. In general, our use of the term 'dinosaur' is intended to be synonymous with the group name Dinosauria: that is, birds and all.

When new fossil dinosaurs are found, the initial priority for palaeontologists is to see the fossils described and published in the technical literature. If enough of the animal is known, it might reveal information on the animal's proportions, body shape or lifestyle. Substantial attention is paid to anatomical details. If the fossil reveals features that are unique and not seen in related species, it may well require a new name. By comparing anatomical details observed in a new dinosaur with those seen in related species, experts can get some idea of where a fossil belongs on a family tree, and they can then use the fossil to formulate a working idea – a hypothesis – on the evolutionary history of the group of animals concerned. The study of evolutionary history is called phylogeny and a substantial amount of work on dinosaurs is phylogenetic in theme.

But of course there's a great deal more to palaeontology than describing an animal and putting it in its place on the family tree. Palaeontologists also study how bones work and what bones tell us about dinosaur biology. Bones are more than just struts or beams that anchor muscles – they are growing,

Excavating fossils, especially large ones like this near-complete *Stegosaurus* skeleton, is gruelling, difficult work. Finding and removing such fossils is merely the first step in a long scientific process.

WHAT'S IN A NAME?

In contrast to living animals, extinct species don't have common names. We only use so-called scientific names for these animals: names like *Tyrannosaurus rex*, *Triceratops horridus* or *Archaeopteryx lithographica*. These names are always written in italics. All animals, plants and fungi, including extinct ones, are allocated these two-part names, or binomials. This binomial system was established in 1758 by Swedish biologist Carl Linnaeus. The second part of the binomial is the specific name (or species, which refers to a set of populations that are similar in appearance and genetics and can interbreed with one another). These species are grouped together in genera (singular genus). The first part of the binomial, or generic name (which is sometimes abbreviated), refers to a set of species that are all broadly similar and more closely related to one another than they are to the species of other genera. For example, *Triceratops horridus* is one of two species included in the genus *Triceratops* (the other is *Tr. prorsus*). Note that not all genera contain more than one species. The vast majority of fossil dinosaur genera only contain a single species, meaning that it's typical when writing about them to use the generic name alone.

An unfortunate consequence of the binomial system is that these names encapsulate a hypothesis about an organism's position on the tree of life. We put *Tr. horridus* and *Tr. prorsus* together in the genus *Triceratops*, for example, because both are regarded as especially close relatives, but if future studies were to show that either one of them was more closely related to a species in another genus than it was to the other species of *Triceratops*, one or both of them would need their names to be changed. Binomials are destined to change as long as we keep making discoveries about the evolutionary relationships between species.

Linnaeus didn't just establish the use of binomial names, he also formalized a system whereby species and genera were grouped into a ranked hierarchy

Carl Linnaeus (1707–1778) was a Swedish biologist who became an expert on classifying plants and animals. He invented the binomial system still in use today.

of increasingly inclusive sets. Genera are grouped into sets called families, families into orders, orders into classes, and classes into phyla. This forms the foundation for the way species and genera are classified. Traditionally, a genus – let's stick with *Triceratops* – is grouped, with other genera, in a family (in this case, Ceratopsidae). This family (with other families) is grouped within an order (in this case, Ornithischia), and so on.

The problem with Linnaean ranks is that people, scientists included, tend to assume that the amount of anatomical variation across different groups of animals is the same – that a non-bird dinosaur and archaic bird 'family' or 'order', for example, is similar in terms of the amount of anatomical variation it includes to, say, a modern mammal 'family' or 'order'.

But this isn't so – the Linnaean ranks recognized for different animal groups are radically different, as is the variation they encompass. Partly for this reason, many biologists and palaeontologists have given up on Linnaean ranks and have found it more useful to simply name the appropriate clades. Scientists have adopted a system called phylogenetic systematics or cladistics. Within this system, any group can be named so long as it's a clade – this being any group of organisms where all the species descend from the same, single ancestor.

The clade names used for non-bird dinosaurs and archaic birds range from small groups containing a handful of species to enormous groups that contain thousands of species. Small clades that essentially correspond to the 'families' of the Linnaean system are still used – examples include Tyrannosauridae and Ceratopsidae. But named clades that include these clades as well as additional, related species are also commonly used – the clade that includes Tyrannosauridae and its close relatives is called Tyrannosauroidea, while the clade that includes Ceratopsidae and its close relatives, like *Zuniceratops* and *Turaceratops*, is called Ceratopsoidea, for example. An enormous number of clade names are now in use for dinosaur groups, and new ones are constantly created as more is learnt about the shape of the dinosaur family tree, and as evidence for new evolutionary relationships is uncovered.

Clade names have both technical and vernacular versions, and we switch between the two depending on the way in which they're being used. Members of Dinosauria, for example, are most often termed dinosaurs. Similarly, members of the groups Ornithischia, Thyreophora and Coelurosauria are most often termed ornithischians, thyreophorans and coelurosaurs, respectively.

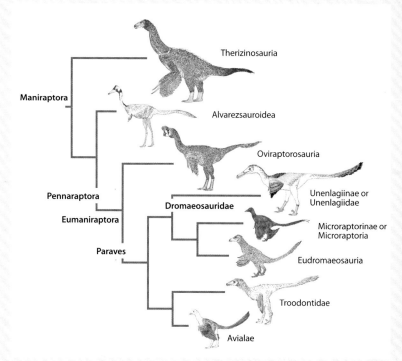

A cladogram is a way of illustrating the evolutionary relationships between organisms – in this case, maniraptoran theropod dinosaurs. A cladogram shows how the groups fall together into clades, and many clades are given names. In this example, Maniraptora, Pennaraptora and Dromaeosauridae – among others – are all clades.

shape-shifting structures that are constantly being rebuilt on the inside. Palaeontologists routinely take fine slices or segments of bone and look at them under the microscope, the results revealing much about how dinosaurs grew and even about their reproductive lives. They also study teeth, muscles and other structures to work out how extinct animals functioned when alive, how they moved, breathed and ate. The study of how anatomy relates to movement, function and behaviour is termed functional morphology. Computer-assisted techniques are now routinely used in the study of dinosaur anatomy and functional morphology, including three-dimensional (3D) imaging, CT-scanning and the digital reconstruction of multiple images and measurements (a technique called photogrammetry). We look more at the functional morphology of dinosaurs in Chapter 3, and we discuss what these studies mean for dinosaur biology and behaviour in Chapter 4.

We also have direct evidence on how fossil dinosaurs walked and ran, in the form of fossil tracks. Millions of Mesozoic dinosaur tracks are known, providing data on dinosaur locomotion and behaviour. We also know of dinosaur droppings, stomach and gut contents, and skin patches, all of which provide us with crucial extra pieces of information on dinosaur biology and behaviour. We look further at these kinds of fossils in Chapter 4.

Many questions about dinosaur biology and behaviour remain unanswered. Trackways and accumulations of skeletons show that dinosaurs of many species were social animals that lived, moved and nested in groups. Modern animals that spend time with other members of their species engage in all sorts of social behaviours. This goes for lizards, turtles and crocodylians, as well as birds and mammals. While we assume that non-bird dinosaurs were similarly complex, the fossil record is mostly silent on these issues, limiting us to speculation. Dinosaurs must have courted one another and fought with enemies, they had to find food and water and avoid bad weather, and perhaps they tussled with friends, helped and cared for their babies and relatives, and interacted with other species.

Technology has changed the way dinosaur fossils are studied, and CT-scanning is now routinely used by palaeontologists. Until recently, palaeontologists relied on CT-scanners in hospitals and clinics. Today, many palaeontology research groups have scanners of their own. Here, a researcher at the Natural History Museum, London examines scans of *Stegosaurus*.

BUILDING FAMILY TREES

A standard way of depicting the evolutionary relationships between animal species is to show those species in a tree-like diagram. As more fossils and more data have been discovered, our family tree diagrams have become more complicated. And the way in which we create these diagrams has become more complicated too.

Prior to the 1980s, it was common for palaeontologists to group sets of animal species together because they possessed features that were absent from other sets of species, and to consider just a handful of anatomical features when trying to work out how species might be related to one another. This traditional way of reconstructing evolution was abandoned during the last few decades of the 20th century as more and more researchers adopted the philosophy and techniques of the biologist Willi Hennig. Hennig founded a school of thought termed phylogenetic systematics, now usually called cladistics. Hennig argued that species should only be grouped together when they share recently evolved features that are unique, and that the only groups we should recognize and name are those where all the included species share the same single common ancestor – these groups are termed clades.

Scientists collect a vast amount of information when studying a group of organisms. So whereas previously only a handful of characters were used to try to reconstruct evolution, now hundreds – or even thousands – of pieces of information are considered. By identifying lists of characters that vary within the group of interest, and then identifying which species included within the study have which primitive and derived character states, scientists produce huge tables of data that describe how the characters being analysed are distributed within a group. For fossil animals, the characters available for analysis are distinct aspects of anatomy. When living animals are studied, characters can be parts of the genetic code, aspects of

behaviour, or even features like distribution, odour or voice. For example, in primates, the presence of a tail is a primitive character state – it's present in ancient fossil primates, in living primates that evolved early on in the group's history, and also in the closest relatives of primates, like tree-shrews – whereas the absence of a tail is a derived character state. Several different computer programs are then used to analyse this data. The program looks at all the data and then arranges it so that the species that share the greatest number of character states are grouped together.

A tree-like diagram – typically termed a cladogram or phylogenetic tree – is the result. The tree shows not just how the species might be arranged, but also how well supported its branching points or nodes are. Some nodes will be supported by many derived character states that point to the same relationship between the same set of species, but others will be weakly supported. Indeed, the more data there is, the more complicated the tree is. And studies tend not to produce a single tree – a program will usually find that there are other, alternative, equally sensible ways in which the character data can be arranged, and it will therefore show several different trees (sometimes numbering in the hundreds, thousands or more).

People who work on phylogeny never lose sight of the fact that cladograms are hypotheses; they're explanations for data that can be tested and changed as new evidence comes in, or as mistakes are identified or reinterpretations occur. By generating cladograms that take account of as much information as possible, we can hope to accurately reconstruct the pattern of evolution. Only with such patterns in front of us can we hope to understand the actual changes that organisms underwent during their history.

Dinosaurs like these Late Cretaceous crested hadrosaurs were social animals, and members of several species occupied the same habitats. These animals probably used body language, vocal signals and odours in communication.

It would be wrong to imply that the fossil record is completely silent on these issues. Enormous numbers of dinosaur eggs and nests are known, revealing much about dinosaur nesting and breeding behaviour, and cases where juveniles are preserved together with adults reveal glimpses of parental behaviour. Variation present within certain dinosaur species can show us how the sexes or growth stages differed and hence what sort of social structure was present. And bite marks and injuries show where dinosaurs interacted with predators or

members of their own species. Again, we will return to these issues later on (see Chapter 4).

So, for many issues concerning behaviour and lifestyle we're forced to rely on indirect methods of inference, comparing dinosaurs to modern animals that are thought to be similar to these dinosaurs in lifestyle or ecology. We also rely heavily on a technique in which members of an extinct group are compared to living, related animals that are close to the extinct animals on the family tree. This technique is termed phylogenetic bracketing (see p.19).

GEOLOGICAL TIME AND THE GEOLOGICAL TIMESCALE

When referring to extinct dinosaurs and other fossil organisms, we frequently need to refer to the fossil's geological age - *Tyrannosaurus rex*, for example, is from the Cretaceous Period, a unit of time that extended from 145 to 66 million years ago. More specifically, *Tyrannosaurus* is from the Late Cretaceous, a segment of the Cretaceous that extended from 100 to 66 million years ago. More specifically still, it's from the Maastrichtian stage, the segment of the Late Cretaceous that extended from 72 to 66 million years ago. As a rule, dinosaur species tended to last for somewhere between 1 and 3 million years before they became extinct – no one species persisted for the whole of the Late Cretaceous, let alone for the whole of the Cretaceous. Experts therefore find it most useful to use stage names, such as the Maastrichtian, when referring to a dinosaur's geological age. Stage names are generally not used here.

In referring to a fossil's age we combine two pieces of information. Terms like 'Cretaceous' and 'Maastrichtian' were originally applied to layers of rock, but they're also understood to correspond to specific sections of geological time. So, our understanding of the geological record combines the identification of rock layers and how they're arranged relative to one another, and our understanding of geological time as established by chemical and radioactive data.

The rocks and sediments of our planet are arranged in layers that can be distinguished on the basis of colour, consistency, structure and the fossils they contain. These layers are arranged in a sequence termed the geological column with a corresponding system of names for the layers within the column. Individual beds belong to larger units termed formations, and numerous formations together form a system. Systems, in turn, are grouped together into gigantic collections of systems called erathems. The vast majority of rock layers on the surface of the Earth belong to one of three erathems, each of which contain very different fossils: the Palaeozoic (the 'age of ancient life'), Mesozoic (the 'age of middle life') and Cenozoic (the 'age of new life'). Mesozoic rocks are the ones that contain non-bird dinosaurs (and early birds too, of course). Three systems are recognized within the Mesozoic: the ancient Triassic, the much thicker Jurassic, and the even thicker Cretaceous. Systems sometimes have distinct Lower and Upper sections, and some have a distinct Middle section as well. The rock layers of the Jurassic System, for example, belong either to the Lower Jurassic, Middle Jurassic or Upper Jurassic.

Because sediments are laid down over long periods, and because it takes hundreds or thousands of years for sediments (like sand or mud) to turn to rock, it has long been clear that the geological column represents a long period of time. But a precise understanding of the timeframe involved was not developed until a technique called radiometric dating was developed in the early 1900s. This is based on the principle of radioactive decay - that the composition of radioactive elements (like

A BRIEF HISTORY OF DINOSAUR DISCOVERIES

The group of animals that we today call dinosaurs was first recognized scientifically during the 1840s. At this time, British anatomist Richard Owen proposed that three large fossil reptiles, all from southern England, shared features of the hip region lacking in other reptiles. The animals that possessed these unusual features were all large, and the key potassium, uranium and argon) decays at a constant, measureable rate over time. By looking at the amount of decay that elements preserved in rock layers have undergone, the rock itself can be dated with precision.

The results of radiometric dating show that the Earth is about 4.5 billion years old, that life originated about 3.7 billion years ago, that the Palaeozoic started about 541 million years ago, and that the Mesozoic started about 252 million years ago. Dinosaurs first appear in Mesozoic rocks dated to about 230 million years ago. Radiometric dating has been applied to rocks from right across the geological column. The boundaries between layers have been precisely dated, as have specific events preserved in the geological record, like extinctions. This system is constantly improved and refined as technology and knowledge improves, so boundaries in the geological column are sometimes given new dates. The boundary between the Cretaceous and the start of the Cenozoic, for example, was previously dated to 65 million years ago but, in 2012, was shown to actually date to 66 million years ago.

A knowledge of the names used in the geological column and of the more important dates is essential for people interested in ancient life and the history of evolution. A consequence of the fact that technical terms like Mesozoic and Cretaceous apply both to layers of rock and to sections of geological time is that we have two, parallel sets of terms – *Tyrannosaurus* was alive during the Late Cretaceous, but its fossils come from Upper Cretaceous rocks. We've been careful to distinguish these two naming systems throughout this book.

Eon	Era	Period	Epoch	Age	
Phanerozoic	Mesozoic	Cretaceous	Late		66
				Maastrichtian	72.1
				Campanian	83.8
				Santonian	86.3
				Coniacian	89.8
				Turonian	93.9
				Cenomanian	100.5
			Early	Albian	113.0
				Aptian	126.3
				Barremian	130.8
				Hauterivian	133.9
				Valanginian	139.4
				Berriasian	145.0
		Jurassic	Late	Tithonian	152.1
				Kimmeridgian	152.3
				Oxfordian	163.5
			Middle	Callovian	166.1
				Bathonian	168.3
				Bajocian	170.3
				Aalenian	174.1
			Early	Toarcian	182.7
				Pliensbachian	190.8
				Sinemurian	199.3
				Hettangian	201.3
		Triassic	Late	Rhaetian	208.5
				Norian	229.4
				Carnian	237.0
			Middle	Ladinian	241.5
				Anisian	247.1
			Early	Olenekian	250.0
				Induan	252.2

Geological time is split up into a tiered system of subdivisions. Dinosaurs dominated the part of the Phanerozoic (the age of 'visible life') termed the Mesozoic (meaning the age of 'middle life').

features that Owen regarded as important showed how their bodies and limbs were specialized to carry great weight. He essentially regarded them as 'super-reptiles' – as reptiles that, in contrast to the mostly small, sprawling reptiles of modern times, resembled giant mammals like elephants and rhinos. Owen named them dinosaurs, a name meaning something like 'terrible reptiles', but with 'terrible' intended to mean 'awesome'.

Richard Owen was one of the most influential biologists and palaeontologists of the Victorian age and made an extraordinary number of discoveries. Among these was that several English fossil reptiles could be classified together in a group that Owen named Dinosauria.

The three animals that Owen regarded as founder members of the Dinosauria are the predatory theropod *Megalosaurus* and the plant-eaters *Iguanodon* and *Hylaeosaurus*. All had been discovered a few decades beforehand, but it hadn't been realized that all three were close relatives. Indeed, a confusing number of large, ancient fossil reptiles were being documented by scientists at this time, and many were exciting, strange and without any obvious close relationship to modern turtles, snakes, lizards or crocodylians.

People had actually been finding and wondering about the fossil bones of dinosaurs and other long-extinct animals for centuries beforehand. Some of these people, including the ancient Greeks, Romans and Chinese, interpreted fossil bones as the remains of mythological heroes or monsters. Indeed, some experts have proposed that certain mythological creatures – most famously the griffin of central Asia – were invented as a result of people's attempts to interpret the fossils of long-extinct animals.

Owen's idea that dinosaurs were pachyderm-like animals was challenged by additional discoveries made in Europe during the latter half of the 19th century. Some of these fossils – namely the small, two-legged plant-eater *Hypsilophodon* in England, and the even smaller bipedal predators *Compsognathus* and *Archaeopteryx* in Germany – demonstrated a close evolutionary link between dinosaurs and birds. *Archaeopteryx*, famously

Of the three fossil reptiles included within Owen's Dinosauria, *Megalosaurus* is the only predator. It is known from many bones, but the most spectacular is this large lower jaw containing both fully erupted and partially erupted sabre-like teeth.

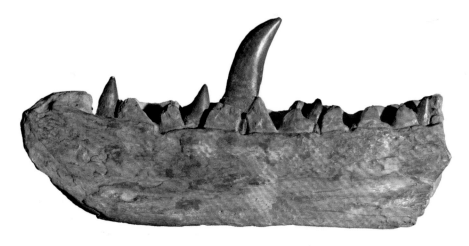

preserved with feather impressions, was significant in showing that birds existed as long ago as the Late Jurassic, about 150 million years ago.

Europe continued to yield new dinosaurs throughout the rest of the 19th century and beyond, but it was North America that then became the centre of attention. Numerous spectacular dinosaur remains from the Late Jurassic and Late Cretaceous of Colorado, Montana and elsewhere resulted in a golden age of discovery as scientists, prospectors and professional fossil collectors found and excavated scores of new dinosaurs. The most familiar non-bird dinosaurs of all – *Tyrannosaurus*, *Triceratops*, *Diplodocus*, *Apatosaurus* and *Stegosaurus* among them – were found at this time, their skeletons transported to the great museums of the eastern USA.

After this phase of enormous interest, things quietened down substantially during the first few decades of the 1900s, so much so that

During the early 1900s, industrialist and philanthropist Andrew Carnegie paid to have replica skeletons of *Diplodocus* sent to London, Paris and elsewhere. This photograph shows the unveiling of the London skeleton – today often known as 'Dippy' – in May 1905.

The English dinosaur *Hypsilophodon* was discovered during the 1840s. Today we know that it was a biped that inhabited woodlands and plains. However, it was incorrectly regarded as a quadruped and even as a tree-climber during the late 1800s and early 1900s.

research on dinosaurs had mostly ground to a halt by the 1930s. A long 'quiet phase' characterized the middle part of the 20th century. Work did continue during this time – Indian dinosaurs were discovered and described during the 1930s, and Russian expeditions went in search of Mongolian dinosaurs during the 1940s, for example – but it was much overshadowed by work on other animal groups. Indeed, during the 'quiet phase' it was generally thought that mammals (especially those belonging to modern groups, like

Scientific interest in dinosaurs waned during the early decades of the 1900s but demand for museum showpieces remained. This specimen of the long-necked sauropod *Diplodocus* was excavated at Dinosaur National Monument, USA, during the 1920s.

PHYLOGENETIC BRACKETING

Imagine that you have a particular question about the anatomy, biology or behaviour of a fossil animal species, a question that simply cannot be answered directly based on the fossils discovered so far. One way of answering the question (at least, answering it to the best of current knowledge) is to look at the position of the species on the tree of life, and to see which living animal species surround it on the tree. A tree that contains *Tyrannosaurus*, for example, shows the lineage leading to crocodylians splitting off from one side, and the lineage leading to birds splitting off from the other. In other words, *Tyrannosaurus* is 'bracketed' on the family tree by living crocodylians and by living birds.

This technique is termed 'phylogenetic bracketing' (or simply 'bracketing'), and it's routinely used to provide answers on the anatomy, biology or behaviour of fossil animals. To take a simple example, let's think about the vision of *Tyrannosaurus*. Did *Tyrannosaurus* have good eyesight, and could it see in colour? If we look at living crocodylians and living birds, we see that members of both groups have excellent eyesight, and both also have good colour vision. So, in the absence of better information,

we can conclude that these traits were true of *Tyrannosaurus* as well.

While bracketing serves as a rough and ready guide to basic questions of this sort, it does have limitations. Let's ask another question: did *Tyrannosaurus* have an oil-secreting gland under its tail? This time, bracketing gives us ambiguous answers, since crocodylians and birds differ with respect to this feature (birds have such an organ, crocodylians don't), and we can't say whether *Tyrannosaurus* retained the primitive condition present in crocodylians or possessed the advanced one present in birds. In cases such as this, bracketing leaves us guessing and only exceptional fossil evidence can provide the answers we seek.

The living animals that 'bracket' fossil ones provide us with otherwise unobtainable information on the biology and anatomy of the fossil species. Obviously, we can only form such ideas when we have a working idea of the phylogenetic relationships between the animals concerned.

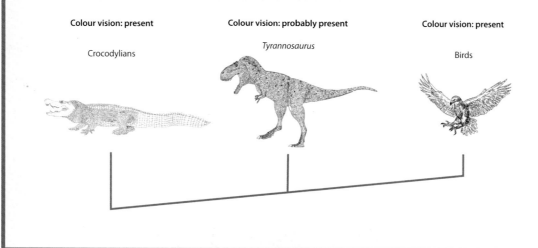

Colour vision: present — Crocodylians

Colour vision: probably present — *Tyrannosaurus*

Colour vision: present — Birds

rodents and horses) were more deserving of study than dinosaurs, and that dinosaurs were dead-ends, uninteresting with respect to our understanding of life on Earth as a whole, and generally not all that worthy of attention. By the 1950s and early 1960s, non-bird dinosaurs were often cast in a negative light – they were said to be failures destined for extinction, inferior to the mammals that replaced them, and only able to survive because the Mesozoic Earth was a vast tropical swampland.

It's often assumed that this old-fashioned view of dinosaurs as failures developed directly from the ideas that scientists held during the 19th century. But this is not really true since it was actually a 20th-century invention that emerged from a phase of apathy about dinosaurs. If anything, the scientists who worked on dinosaurs during the late 1800s and early 1900s frequently imagined them as active creatures related to birds.

OSTROM, BAKKER AND THE DINOSAUR RENAISSANCE

Whatever the cause of the 'quiet phase', it came to an end during the late 1960s when a handful of palaeontologists began to look at dinosaurs anew. In a way, they revived the more active view of non-bird dinosaurs and archaic birds that had existed during the 19th century. This event is termed the Dinosaur Renaissance and it involved equal amounts of careful, detailed science and rash, poorly supported speculation. Two scientists, both based in the USA, are most famously associated with the Renaissance. The first is John Ostrom of the Peabody Museum of Natural History at Yale University.

Ostrom's early scientific work concerned the teeth and jaws of the duckbilled hadrosaurs and of horned dinosaurs like *Triceratops*, two important plant-eating groups of the Late Cretaceous. He argued that hadrosaurs were not swamp-dwellers as thought during the 'quiet phase', but land-living browsers that ate from conifers. He also saw evidence indicating that non-bird dinosaurs were more social and more complex in behaviour than thought. And he pointed to indications of fast growth and a more active, 'warm-blooded' physiology for non-bird dinosaurs than was considered likely during the 'quiet phase'.

But outshining this work were his studies of the bird-like theropod *Deinonychus* (discovered in Montana in 1964) and the Jurassic bird *Archaeopteryx*. Not only did Ostrom describe the extraordinary anatomy of the sickle-clawed, highly agile *Deinonychus*, he was also able to document the many features shared by *Deinonychus* and *Archaeopteryx* – so many that they provided clear evidence of a close evolutionary relationship. *Deinonychus* is a Cretaceous fossil (dating to about 115 million years ago) while *Archaeopteryx*

THE

DINOSAUR

H E R E S I E S

**COLD-BLOODED, DIM-WITTED
MONSTERS OR ONE OF EVOLUTION'S
GREATEST SUCCESS STORIES?**

ROBERT BAKKER

Robert Bakker's ideas about dinosaur biology and evolution, many of them explained and illustrated in his famous 1986 book *The Dinosaur Heresies*, have been extremely influential to the modern generation of dinosaur experts.

is a much older, Jurassic one (dating to about 150 million years ago), meaning that *Deinonychus* is surely a late-surviving relict of an earlier phase in evolution. Far older, smaller *Deinonychus*-like theropods awaited discovery, Ostrom proposed. This view has since been confirmed by numerous discoveries (a story we return to in Chapter 5).

Ostrom's ideas and observations received widespread coverage in magazines and TV shows. They were vigorously promoted even further by one of his students, the famously iconoclastic Robert Bakker. He argued that the microscopic structure of dinosaur bone revealed evidence for rapid growth similar to that present in mammals and birds, and that dinosaur trackways provided evidence for rapid walking and running speeds like those seen in living mammals and birds. He also looked at the pace of dinosaur evolution, their overall anatomy, and the ratio of dinosaur predators to herbivores. All these lines of evidence, Bakker said, provided strong support for the idea that dinosaurs were 'warm-blooded' animals whose bodies and organs worked more like those of birds and mammals than those of lizards and crocodylians. He also championed Ostrom's work on bird origins, and argued that the traditional idea then prevalent – that non-bird dinosaurs were evolutionary failures, inferior to mammals – was wrong, and that dinosaurs were a phenomenal success story, superior in evolutionary terms to other animal groups.

It is simply wrong to imagine the spectacular giant dinosaurs of the past – like the plate-backed herbivore *Stegosaurus* and the horned theropod *Ceratosaurus* shown here – as failures of evolution. On the contrary, dinosaurs are one of the most successful animal groups that have ever evolved.

DINOSAUR RESEARCH IN THE MODERN ERA

Ostrom's and Bakker's ideas and publications encouraged other scientists to pay closer attention to what was going on in the world of non-bird dinosaur research. But it would be wrong to say that Ostrom and Bakker were the only ones generating interest in non-bird dinosaurs at this time. In fact, research programmes in Poland, Russia, China, South Africa, Argentina and elsewhere meant that scientists outside the USA were making spectacular discoveries at the same time. Some of this research was occurring as a consequence of post-war economic recovery, while much of it was the continuation of research that had started during the 'quiet phase' but had previously failed to win attention, or produce exciting results.

Whatever happened, the ideas and discoveries put forward by Ostrom and Bakker coincided with the announcement of amazing new dinosaurs

from many places, including *Deinocheirus* from Mongolia (famous for its gargantuan arms), fang-toothed *Heterodontosaurus* from South Africa, the sail-backed plant-eater *Ouranosaurus* from Niger, and the enormous long-necked *Supersaurus* from Colorado. Add *Deinonychus* to this mix, and it seems that many things came together at just the right time, enough to capture the attention of journalists and the public alike. The Dinosaur Renaissance marked a shift in how much attention dinosaurs received relative to other fossil animal groups.

Since that time, an increasing number of scientists have been attracted to the study of dinosaurs. Ostrom's hypothesis of bird origins is now so well supported that it can be considered one of the best supported hypotheses in the history of vertebrate evolution. The old idea that non-bird dinosaurs were evolutionary dead-ends is therefore woefully wrong. Indeed, an understanding of dinosaur biology and anatomy is crucial if we want to investigate how and where the many features of birds evolved.

The vast numbers of new dinosaurs that have been documented since the 1960s are equally exciting. New dinosaurs have of course been discovered ever since the first fossil dinosaur (*Megalosaurus*) was named in 1824, but an incredible surge in discoveries mean that more than 85% of recognized non-bird dinosaurs have been named since 1990.

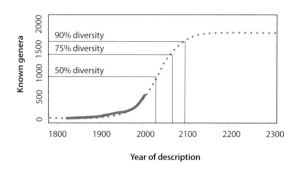

The soft tissues of fossil dinosaurs – the structures that covered the outsides of their bodies – are becoming better known thanks to amazing discoveries. We now have substantial information on the feathers, filaments and other structures that grew from the skin of non-bird dinosaurs, and a few specimens even have muscles, guts and other internal organs preserved. These new ideas about dinosaur biology and evolution and the many new discoveries have, combined with technological advances, made the study of non-bird dinosaurs and archaic birds one of the most ground-breaking, active areas of palaeontology. The face of dinosaur science today is a world away from that which existed just a few decades ago.

This work on non-bird dinosaurs and archaic birds has also made it obvious that all too little research has been done on the anatomy of living animals, specifically on functional morphology. Work on dinosaurs has inspired palaeontologists to test many ideas about the patterns and trends of evolution using techniques originally devised to test ideas relevant to dinosaurs alone. Questions asked by palaeontologists have therefore driven an 'anatomical revolution' in which scientists have studied modern animals anew, including elephants, lizards, crocodiles and birds.

An enormous number of new non-bird dinosaur species have been named in recent decades, and all indications are that many more species have yet to be found. These graphs show that we have a long way to go before we've properly sampled the full range of dinosaur diversity. The thick line shows the actual rate of discoveries made so far, and the dotted line shows the rate of discoveries predicted for the future.

DINOSAURS AND THE MESOZOIC WORLD

Dinosaurs evolved in a complex world where continents collided, mountains rose, seas rose and fell, climates changed, and animal and plant groups came and went. All of these events influenced dinosaur evolution, why they looked like they did, and why they evolved the lifestyles and behaviours that they did. It's often imagined that non-bird dinosaurs and archaic birds inhabited a verdant, tropical planet, covered by hot forests and swamps, and that Mesozoic animals were suited for life in constantly warm, lush conditions. Areas of the world were like this during parts of the Mesozoic and some dinosaurs, at least, did live in conditions of this sort. However, dinosaurs were around for such a incredible span of time that it's difficult to make generalizations about the conditions they encountered across their history.

When dinosaurs first evolved during the Triassic, all the continents were united in a supercontinent termed Pangaea (a name that means 'whole Earth'). Pangaea is sometimes imagined as a 'prototype continent' that only existed because continental fragmentation hadn't yet occurred. Actually, its existence was due to the coalescence of several previously separate landmasses. The continents had collided and split apart several times before Pangaea formed around 300 million years ago.

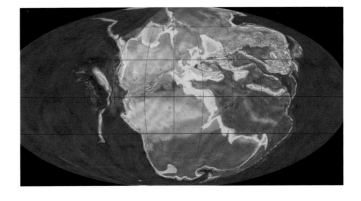

The existence of supercontinents has a major impact on global climate. A relatively small coastline and the existence of a vast continental interior mean that little humidity from the oceans reaches inland, resulting in extremely dry conditions and the existence of vast deserts. Animals and plants that evolve on supercontinents have, in theory, the chance to occur virtually worldwide, since there are no seaways or oceans to prevent their spread. In practice, things are not this simple – conditions vary from one region to another and there might still be barriers that slow or prevent spread, like mountain ranges and places of exceptional heat or cold. This view matches what we know of the fossil record, since Triassic dinosaurs and other animals generally don't seem to have occurred right across Pangaea. Instead, they were restricted to particular climatic zones.

About 200 million years ago, Pangaea began to break apart along an east–west fault. It split into two new continental masses: Laurasia in the north and Gondwana in the south. From this point onwards,

When dinosaurs first appeared about 230 million years ago, all of the world's continents were united into a supercontinent called Pangaea. This stretched from north to south and was surrounded by the gigantic Panthalassic Ocean.

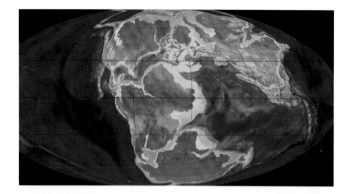

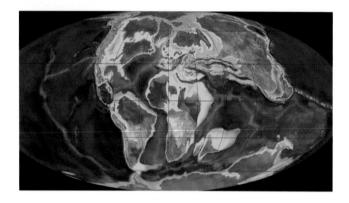

By about 150 million years ago (top), during the Jurassic, Pangaea had split into a northern landmass (called Laurasia) and a southern landmass (called Gondwana). This meant more coastline, and a cooler, more moist climate.

By the Late Cretaceous, the world looked essentially modern (bottom). The Atlantic Ocean divided Europe and Africa from the Americas, and the Gondwanan continents had mostly split apart. High sea levels meant that shallow seas covered low-lying regions.

animals of the north and south embarked on different evolutionary trajectories, becoming increasingly more distinct from one another. Both landmasses later split up still further. The formation of the North Atlantic Ocean about 80 million years ago caused Laurasia to break into a western section (consisting of North America) and eastern section (consisting of Greenland, Europe and Asia). Gondwana's history is more complex, with South America, India, Madagascar and Australasia all splitting away from Antarctica, and from each other, at various times between 110 and 40 million years ago. Most of these Gondwanan landmasses moved north, with Africa and India eventually colliding with Europe and Asia, and South America joining North America via a landbridge.

One of the great questions about dinosaur history is how their evolution was affected by this continental break-up. Did many of the main events of dinosaur evolution occur because dinosaur populations were separated and moved by continental splitting? Questions of this sort remain at the core of the science of biogeography, the study of animal and plant distribution.

In recent years, newly discovered dinosaur species have shown that continental movement probably was the main driver of dinosaur distribution. Dinosaurs of most groups now have fossil records that extend back into the Jurassic, to a time when continental connections meant that the groups alive at the time could become widely distributed. A classic example is provided by the long-necked herbivores called titanosaurs. For years, titanosaurs were mostly known from the Upper Cretaceous rocks of South America, Madagascar and India, with rare occurrences in Europe, Asia and North America interpreted as showing how members of the group had island-hopped north during the closing years of the Late Cretaceous.

More recently discovered fossils somewhat contradict this view by showing that titanosaurs were present in Laurasia from the start of the Cretaceous at least. This distribution supports the idea of them becoming widely distributed early on in their history thanks to the presence of continental connections, their later distribution being the result of continental splitting and movement. Of course, there were probably cases where dinosaur lineages spread to new regions by crossing landbridges too.

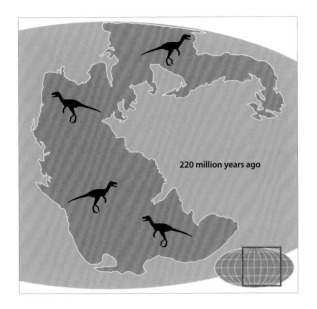

220 million years ago

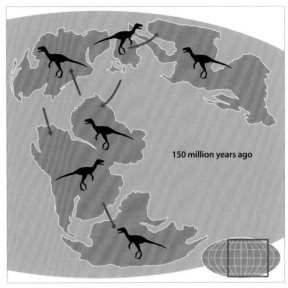

150 million years ago

90 million years ago

The distribution of dinosaurs (and other land animals) can be influenced by continental movements, and also by the fact that animals themselves move across landbridges and even swim across stretches of sea. The two maps at the top show how the distribution of an imaginary dinosaur group might have been controlled by continental movement – a group present across a continuous landmass might eventually occur across separate landmasses as the landmasses split apart and move away from one another, taking the animals with them. The map at the bottom depicts the way in which animals can use landbridges and short swimming trips between islands to move from one region to another.

Because the Mesozoic world was mostly warm, scarcely any water was locked up in ice. As a consequence, sea levels were at an all-time high and low-lying areas of land were under water. Much of Europe is low-lying, meaning that large areas were flooded during the Jurassic and Cretaceous, the exposed portions existing as island archipelagos and isolated mini-continents. A large area of central Asia was covered by a shallow sea at the same time, meaning that eastern Asia was cut off from eastern Europe. North America was also strongly affected by high sea

The archaic hadrosaur *Telmatosaurus* is one of several unusual, island-dwelling dinosaurs that inhabited what's now Romania during the Late Cretaceous. It was most similar to animals otherwise typical of the Early Cretaceous.

levels, with a great seaway cutting the continent in half during the latter half of the Cretaceous.

A result of these high sea levels is that the dinosaurs that lived during several segments of Jurassic and Cretaceous time were unique to island landmasses and mostly evolved in isolation. Familiar Late Cretaceous dinosaurs like *Tyrannosaurus* and *Triceratops* were not widely distributed; instead, they were unique to a long, narrow continent – called Laramidia – that today forms western Canada and much of the far west of the USA. Very different dinosaurs lived in Appalachia, the landmass to the east that today forms eastern Canada and the eastern part of the USA. Weird, island-dwelling dinosaurs also inhabited the islands of Late Cretaceous Europe. Some – including various sauropods, ankylosaurs and hadrosaurs – were dwarves, only half or one-third the size of related species elsewhere. Others, like the Romanian hadrosaur *Telmatosaurus*, were late-surviving relics of a sort that had gone extinct elsewhere. And others were peculiar and unique denizens of the islands where they occurred.

CLIMATE AND WEATHER

Throughout the Mesozoic, the world was in a hothouse or greenhouse phase. Average global temperatures were high, polar ice was generally absent, and forests occurred well within the polar circles. The Triassic world, as we've already seen, was subject to extreme aridity and heat, with desert conditions dominating the Pangaean supercontinent. At the start of the Triassic, temperatures in the hottest parts of Pangaea almost certainly exceeded the land temperatures of today and were probably the hottest temperatures of the last several hundred million years. The average global temperate during the Early Triassic was close to 30°C (86°F) (average global temperature today is 14°C/57°F) and sea surface temperatures may have exceeded an incredible 40°C (104°F) (today, the average sea surface temperature is about 17°C/62°F). These exceptionally high temperatures were also the case at the end of the preceding geological age – the Permian – and may have made life impossible for many plant and animal groups.

Conditions cooled during the later parts of the Triassic but the climate remained hot overall, so desert-dwelling adaptations were surely widespread across the land-living animals of the time. This long period of heat and dryness finally ended during the Jurassic as continental break-up meant that more coastline was created. This resulted in cooler, moister conditions, and enormous forests spread throughout the world's tropical regions. By the Late Jurassic, average global temperatures seem to have been only 3°C (37°F) higher than those of today. Continental interiors remained arid, but the huge cells of moving air that existed over the giant, warm oceans are in keeping with evidence from fossils for annual wet seasons.

Similar conditions to those of the Jurassic were also present across part of the world during the Cretaceous. Things changed when a phase of profound global warming termed the Cretaceous Thermal Maximum occurred between about 120 and 80 million years ago (a span of time extending from the middle of the Early Cretaceous to the middle of the Late Cretaceous). This caused average land temperatures to be about 6°C (10.8°F) higher than those of today, and sea surface temperatures to be as much as 9°C (16.2°F) higher than those of today. A result of these conditions was that lush forests stretched from the equator to the poles. Some computer models indicate that the amount of vegetation present worldwide

Many dinosaurs alive during the Late Triassic must have been adapted for dry desert conditions, since these were widespread at the time. But lakes, rivers and marshes existed in some places, and they were surely visited by dinosaurs that drank and foraged at the water's edge.

was much greater than that present during the rest of the Mesozoic. Larger quantities of vegetation weaken air currents and so reduce the amount of mixing that occurs between different parts of the atmosphere. They also have impacts on rainfall and where it occurs. Quite why this Cretaceous warming phase occurred is controversial. One idea is that high carbon dioxide (CO_2) levels – released by a prolonged phase of volcanic activity – were behind this climatic event. Whatever happened, these lush, super-greenhouse conditions surely had an impact on animal evolution.

Despite these high temperatures, Mesozoic Earth was not in a perpetual tropical state across its entire surface. Modelling work has shown that even a greenhouse world can have cool continental interiors, upland regions and poles. Indeed, data from several parts of the Mesozoic world indicate cool conditions, with climates similar to that of modern Britain, New York or northern Japan. This is the case for Liaoning in western China, a location famous for its hundreds of fossils of early birds and other feathered theropods. Here, the average annual temperature during the Early Cretaceous seems to have been about 8–11°C (46–60°F). Perhaps this explains why some of the feathery dinosaurs found at Liaoning look so well insulated (some even have feathering on their feet that extends all the way to the tips of their toes). The possibility exists that these animals were specially adapted for life in a cool climate.

Non-bird dinosaurs of many sorts also inhabited Australia, Alaska and Antarctica when these parts of the world were within the polar circles and subject both to prolonged winter darkness and cool temperatures. None of these places were as cold during the Mesozoic as they are today, but they were cool, and yet dinosaurs occurred in these places year-round.

Dinosaurs were around for a long span of time and during that time all manner of changes happened to the world's surface. A supercontinent split apart, sea levels rose and fell several times, and temperatures soared, sometimes to super-greenhouse conditions. There is no doubt that these many changes had major impacts on dinosaur evolution, on where and how dinosaurs could live. In recent years, an improved understanding of Mesozoic temperatures and fossil occurrences has meant that

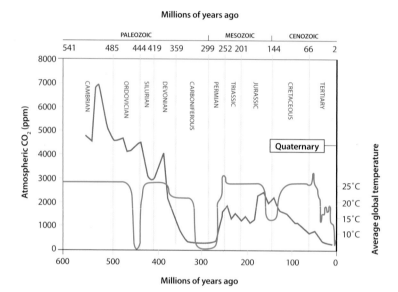

The composition of the atmosphere has fluctuated considerably over the past 600 million years, and climates have too. This graph shows how global temperatures (light blue line) were mostly high during the Mesozoic, in part because atmospheric carbon dioxide levels (grey line) were too.

palaeontologists have been able to better match evolutionary events in dinosaur history with changes in climate and continental shape. Our understanding of the interplay between these factors is set to improve the more we study this record.

DINOSAURS IN THE TREE OF LIFE

Dinosaurs are reptiles and part of the same major group of animals as turtles, crocodiles, snakes and lizards. Like living reptiles, dinosaurs had scaly skin and were capable of living in dry, arid environments well away from water. Based on what we know about living reptiles, we can use bracketing (see p.19) to infer that dinosaurs had excellent eyesight and good colour vision, and that they had a chambered heart, practised internal fertilization, and had a digestive and reproductive system essentially similar to that of modern reptiles.

While this is technically correct and not controversial, the problem is that the term 'reptile' as commonly used is associated with animals like turtles, lizards, snakes and crocodylians. These animals all share a so-called cold-blooded biology, they generally have low energy demands, and they tend to be less active than so-called warm-blooded birds and mammals (as

Dinosaurs of the Late Jurassic – like this *Stegosaurus*, predatory *Allosaurus* and long-necked *Supersaurus* – evolved in a world where average temperatures were somewhat higher than those of today. Flowering plants had yet to spread, but modern-looking conifers, cycads and ferns dominated the enormous forests.

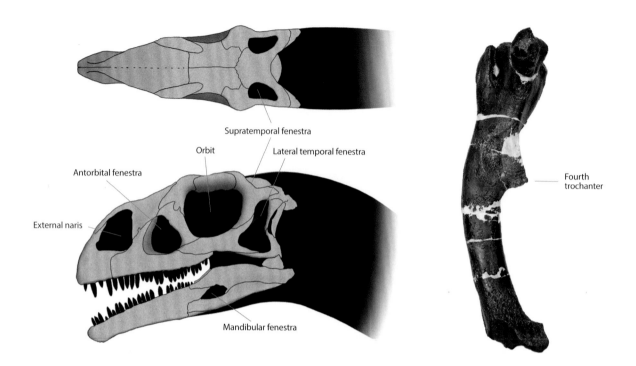

Supratemporal fenestra

Orbit

Lateral temporal fenestra

Antorbital fenestra

External naris

Fourth trochanter

Mandibular fenestra

Dinosaurs possess a key feature in the skull typical of archosaurs – an accessory opening between the nostril and eye called the antorbital fenestra shown above. This structure was occupied by an air-filled sac.

The rear surface of the archosaur femur possesses a raised ridge called the fourth trochanter (above right). Still present in living crocodylians, this is the attachment site for a huge muscle that attaches to the tail.

we'll see in Chapter 4, use of the terms 'cold-blooded' and 'warm-blooded' is misleading and even inaccurate in places). People therefore tend to assume that any animal called a 'reptile' shares this set of attributes. But when used in the scientific sense, the term 'reptile' simply applies to that group of animals that includes turtles, lizards, snakes and crocodylians and all animals that share the same common ancestor as these four groups. The fact that dinosaurs are reptiles doesn't, therefore, mean that they were similar to living reptiles like lizards or crocodylians in all aspects of their biology. (As birds are part of Dinosauria, they should also be considered a sub-group of reptiles from an evolutionary point of view.)

Dinosaur skeletons reveal a set of anatomical features unique to a group of reptiles called archosaurs, sometimes called the 'ruling reptiles'. These features include the presence of a large window-like opening on the side of the snout called the antorbital fenestra, and a prominent muscle attachment site on the back surface of the thigh bone, called the fourth trochanter. Both structures are linked to important features of archosaurian soft tissue anatomy. The edges of the antorbital fenestra anchored certain jaw-opening muscles, but it was also filled with a large, air-filled sac that perhaps had an important role in lightening the head and in temperature control. The fourth trochanter, meanwhile, is the main anchor site for the giant caudofemoralis longus – a huge muscle connected to the side of the tail and used to pull the thigh backwards during the walking or running cycle.

Archosaurs consist of two major lineages. One includes living crocodylians and their relatives and is called the 'crocodile-line' group. Archosaurs that belong to this group have a complicated ankle joint and usually have bony plates running along the top of the neck, back and tail. The second major archosaur lineage includes birds (and hence all other dinosaur groups as well) and their close relatives and is called the 'bird-line' group (the scientific name most often used for this group is Ornithodira). Bird-line archosaurs have a simple ankle joint and generally lack the bony plates seen in their crocodile-line cousins. They also have a longer, more slender neck and a narrower, longer foot.

Fossils show that the split between these two groups happened early in the Triassic, about 247 million years ago. This is not long after an enormous mass extinction event that ended the preceding Permian age. It would seem that archosaurs evolved quickly to take advantage of the new, relatively empty animal communities that existed in the wake of the extinction.

Early evolution among bird-line archosaurs occurred among very small animals. A Late Triassic bird-line archosaur from Scotland called *Scleromochlus* seems to be a good example of what the earliest bird-line archosaurs were like. Less than 20 cm (8 in) long, it was a long-legged, slender predator that probably preyed on insects. Its long leg and foot

Dinosaurs are close relatives of pterosaurs, forming with them the clade Ornithodira. And ornithodirans are close relatives of crocodile-line archosaurs, the two groups together forming Archosauria.

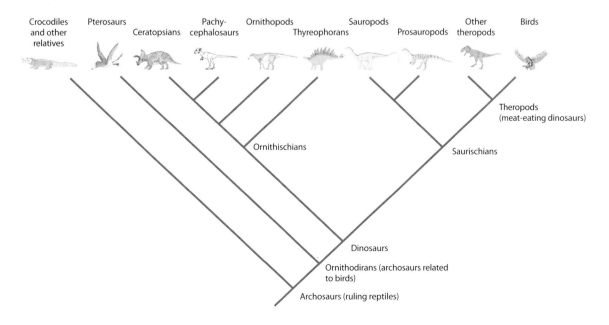

Tiny *Scleromochlus* from the Late Triassic of Scotland was probably close to the ancestry of both pterosaurs and dinosaurs. It's known from seven specimens, none of which are especially well preserved.

bones have led some experts to suggest that it might have been specialized for a hopping or leaping lifestyle. Animals like *Scleromochlus* seem to have been ancestral to pterosaurs – the membranous-winged flying reptiles of the Mesozoic – and also to a second group, the also small, lightweight dinosauromorphs. As suggested by their name (which means 'dinosaur forms') dinosauromorphs would eventually give rise to dinosaurs and thereby spawn a dynasty that included the largest and most successful land-living animals of all time. It would take some considerable time – perhaps more than 30 million years – before dinosauromorphs evolved large size and took to filling important, conspicuous roles in animal communities. Why this slow, drawn-out rise to success? Was something preventing bird-line archosaurs from becoming big, important animals?

REIGN OF THE CROCODILE-LINE ARCHOSAURS

Today, crocodile-line archosaurs are represented only by crocodylians: the crocodiles, alligators and gharials. These are the tip of the iceberg when it comes to the diversity present among the more ancient crocodile-line archosaurs of the Triassic, and Triassic crocodile-line archosaurs filled many roles that were later occupied by dinosaurs during the Jurassic and Cretaceous. Four-legged, armour-plated omnivorous or herbivorous crocodile-line archosaurs walked the land, as did predatory species equipped with deep, massive skulls and blade-like teeth. The former are termed aetosaurs, and the latter rauisuchians.

The biggest rauisuchians were gigantic animals 8 m (26 ft) or more in length. They were very obviously the top predators of the day. Many walked on all fours but others had short forelimbs and appear to have been bipedal. We also know of quadrupedal rauisuchian relatives that had sails on their backs. One of these, a Chinese animal called *Lotosaurus,* has a toothless beak and was probably omnivorous or herbivorous. Then there are those members of the rauisuchian group that walked on two legs, had slim forelimbs, a long neck, and a short, toothless skull. *Effigia* from the USA is the best known of these.

During Triassic times, diverse members of the crocodile-line group were occupying many of the roles filled by dinosaurs later on, and were the dominant consumers and predators in most Triassic animal communities. For as long as these crocodile-line archosaurs were around, dinosaurs could probably never become an important group of animals. What does this tell us about the early history of dinosaurs and their rise to success? We'll come back to this issue in a moment.

Crocodile-line archosaurs of several groups evolved omnivorous or herbivorous habits. One of the strangest is the Middle Triassic Chinese animal *Lotosaurus*. It was a sail-backed, toothless quadruped.

DINOSAUR BEGINNINGS

Dinosaurs dominated life on land during the Jurassic and Cretaceous periods, between approximately 200 and 66 million years ago. They probably originated some considerable time beforehand, about 240 million years ago during the Middle Triassic. Early dinosaurs are rare and only a small number of species are known.

We saw earlier how dinosaurs belong to a group of bird-line archosaurs called dinosauromorphs. Several lineages evolved within this group, of which dinosaurs were the last to emerge and the only one that would persist beyond the Triassic and go on to evolve a diversity of lifestyles and body shapes. What do these early dinosauromorphs tell us about dinosaur origins? All are small, lightweight animals. A group called the lagerpetids – known from Argentina and the USA – possess an unusual foot structure where the two toes on the inner side were greatly reduced, the result being a strongly asymmetrical foot that looks suited for rapid running or perhaps even leaping or hopping. A dinosauromorph from Argentina – *Marasuchus* – lacks this weird foot anatomy and the shapes of its neck bones, hips and hindlimb bones show that it was more closely related to dinosaurs. The proportions of the *Marasuchus* skeleton suggest that it was a biped, and it has the sharp, backward-curved teeth of a predator. Both lagerpetids and *Marasuchus* were small, at less than 70 cm (28 in) in total length.

Next, we come to the silesaurids, a dinosauromorph group from the Middle and Late Triassic, which are even more dinosaur-like than *Marasuchus*. Most silesaurids were between 1.5 and 3 m (5 and 10 ft) in total length. They were slender, long-necked animals, their long forelimbs perhaps indicating a quadrupedal way of life. Silesaurids are named for

Marasuchus was a close relative of dinosaurs from the Late Triassic of Argentina. The proportions of its limbs suggest that it was bipedal, and its teeth show that it was most likely a predator. However, other close relatives of dinosaurs were quite different. Some were omnivores or herbivores that walked quadrupedally.

Silesaurus from Poland, but members of the group have now been reported from the USA, Brazil, Argentina, Tanzania, Zambia and Morocco, so they were obviously widespread across the Triassic world.

One especially interesting thing about silesaurids is that their teeth and jaws suggest a herbivorous or omnivorous lifestyle. The teeth are leaf-shaped with large serrations along their edges, and a toothless, beak-like region is present at the front of the lower jaw. Prior to the discovery of this group, it was assumed that dinosaurs evolved from sharp-toothed predators like *Marasuchus*. The fact that silesaurids were herbivores or omnivores might mean that dinosaurs actually evolved from herbivorous or omnivorous ancestors. Support for this possibility comes from the fact that two of the three main dinosaur groups include herbivorous or omnivorous species, not predatory ones. An alternative possibility is that silesaurids were doing their own weird thing, and that the common ancestor they shared with dinosaurs was a predator after all. As always with discussions of this sort, we need more fossils before we can get a better idea of what happened.

Another dinosauromorph deserves mention. This is *Nyasasaurus* from Tanzania, an animal currently known only from an arm bone and vertebrae from the hip region. *Nyasasaurus* seems to be even more closely related to dinosaurs than are the silesaurids. The possibility exists that it might be an early dinosaur, something we can neither confirm nor deny until we have better fossils. *Nyasasaurus* is also interesting in being especially old. It dates to about 243 million years ago, and demonstrates how the different dinosauromorph groups, including dinosaurs themselves, had diversified by the Middle Triassic.

All early dinosauromorphs possess features of their limbs and limb girdles which show that they had long, erect legs positioned directly beneath the body. They all look like swift, efficient runners, capable of fast movement. If we look a bit further, we see that other bird-line archosaurs were similarly adapted for fast, efficient locomotion, as were the vast majority of early crocodile-line archosaurs. The reason that this is important is that it shows that dinosaurs were not unusual or remarkable when it comes to their walking and running abilities.

This brings us to one of the main issues surrounding dinosaur origins. For much of the 20th century it was thought that dinosaurs came to dominate Mesozoic life on

Several dinosaur-like archosaurs from the Middle and Upper Triassic – the lagerpetids, *Marasuchus* and silesaurids – belong with dinosaurs in a clade called Dinosauromorpha. All were small, lightly built animals.

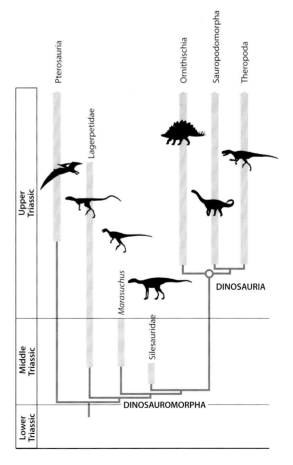

Nyasasaurus, from the Middle Triassic of Tanzania, was a very dinosaur-like dinosauromorph – it might even be an early dinosaur. It lived in a world dominated by animals of other sorts, among them the rhynchosaurs like those shown in the background.

land because they out-competed the other land-living animals of the time. In other words, it was thought that dinosaurs were better at running, better at exploiting prey and other resources, and better at breeding than contemporary animal groups. But the more we've learnt about Triassic animal life on land, the more unlikely this view of dinosaur superiority has appeared.

We've already seen that the crocodile-line archosaurs of the Triassic occupied ecological roles normally regarded as typical of dinosaurs. The idea that small, lightly built dinosauromorphs and early dinosaurs were able to compete directly with their giant crocodile-line cousins is extremely unlikely. If anything, dinosauromorphs and early dinosaurs were probably secretive animals that stayed out of the way of these much larger, more formidable creatures and were at risk of being killed and eaten by them. The fossil record also seems to show that neither dinosaur-like dinosauromorphs nor early dinosaurs were abundant relative to the other animal groups of the time, nor were early dinosaurs widely distributed – virtually all species come from western Gondwana alone. Also important is that fossils from the Middle Triassic (like *Nyasasaurus*) show that the rise of dinosaurs was a slow, protracted affair rather than a swift and immediate dominance.

In summary, the whole idea that dinosaurs managed to take over the world because they were ecologically, physiologically or anatomically superior to other animal groups is not supported by the evidence. So, what really happened? The Late Triassic was a tumultuous time when large-scale extinction events drastically affected life on land and saw the decline and disappearance of several animal groups. As is the case for the far more famous mass extinction event at the end of the Cretaceous, the exact cause of the end-Triassic mass extinction has been the subject of much speculation and disagreement, though major sea-level changes and a violent phase of volcanic activity seem to be the primary catalysts. More than one extinction event seems to have happened – one at about 220 million years ago, and another at the end of the Triassic, 201 million years ago. Whatever happened, crocodile-line archosaurs were severely affected and all perished except for

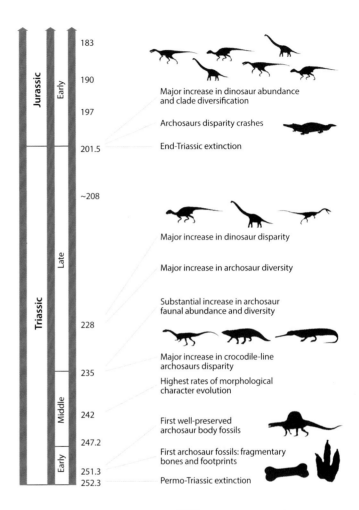

one lineage – the one (termed Crocodylomorpha) that ultimately led to modern crocodylians. Dinosaurs did not perish, perhaps because they were small and therefore better able to withstand changes in climate and a decline in available resources, and better at replacing their numbers due to shorter lifespans and faster growth. With crocodile-line archosaurs gone, dinosaurs were now able to inherit an Earth where the spaces previously occupied by large, land-living animals were empty. According to this view, dinosaurs were 'victors by accident' – they inherited the Earth thanks to the bad luck that befell other animals, not because they were superior or better adapted than those other groups.

Finally, the stage was set for the development of a world ruled by dinosaurs.

This diagram charts the main events in Triassic archosaur evolution. Crocodile-line archosaurs were dominant for much of the Triassic and may have prevented dinosaurs from evolving larger size.

2

THE DINOSAUR FAMILY TREE

ONE OF THE AIMS OF SCIENTISTS interested in dinosaurs is to reconstruct the dinosaur family tree – to understand how species are related to one another, and to arrange the different groups into a sequence that matches the pattern of their evolution. The study of the evolutionary process – also termed phylogeny – is known as phylogenetics and a vast amount of work on dinosaur phylogeny has been performed. Building a good, working model of phylogeny is key to understanding patterns and processes in nature. Once we have an idea of how a family tree is shaped, we can begin to understand the evolutionary trends within a group, such as those involving body size or the features associated with plant eating. These trends can then be linked with other events, like climatic changes or the splits that occurred between landmasses. These studies also highlight the gaps that still exist in our knowledge.

Today, most scientists agree upon the overall shape of the dinosaur family tree. Areas of controversy and uncertainty remain, but the interpretations of different scientific teams are mostly becoming more similar over time as more work is done, and as more data is analysed.

A large number of bony anatomical features have been identified that are unique to dinosaurs. Many are features that can only really be appreciated by people with a good understanding of anatomy. They include enlarged attachment sites for the jaw muscles that wrap on to

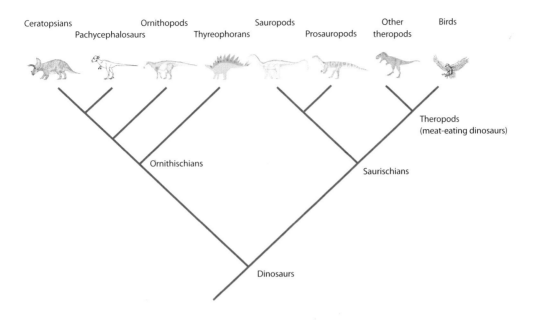

Ceratopsians Ornithopods Sauropods Other theropods Birds
Pachycephalosaurs Thyreophorans Prosauropods

Theropods
(meat-eating dinosaurs)

Ornithischians

Saurischians

Dinosaurs

the top of the skull, raised bony mounds on the upper parts of the neck vertebrae termed epipophyses, an especially long muscular crest on the upper part of the humerus, a fully open, window-like hip socket, and an especially narrow fibula in the lower leg that has a very small area of contact with the ankle bones further down. Because these features are unique to dinosaurs and not present in other archosaurs, they prove that Dinosauria is a clade – that is, a group of organisms where all the species descend from the same, single ancestor.

Early in its history, the dinosaur family tree split into two main branches: Saurischia and Ornithischia. Both groups are clades too. Key features unique to saurischians include a heavily built thumb with an enlarged claw, and key features unique to ornithischians include a back-turned pubic bone in the hips and a V-shaped or U-shaped bone at the tip of the lower jaw, called the predentary. We know that the split between saurischians and ornithischians occurred some time before 230 million years ago (the early part of the Late Triassic) because early members of both groups are known from rocks of this age. Saurischia split early in its history into Theropoda (the predatory dinosaurs and birds) and Sauropodomorpha (the sauropods and their relatives). Early members of all three groups were similar. All were small, bipedal, lightly built omnivores or predators with grasping hands.

Dinosauria consists of two main clades – Ornithischia and Saurischia, one of which (Saurischia) survived to the present. This simple cladogram depicts the main groups within those two clades.

41

THEROPODS: THE PREDATORY DINOSAURS AND BIRDS

Predatory dinosaurs and birds, collectively termed theropods, form one of the three great dinosaur groups. Note that the term 'predatory dinosaur' is merely a convenient catchall name for theropods, since we know that many non-bird theropods were omnivorous or even herbivorous. Birds, of course, evolved omnivorous and herbivorous lifestyles on many separate occasions.

As a generalization, all theropods – even the very oldest ones known – are bird-like. Bipedality is a nearly universal feature of the group, and the majority of species have a narrow, bird-like foot where the first metatarsal bone does not contact the ankle (metatarsals are the bones that make up the long part of the foot). This first metatarsal is connected to the first toe (called the hallux), and this is typically reduced in size or positioned higher up on the side of the foot in theropods than it is in other dinosaur groups. Later on in evolutionary history, birds evolved an enlarged hallux. We'll talk more about that story in Chapter 5.

Theropods tend to have hands specialized for a predatory way of life. The bones at the ends of their fingers are long, and the bones that supported the claws have strongly curved tips and large bulges on their lower surfaces. These bulges, known as flexor tubercles, show where powerful muscles and ligaments attached – muscles and ligaments that would have been used by these animals in digging their claws into the bodies of prey animals. Old reconstructions often show theropods with their palms facing the ground. Articulated skeletons and detailed studies of the movements possible at theropod limb joints actually show that their hands were fixed in a 'palms-inwards' pose. We explore what this means for theropod behaviour in Chapter 4.

Even when birds are excluded from consideration, theropods are very diverse, containing more than a third of all dinosaur species. Birds – with about 10,000 living species – outnumber all other dinosaur groups by a huge margin, meaning that Theropoda is the largest, most successful

Herrerasauridae

Coelophysoidea

Dilophosaurus

Neoceratosauria

Megalosauridae

Megalosauroidea

Spinosauridae

Allosauridae

Allosauroidea

Carcharodontosauria

Coelurosauria

Early theropods (those towards the top of this cladogram) were mostly small, lightly built predators that lacked the many bird-like features typical of later groups. Giant size evolved several times independently within Theropoda.

dinosaur group that ever evolved. Becoming small and evolving a sophisticated flight ability made birds – and therefore theropods – one of the greatest success stories in the entire history of vertebrate animals.

We can imagine theropods as consisting of three main assemblages, each of which we'll look at in turn. The first includes those groups that evolved early in theropod history. These theropods are less bird-like than later ones and we'll call them the 'archaic theropods'. The second group includes the megalosaurids, spinosaurids and allosauroids, a collection of mostly large theropods that include deep-headed super-predators as well as long-snouted fish-eaters. Finally, the third group includes the birds and all of the essentially bird-like groups, and is termed Coelurosauria.

'Archaic theropods': herrerasaurs, coelophysoids, neoceratosaurs

The oldest theropods come from the Late Triassic of Argentina and date to about 230 million years ago. *Eodromaeus* is small (just 1.2 m or about 4 ft long) and lightly built, as is typical for the oldest members of all three main dinosaur groups. It's similar to another small Argentinean dinosaur called *Eoraptor*, so much so that *Eoraptor* has often been identified as an early theropod too. Actually, *Eoraptor* possesses a few features of tooth anatomy which suggest that it might be a sauropodomorph. Similarly, *Nyasasaurus*, from even older Middle Triassic rocks in Tanzania, is theropod-like in some details and has also been suggested to be an early theropod. In other respects though, *Nyasasaurus* looks more likely to be a non-dinosaurian dinosauromorph, as we saw on p.37.

With this uncertainty about classification in mind, how can we distinguish early theropods from early sauropodomorphs and ornithischians? Several details of the skeleton seem to be unique to theropods. They have air-filled pockets in the skull and neck bones that the earliest members of the other dinosaur group do not have, and they also have particularly long bones at the ends of the fingers and a foot-shaped bony swelling at the end of the pubic bone in the pelvis. Over time, theropods evolved larger body size and became better able to tackle large prey. *Eodromaeus* and its relatives probably ate insects and mouse-sized animals, but *Herrerasaurus* – a much bigger, more heavily built Late Triassic predator that reached 4.5 m (nearly 15 ft) and perhaps more – was able to kill far larger animals.

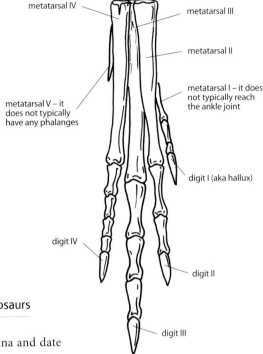

metatarsal IV

metatarsal III

metatarsal II

metatarsal I – it does not typically reach the ankle joint

metatarsal V – it does not typically have any phalanges

digit I (aka hallux)

digit IV

digit II

digit III

Theropods are characterized by a narrow, bird-like foot where the weight is carried on digits II, III and IV. Digits I and II were modified, shortened or even lost entirely in some theropod groups. This is a right foot, the inner edge of the foot being on the right.

Eodromaeus is a very early theropod from Argentina. It would have been a small, lightly built predator, its curved hand claws and serrated teeth suggesting a diet of lizard-sized prey. It remains uncertain whether early dinosaurs like this had a fuzzy covering or not. Only new, well-preserved fossils will resolve the debate.

Some descendants of *Herrerasaurus*-like animals became much larger (as we'll see shortly) but others evolved slender, delicate skulls. The majority of these belong to a group called Coelophysoidea. All are slender, lightweight dinosaurs, mostly between 2 and 3 m (6½ and 10 ft) long. A shallow toothless notch, termed the subnarial gap, is present in the upper jaw and looks suited for the grabbing or holding of small prey. These prey probably included large insects, lizard-like reptiles and baby dinosaurs, and it's also plausible that coelophysoids were waders that caught fish and other aquatic animals on occasion. Hundreds of coelophysoid specimens are known from fossil sites in the USA and southern Africa, most famously from the Upper Triassic rocks of Ghost Ranch in Arizona. These animals seem to have died together while assembled in one or several mega-groups, but why they all died together is unknown.

Coelophysis and kin had some much larger relatives, the most famous of which is the 7 m (23 ft) long *Dilophosaurus* from the Lower Jurassic of the USA. *Dilophosaurus* resembles *Coelophysis* in having a subnarial gap, and in being slender and lightly built. But what makes it special is the presence of twinned, plate-like crests on its snout. Right now, both the function of the crests and the forces that drove their evolution are unknown but it seems likely that they had a display role. Maybe they were used in advertising sexual maturity or breeding condition. As will become clearer as we look at other dinosaur groups, features such as elaborate bony crests, frills, sails and horns were widespread.

Finally among the 'archaic theropods' are a large group of species best termed the neoceratosaurs. Large, heavily built predators belong to this group, the best examples of which are *Ceratosaurus* from the Late Jurassic and a group known as the abelisaurids from the Late Cretaceous. The abelisaurids include *Carnotaurus* from Argentina and *Majungasaurus* from Madagascar. In addition to these robust predators, some lightly built, small theropods called noasaurids also belong among the neoceratosaurs. *Ceratosaurus* means 'horned lizard' and is a reference to its large nasal horn. It also has hornlets in front of its eyes, bony studs running along the midline of its neck, back and tail, and especially long teeth in the upper jaw.

Some abelisaurids also had horns. In *Carnotaurus* these are rounded bosses that project from above its eyes, while *Majungasaurus* has a blunt-tipped horn on its forehead. Several features of abelisaurid anatomy are unusual. Short, broad faces are typical. Several species have reduced arms where the hand and lower arm is short and the fingers are reduced to blunt, clawless stumps. And while some species are long-legged and look like many other large theropods, others – like *Majungasaurus* – had short, robust legs. These features suggest that abelisaurids were behaving in different ways to other big theropods.

Coelophysis is one of the best known early theropods and is known from hundreds of specimens, some of which are complete skeletons. Its shallow, narrow skull suggests a lifestyle that involved the grabbing of small, fast-moving prey.

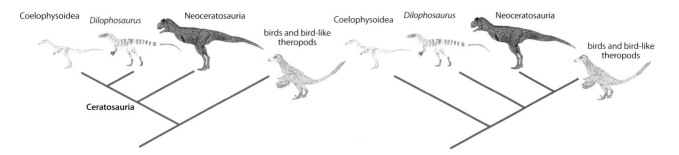

During the 1980s and 1990s most experts thought that coelophysoids, dilophosaurs and neoceratosaurs formed a clade, termed Ceratosauria. Supposedly, all ceratosaurs could be put in a group because they share leg bones that fused together during growth, had fused hip bones and a list of other features. Many of these theropods have horns and head crests, many look 'old-fashioned' relative to the more bird-like theropods, and most are unique to the Gondwanan continents. For these reasons, the idea of Ceratosauria as a distinct theropod clade was an appealing one.

Studies eventually showed however, that the features thought to unite ceratosaurs are found more widely among theropods as a whole. Current evidence indicates that the dilophosaurs and neoceratosaurs are more closely related to the much larger theropod clade that includes *Allosaurus*, *Tyrannosaurus* and birds than they are to the more 'archaic' coelophysoids.

Megalosaurids, spinosaurids and allosauroids

Moving now to the second great assemblage of theropods, we come to a set of groups that are best known for including giant, spectacular predators, some of which are among the largest land-living predators that ever existed. The two main clades from this part of the family tree are the megalosauroids and the allosauroids.

Megalosauroids are named for *Megalosaurus* from the Middle Jurassic of England, the first non-bird dinosaur to be scientifically named. Even today, *Megalosaurus* is known only from fragmentary remains, but certain closely related theropods – *Eustreptospondylus* from the Late Jurassic of England and *Torvosaurus* from the Late Jurassic of the USA and Portugal – are represented by more substantial skeletons. These animals are grouped together in a megalosauroid clade called Megalosauridae. They seem to have been land-living predators that killed other dinosaurs, most probably by inflicting slashing wounds with their large, serrated

Experts have disagreed over the way in which the main theropod groups are related to one another. The cladogram on the left shows several archaic theropod groups clustering together in a clade termed Ceratosauria. Newer studies have overturned this idea, as shown in the cladogram on the right.

Ceratosaurus (opposite right) is a large theropod known from the Late Jurassic of USA and Portugal. Its named means 'horned lizard'. It lived alongside a diverse array of herbivorous dinosaurs, among which were gigantic brachiosaurs like the one shown here.

47

Knife-like, gently curved teeth like this one above are typical of big theropods like megalosauroids and allosauroids. Fine serrations run along the front and rear edges of the tooth's crown. These teeth are built to slice through flesh.

The great sail-backed North African theropod *Spinosaurus* (opposite) – the largest theropod yet discovered – was a fish-eater that frequented estuaries and river deltas. It might have been an especially good swimmer.

The first part of the European spinosaurid *Baryonyx* to be discovered was this giant thumb claw (opposite), 30 cm (12 in) long along its upper curve. Giant curved hand claws like this were typical of spinosaurids.

teeth and perhaps by also making stabbing and raking wounds with their hand claws.

Another group of megalosauroids evolved in a very different direction. These theropods possess an elongate, narrow, crocodile-like snout, and several species have cone-like, unserrated teeth and especially muscular forelimbs. These are the spinosaurids, a Cretaceous group specialized for amphibious, fish-catching lifestyles.

Spinosaurids were first recognized in 1915 when the giant, sail-backed *Spinosaurus* was described from Egypt. Alas, the remains known at the time made it difficult for experts to make sense of this dinosaur, and *Spinosaurus* was imagined as a *Megalosaurus*-like predator with a sail on its back. To make matters worse, the only known specimen was destroyed in a bombing raid during the Second World War. Since the 1970s, tantalizing fragments from Morocco, Libya and elsewhere in northern Africa have built up our view of this dinosaur. Today, enough is known for us to reconstruct *Spinosaurus* with confidence. It was gigantic, perhaps reaching 14 m (46 ft) and 10 t – a size that makes it the biggest theropod we know of. It had short hindlimbs, spreading and probably webbed feet, and a flexible tail. These features suggest that it spent some or even much of its time hunting in the rivers and estuaries that covered North Africa when it was alive. Close relatives of *Spinosaurus* inhabited South America, a distribution which reflects the fact that Africa and South America were connected during the early part of the Cretaceous.

Most of our knowledge of spinosaurids comes not from *Spinosaurus*, but from a group termed the baryonychines, named for *Baryonyx* from the Early Cretaceous of Surrey in England. This was the first spinosaurid which demonstrated the presence of a long, crocodile-like snout in these dinosaurs. Its discovery in 1983 was a sensation, as it was such a spectacular, radically new dinosaur. *Baryonyx* fossils (mostly isolated teeth) have since been discovered at many locations in England, Spain, Portugal and elsewhere, indicating that it occurred widely across the swampy, flooded lowlands of Early Cretaceous Europe. Baryonychines also inhabited Laos and Niger.

Living alongside megalosaurids and spinosaurids in many animal communities of the Jurassic and Cretaceous were the allosauroids, another group of large-bodied theropods. The most familiar member of this group is *Allosaurus* from the Late Jurassic of the USA and Portugal. This large predator – big individuals were 8.5 m (nearly 28 ft) long and weighed over 1.5 t – had tall, triangular horns in front of its eyes, and a deep, narrow snout. *Allosaurus* was one of the first dinosaurs in which computer-assisting modelling techniques were used to examine its behaviour and biology – a subject we discuss further in Chapter 4.

Towards the end of the Jurassic, an allosauroid group termed Carcharodontosauria evolved from an *Allosaurus*-like ancestor. The group name means '*Carcharodon*-toothed lizards' and is a reference to the fact that their teeth are vaguely similar to those of *Carcharodon*, the great white shark. *Carcharodontosaurus* – the first member of the group to be named – was originally discovered in the same Late Cretaceous location in Egypt that also yielded the original *Spinosaurus* specimen, but better fossils have since been found in Morocco.

Close relatives of *Carcharodontosaurus* come from Argentina and Brazil, and include *Mapusaurus*, *Giganotosaurus* and *Tyrannotitan*. All were gigantic, heavily built predators, in some cases reaching 13 m (42 ft) and 6 or 7 t. In other words, they were similar in size to (or even larger than) *Tyrannosaurus*. The size, heavily built proportions and big, blade-like teeth of these giants suggest that they attacked and killed big dinosaurs like sauropods and may even have evolved in step with them. Not all carcharodontosaurians were like this. A Cretaceous group termed the megaraptorans were small and lightly built, and possessed slender, elongate hindlimbs, long arms and large hand claws. Members of this small, lightweight group survived to the end of the Cretaceous.

Coelurosaurs: tyrants and ostrich mimics

We now come to the third and final theropod group, the clade Coelurosauria. Birds belong here, as do their close relatives the oviraptorosaurs, the dromaeosaurids (the group that includes *Velociraptor*) and the ostrich mimics or ornithomimosaurs. Key features uniting these dinosaurs include an especially large air-filled opening on the side of the snout, an increased number of air-filled spaces in the back of the skull, and arms and hands that are longer than those of other theropod groups. Tyrannosauroids or tyrant dinosaurs are coelurosaurs, and thus more closely related to birds than to earlier giant theropods like allosauroids. Indeed, tyrannosauroids share with other coelurosaurs a large brain, a long, narrow foot, a long pelvis, and a tail that is shorter and more lightweight than that of other theropods. As tyrannosauroids evolved larger size and more strongly built skulls and bodies, they came to resemble megalosauroids and allosauroids. The evolutionary process whereby members of distantly related groups come to resemble one another due to specialization for the same

Several early tyrannosauroids are known from the Late Jurassic and Early Cretaceous of North America, Europe and Asia. *Eotyrannus*, is from southern England. It had long, slender hands and features of the snout and jaw consistent with a powerful crushing bite. This diagram only depicts those bones (or parts of bones) discovered so far.

lifestyle is called convergence. It seems to have been a common occurrence among dinosaurs.

Until the 1990s, all tyrannosauroids known from partial or complete skeletons were members of the giant, short-armed group Tyrannosauridae. We now have good fossils of older tyrannosauroids from the Early Cretaceous and Jurassic. These include *Guanlong*, *Dilong* and *Yutyrannus* from China, and *Eotyrannus* and *Juratyrant* from England. It also turns out that theropods which have been known for much longer – like *Proceratosaurus* from England, first described in 1910 – are additional early members of the tyrannosauroid group.

The majority of early tyrannosauroids are less than 4 m (13 ft) long and are similar in size to related coelurosaur groups. They have longer arms and hands than tyrannosaurids, three fingers, and shallow, lightweight skulls that lack the bone-crunching specializations of tyrannosaurids. At least two of them (*Dilong* and *Yutyrannus*) preserve a fuzzy body covering formed of hair-like filaments. Filaments of this sort are seen widely across coelurosaurs. *Yutyrannus*, at 9 m (30 ft) long, is special in being one of the largest theropods yet discovered with a fuzzy covering.

Ostrich mimics – or ornithomimosaurs – are also coelurosaurs, and they probably emerged from an ancestor that was closely related to the earliest tyrannosauroids. As indicated by the name, ornithomimosaurs are ostrich-shaped overall. The toothless jaws and long, powerfully muscled hindlimbs of the best-known species suggest that they lived in an ostrich-like way. They were probably omnivores that browsed on shrubs

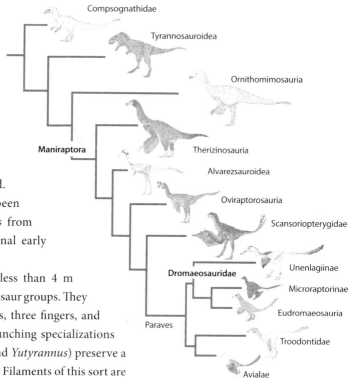

Compsognathidae
Tyrannosauroidea
Ornithomimosauria
Maniraptora
Therizinosauria
Alvarezsauroidea
Oviraptorosauria
Scansoriopterygidae
Unenlagiinae
Dromaeosauridae
Microraptorinae
Eudromaeosauria
Paraves
Troodontidae
Avialae

This simplified phylogeny shows the relationships between the main lineages within Coelurosauria, the theropod clade that includes birds and all of the more bird-like groups. Tyrannosauroids and ornithomimosaurs are outside the clade – called Maniraptora – that includes those more bird-like lineages.

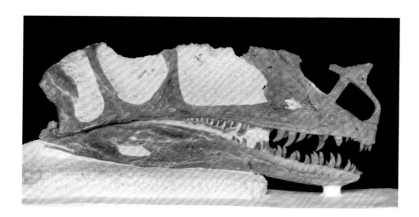

Proceratosaurus from the Middle Jurassic of England is the oldest tyrannosauroid yet discovered. Its skull is just 29 cm (11½ in) long and preserves the base of some sort of nasal crest or horn.

and trees, grabbed small animals, fruits and seeds with their jaw tips, and used speed to escape danger.

But not all ornithomimosaurs were like this. Early species had small teeth lining parts of their jaws. Some only had a few teeth, but one had an incredible 230 or so in total. This multi-toothed dinosaur is *Pelecanimimus polyodon* from the Early Cretaceous of Spain. Its numerous teeth suggest an unusual lifestyle, but we have no additional information on what it was doing or how it was living. Even more remarkable is *Deinocheirus* from the Late Cretaceous of Mongolia, which was long known only from its forelimbs, shoulder bones and a few ribs. Each arm is 2.4 m (nearly 8 ft) long, but the lack of other remains left experts guessing as to the complete appearance of this giant. The answer was revealed in 2014 when the discovery of new remains showed that *Deinocheirus* has a great hump on its back, short, stocky hindlimbs, and a long, duckbilled snout and deep lower jaw. At 11 m (36 ft) long and over 6 t, it was one of the largest theropods of all, though like other ornithomimosaurs it probably mostly ate plants.

More coelurosaurs: the maniraptorans

Finally, we come to the maniraptorans. The name 'maniraptoran' means 'predators that grab with their hands' and refers to the long-fingered, big-clawed hands of these dinosaurs. Some were large, but others were similar in size to chickens or crows. Probably all were covered in a thick, bird-like plumage. The group contains at least six major lineages. The most familiar of these is Avialae, the group that includes birds and their closest relatives,

Small, ground-dwelling theropods were a persistent feature of Mesozoic habitats. This reconstruction shows *Mei long*, an early member of the maniraptoran group Troodontidae. *Mei long* was named in 2004. Its name means 'sleeping dragon' because the first specimen to be discovered was curled up in a sleeping position.

and the group that has to be regarded as the most successful theropod and dinosaur group of them all. We look at bird history and evolution more in Chapter 5.

Beyond Avialae, the most bird-like maniraptorans are the troodontids and the dromaeosaurids. These groups were named for the mid-sized, North American Late Cretaceous dinosaurs *Troodon* and *Dromaeosaurus*, respectively. *Troodon* is a long-legged theropod with big eyes and sensitive ears, and its coarsely serrated teeth suggest a diet that perhaps included leaves and fruit as well as small animals. *Troodon* was similar in weight to a small adult human. Other troodontids – ranging from crow-sized to *Troodon*-sized – inhabited woodlands, shrublands, deserts and other habitats during the Middle and Late Jurassic as well as the Cretaceous.

While fox-sized *Dromaeosaurus* is the namesake member of Dromaeosauridae, it's far from the most familiar member of its group. As we saw in Chapter 1, one dromaeosaurid in particular – *Deinonychus* from the Early Cretaceous of the USA – was instrumental in changing our view of dinosaurs. *Deinonychus* was about 4 m (13 ft) long, similar in weight to a large wolf, and equipped with large, strongly curved hand claws as well as enormous, hooked claws on each of its second toes. Unusually shaped toe bones show us that these 'sickle-claws' were held up off the ground when the animal walked or ran.

Once scientists became familiar with the anatomy of *Deinonychus* it became clear that a Late Cretaceous theropod discovered way back in the 1920s was actually a very close relative. This animal is *Velociraptor* from Mongolia and China, a smaller, desert-dwelling dromaeosaurid. If you're wondering why the scaly creatures in the *Jurassic World* and *Jurassic Park* movies are called *Velociraptor*, it's because the movie-makers decided to follow the (now abandoned) idea that *Deinonychus* and *Velociraptor* are so similar that they should be given the same name.

Thanks to the enormous surge in dinosaur discoveries since the 1980s, our knowledge of dromaeosaurid diversity has increased substantially. In 1993, the discovery of a giant dromaeosaurid, perhaps five times heavier than *Deinonychus*, was announced from the USA. This animal is *Utahraptor*, and it and similar animals show that dromaeosaurids evolved to a large size on several occasions. At the other end of the size scale, the year 2000 saw the naming of crow-sized *Microraptor* from China, good fossils of which preserve long feathers on the forelimbs, on the end of the tail, and

Predatory maniraptorans like *Deinonychus* were built like large, ground-running birds. Backturned pubic bones in the hips were typical, as was an unusual raised second toe with a large, strongly curved claw.

on the hindlimbs too. These feathers are not just long, they're of the shape associated with gliding or flapping. How *Microraptor* flew – and whether it flew at all – has been the subject of substantial investigation, and we look further at *Microraptor*'s behaviour and lifestyle in Chapter 4. We also know of a mostly Gondwanan dromaeosaurid group called the unenlagiines. These have especially long, slender snouts and may have been fish-catching predators of lakes and rivers.

Also closely related to avialans, dromaeosaurids and troodontids are the bizarre scansoriopterygids of Middle and Late Jurassic China. Scansoriopterygids are tiny theropods, with total lengths of 30 cm (12 in) or less as fossils. They were longer than this in life because of streamer-like tail feathers that emerged from the ends of their short tails. Short snouts, sharp teeth that project forwards out of the mouth, and weird hands where the third fingers are far longer than the other two are additional scansoriopterygid features. This hand configuration is very unusual, since in most theropods the second finger is normally the longest. One scansoriopterygid – *Yi qi*, named in 2015 – reveals how these long third fingers helped support a membrane that stretched from the hand to the edge of the body. A rod-like bone emerged from the wrist and also helped to support this membrane. As remarkable as it seems, these small, long-fingered maniraptorans were apparently gliding (or fluttering, or flapping) with membranous wings, despite belonging to a group where feathered forelimbs were otherwise the norm.

Bird-like maniraptorans like troodontids and dromaeosaurids can be considered the most typical members of Maniraptora. We know of other maniraptoran groups that are far less typical, some of which are downright bizarre. Oviraptorosaurs ranged from less than 1 m (3¼ ft) to over 8 m (26 ft) in length, and typically have short, parrot-like skulls, sometimes topped with a hollow crest. Most were toothless, with sharp beaks, and were probably omnivores or herbivores. Several have been found preserved sat on top of egg-filled nests, in a very bird-like brooding pose. Alvarezsaurids were small, lightly built maniraptorans with short, strongly built arms that bore a massively enlarged, thickened thumb and thumb claw. The remaining fingers are either tiny remnants or lacking altogether, depending on the species. These unusual forelimbs look like digging tools, and a popular idea about the behaviour of these animals is that they were ant- or termite-eaters that broke open rotting wood to feed on insects.

Then there are the therizinosaurs. The name *Therizinosaurus* means 'scythe lizard' and was given to the first member of this group to be

Alvarezsaurids must have been fast runners, but their weirdest feature was a shortened, muscular forelimb. *Mononykus* from the Late Cretaceous of Mongolia, described in 1993, was the first member of the group to become well known. It was about 1 m (3¼ ft) long.

Yi qi from the Late Jurassic of China (opposite) shows that one maniraptoran group – the scansoriopterygids – possessed membranous wings. These were small predators or omnivores that probably climbed in trees and ate insects and plant parts.

The beautifully preserved skull of the Late Cretaceous therizinosaur *Erlikosaurus* from Mongolia preserves the toothless beak region, small cheek teeth and large nostril opening typical of this group.

recognized – a giant animal from the Late Cretaceous of Mongolia, originally misidentified as a huge turtle-like reptile. The biggest of its scythe-shaped hand claws is about 70 cm (28 in) long. Additional members of the group discovered since the 1970s have shown that therizinosaurs were not turtle-like at all. They were actually short-tailed, long-necked maniraptorans. Their beaked, toothless jaw tips, leaf-shaped cheek teeth, broad hips, chunky hindlimbs and short, broad feet show that they weren't predators. Instead, they were slow-moving herbivores that perhaps used their giant hand claws to break down or tear at branches. Or maybe those big claws were needed as defence against the predatory theropods that therizinosaurs lived alongside, such as megaraptorans and tyrannosauroids. Like other maniraptorans, therizinosaurs were covered in feathers. *Beipiaosaurus* from the Early Cretaceous of China has filaments covering its body, limbs and tail, and spine-like and strap-like filaments sprouting from its body too. Maybe these functioned as extra protection from predation, or helped provide camouflage.

As mentioned already, the last few decades have seen an explosion in the number of recognized Mesozoic dinosaur species. While these new dinosaurs come from countries across the globe, a great many of them come from China, and especially from the Jurassic and Cretaceous rocks of Liaoning Province in the far east of the country. Many of these new Chinese dinosaurs are maniraptorans, and they have dramatically improved our knowledge of maniraptoran evolution and biology.

Many of these new maniraptoran species are small, primitive, early members of their groups, and one thing they show is that the early members of all of these groups were similar in appearance and lifestyle. If you were to travel back in time and be confronted with these animals, it's highly unlikely that you would be able to work out which one belonged to which group. Ultimately, the only group that survived were the birds, but – back then – birds were simply one among many groups of small, similar, feathered maniraptorans.

SAUROPODS AND KIN: THE SAUROPODOMORPHS

Diplodocus, *Brachiosaurus* and their relatives belong to a major group of saurischian dinosaurs termed sauropods. All were large or stupendously large, long-necked herbivores that walked permanently on all fours, and their jaws and teeth reveal obvious specialization for a lifestyle

Advanced sauropods like *Diplodocus* (opposite below) are unmistakeable, combining pillar-like limbs and an extremely long neck and tail. But many other features of the sauropod skeleton are weird too, like their skulls and columnar hands.

that involved the cropping and eating of leaves, fern fronds and other plant parts. Sauropods are famous for the incredible size they achieved, but we also know them thanks to their fantastically long necks. In some species, the neck was four or five times longer than the body, was formed of as many as 15 vertebrae, and was more than 10 m (33 ft) long. It's generally agreed among scientists that the neck was a food-gathering structure that gave these dinosaurs a competitive advantage over other species when it came to how much foliage they could reach. Despite this agreement, argument continues over the way in which the neck was held, how flexible it was, and how it might have been used.

Sauropods are much more than giant herbivores with super-long necks. They also evolved novel ways of supporting a tremendous amount of weight through unique modifications of their hands, feet and limb bones; they developed an extremely elaborate system of air-filled tubes, pockets and chambers throughout the skeleton; and they evolved a digestive system that enabled them to extract energy from huge quantities of low-quality plant material. Scientists interested in sauropods have looked at living birds, crocodiles and big mammals in their efforts to better understand the biology and anatomy of these extinct giants, but the problem remains that no living animal is that much like a sauropod. We'll return to issues of sauropod biology later on (see pp. 109, 132 and 174).

For years, our knowledge of how the sauropod body form evolved was shrouded in mystery. We've long known of saurischians that are

Eoraptor

Plateosaurus

Melanorosaurus

Shunosaurus

Sauropoda

Cetiosaurus

Mamenchisauridae

Turiasauria

Diplodocoidea

Macronaria

Camarasaurus

Brachiosaurus

Titanosauria

This simplified sauropodomorph cladogram shows how the early members of the group were bipedal and far smaller than the giant sauropods that evolved later on. The majority of sauropod species belong to the advanced lineages Diplodocoidea and Macronaria.

clearly not sauropods but are more closely related to them than they are to other dinosaurs. These animals resemble sauropods in being long-necked and often quite large, but differ from them in mostly being bipedal, in having teeth and jaws suited for an omnivorous way of life, and in lacking those weight-bearing specializations of the limbs. Among the best known of these sauropod relatives are *Plateosaurus* from the Late Triassic of Germany, Switzerland and elsewhere in Europe, and *Massospondylus* from the Early Jurassic of South Africa, Lesotho and Zimbabwe. All of these animals are, together with sauropods, united within a clade termed Sauropodomorpha – a group that originated in the Triassic from the same saurischian ancestor that also gave rise to theropods. For much of the 20th century, sauropodomorphs like *Plateosaurus* and *Massospondylus* were collectively termed prosauropods. This name has fallen out of fashion as it's been discovered that 'prosauropods' are not a clade but a series of lineages, some of which are very closely related to sauropods while others are not.

The very oldest sauropodomorphs were very different from sauropods, and indeed from all big-bodied sauropodomorph species. They were small (less than 1.5 m or 5 ft long in total), lightly built bipeds with blade-like teeth and large, strongly curved hand claws borne on long, slender fingers. *Eoraptor* from the Late Triassic of Argentina is a classic example. It's so unspecialized, relative to later sauropodomorphs, that it was originally interpreted as a theropod, and it remains difficult to be precisely sure where it, and similar forms, belong within the saurischian family tree. *Eoraptor* and similar forms were probably predators that also ate leaves, though it remains unknown how their diet was partitioned – were they mostly eating animals, or mostly eating plants? We can't say until we find a specimen with stomach contents or some other direct evidence for diet.

During the course of the Triassic, *Eoraptor*-like animals gave rise to larger, longer-necked sauropodomorphs that became increasingly dedicated to a diet of plants. *Saturnalia* from the Late Triassic of Brazil looks like a stretched, small-headed version of *Eoraptor*. It has a longer neck and body than *Eoraptor*, and a skull that's smaller relative to the whole length of the animal (*Saturnalia* was about 2 m or 6½ ft long in total). This new, longer-necked, smaller-headed body form proved highly successful, and a dynasty of bipedal, mostly herbivorous sauropodomorphs occurred on most continents for the rest of the Triassic and much of the Early Jurassic.

Until recently, early sauropodomorphs like *Plateosaurus* and *Massospondylus* were often depicted as capable of walking and running on all fours by placing the palms of their hands flat on the ground. Studies

that involve manipulating the bones and joints of three-dimensional skeletons and digital modelling work show that poses of this sort could not be achieved. The forelimbs of these dinosaurs were fixed in a 'palms-inwards' posture, meaning that the arms and wrists could not be rotated to allow the palms to face downwards. This means the hands could not be placed on the ground for support and that these animals must have walked on their hindlimbs alone. A hand posture of this sort is also typical of theropods and is still seen in birds today.

Other pieces of evidence strengthen the view that *Plateosaurus* and its relatives were bipeds and not quadrupeds. For one thing, their hands look better suited to be food-grabbers or weapons than walking aids. And their proportions overall are more in keeping with a two-legged pose – the forelimbs are so short relative to the hindlimbs that the four-legged running pose suggested by some experts looks extremely unlikely.

At some point during their history, sauropodomorphs made the switch from a two-legged, short-armed body shape to a four-legged, long-armed one. We know that this had happened by about 207 million years ago, during the Late Triassic, since we have fossils of big, quadrupedal sauropodomorphs from this time. The animals concerned include *Melanorosaurus* and *Antetonitrus* from South Africa, and *Lessemsaurus* from Argentina. These giant sauropodomorphs overlapped in size with many of the sauropod species that would evolve later on.

The forelimbs of *Antetonitrus* appear to be halfway between the grasping, lightweight arms and hands present in *Plateosaurus*-type sauropodomorphs and the column-like, weight-supporting arms and hands seen in sauropods. It seems that the radius – the arm bone that extends from the 'thumb side' of the wrist to the elbow – changed

Plateosaurus from the Late Triassic of Europe is known from numerous specimens, some of which are essentially complete. Computer modelling has allowed experts to work out how this animal moved and what its range of postures were.

Antetonitrus from South Africa is one of the oldest sauropodomorphs in which the hands and arms were specialized for weight-bearing. It was a large, bulky-bodied, long-necked herbivore or omnivore that perhaps reached 10 m (33 ft) long. This diagram only depicts those bones (or parts of bones) discovered so far.

its position during evolution, forcing the hand to change from a 'palms-inwards' pose to one where the palm was facing backwards. This now meant that the fingers could be planted squarely on the ground, and it seems that they then became better suited for carrying weight.

Sauropod origins and anatomy

If we look back at everything we've just learnt, it's obvious that sauropodomorph fossils reveal an excellent record of the evolutionary changes that occurred during the early history of this group. Small, bipedal, lightly built sauropodomorphs appeared during the Late Triassic and seem to have been mostly carnivorous. From animals like this, far bigger, more heavily built species evolved with longer necks, smaller skulls, and teeth more suited for a leaf-eating diet, though pointed teeth at the front of their jaws show that they were probably still omnivores. Several groups of larger, longer-necked sauropodomorphs spread around the world and were a constant presence in numerous environments for over 30 million years. Through changes in hand, foot, arm and leg anatomy, further increases in body size, and other changes, one lineage evolved into sauropods.

It's obvious from the shapes of sauropod bodies and limbs that they were land-living animals. Their chests are typically deep as well as relatively narrow, their limbs are usually long and slim, and their hands and feet are compact and not all that big compared to the size of the animal. The way in which sauropod teeth were worn down shows that they were eating land-living plants like conifers and ferns, and the majority of sauropod fossils come from environments that were seasonally arid, parkland-style open woodlands. Thousands of sauropod tracks and eggs were preserved in such habitats.

Surprisingly, despite all of this evidence, there was a time during the late 19th and early 20th centuries when sauropods were thought to be aquatic animals, dedicated to a life of eating water plants and lounging and floating in pools and lakes. The long neck was imagined as a special feature that allowed these animals to reach the water's surface while standing on the lake floor, and the nostrils were thought to be positioned on top of the head so that they poked above the surface when the sauropod needed to take a breath. It's not entirely clear where these aquatic ideas came from. One possibility is that Richard Owen's original misidentification of the English Middle Jurassic sauropod *Cetiosaurus* as a whale-like marine reptile influenced those other scientists that followed him. Another is that early misinterpretations of sauropod-yielding rock layers as being deposited in gargantuan tropical swamplands influenced ideas about sauropod behaviour.

As usual though, it's not accurate to imply that all scientists thought the same thing throughout the whole of this timeframe. In the UK, Gideon Mantell in 1852 and John Phillips in 1870 both regarded sauropods as land-living animals, and Othniel Marsh and Edward Cope, the great American dinosaur specialists of the late 1800s, also thought of sauropods as land-living, giraffe-like browsers in their publications of 1877. Elmer Riggs – describer of the new, long-armed Late Jurassic sauropod *Brachiosaurus* – also argued for a dedicated land-living lifestyle for sauropods in several publications during the early 1900s. The final thing worth saying here is that even the modern view of fully terrestrial sauropods doesn't entirely remove the possibility that some species might have lounged in water or swam on occasion, or foraged in lakes and rivers for water plants. For the most part though, sauropods were clearly as terrestrial as modern elephants or giraffes.

Sauropod limbs are a lot stranger than might be assumed. The bones of their forelimbs are long and slender in some species, short and thick in others, but always held in a column-like arrangement ideal for supporting weight. Sauropod hands are especially odd and one of the most interesting evolutionary transformations that occurred in sauropod history concerns how a hand originally adapted for grasping and fighting changed into a weight-supporting, column-shaped structure. Sauropods did not walk with

A few sauropods were very odd and did not conform to the long-necked, long-tailed shape typical of the group. *Brachytrachelopan* from the Late Jurassic of Argentina is an unusual short-necked sauropod. However, it still had the column-like limbs and distinctive, weight-supporting hands.

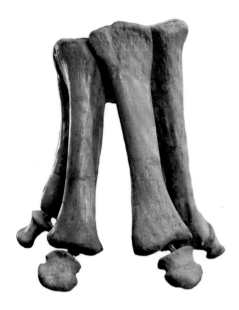

their fingers spreading out, or with the palm touching the ground. Instead, the long bones that form the palm of the hand – the metacarpals – were arranged in a semi-circular, vertical block that was concave at the back. The bones of the fingers were short, reduced in number and even missing altogether in the members of most sauropod groups. This includes claws: advanced sauropods lacked hand claws altogether except for the one on the thumb, and even this was missing in a great many species.

In contrast, sauropod feet are broader, longer structures where the five toes are continuous with the massive, oval or rounded foot sole. The ankle joint was close to the ground, and both footprints and articulated skeletons show that a giant fatty pad cushioned the underside and kept the metatarsals raised up off the ground. Three or four large, curved claws projected from the toes on the inside of the foot. This type of foot is very clearly a weight-supporting structure, and the fact that sauropod feet are almost always much larger than the hands matches other evidence showing that most of their weight was carried in the back part of the body, close to the hips.

The sauropod hand is unique. Claws and hooves were often absent, and the metacarpals – the bones that form the palm of the hand – were arranged in a tube or column. This is the hand of the African brachiosaur *Giraffatitan*.

Plateosaurus and its relatives were not as specialized for plant-eating as the sauropods that evolved later on. Sauropods had wider mouths than animals like *Plateosaurus*, and teeth more suited for the chopping and slicing of plants.

Archaic sauropods

Early sauropods from the Late Triassic and Early Jurassic show how *Melanorosaurus*-like animals evolved a limb anatomy supremely adapted for the supporting of great weight. At the same time, changes in the skull meant that these dinosaurs became better able to crop large mouthfuls of food. Sauropod snouts are far broader than those of earlier sauropodomorphs, their lower jaws are U-shaped rather than V-shaped, and unusual bony plates grew alongside the bases of the teeth, to reinforce the teeth during biting. Massively enlarged bony nostrils are also an obvious feature of early sauropods. We aren't sure why sauropods evolved such giant noses. Perhaps they were related to temperature control, an ability to make loud, resonating calls, or an enhanced sense of smell. Even before the start of the Jurassic, some of these earliest sauropods had become giants with column-like arms and legs. *Isanosaurus* from the Late Triassic of Thailand, for example, might have reached 15 m (50 ft) in length.

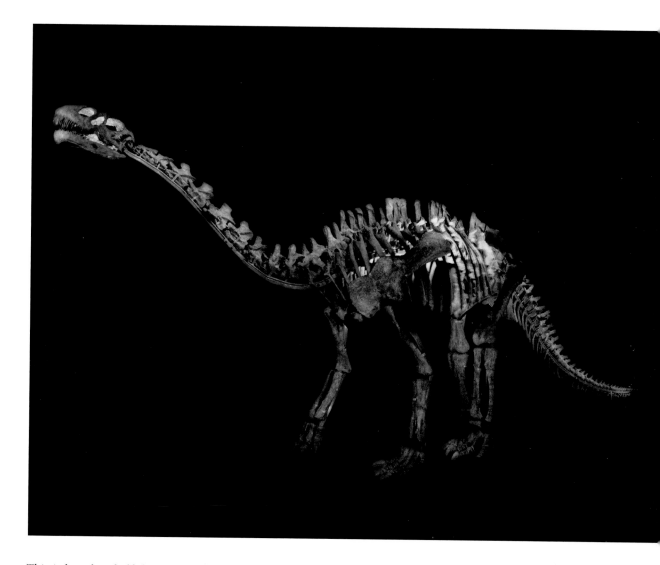

This is less than half the size of the sauropods that evolved later on, but was gigantic compared to earlier sauropodomorphs.

By the Early and Middle Jurassic, sauropods similar to those of later times had evolved. These include *Vulcanodon* from Zimbabwe and *Shunosaurus* from China. *Shunosaurus* is unusual because it had a spiny club at the end of its tail. Several sauropod species possess bony tail clubs or tail spines of this sort. Perhaps these were used as a defence against theropods, or maybe they were used in mating or territorial battles. Wear marks show that the teeth of these early sauropods met at their tips – an unusual feature that isn't typical for dinosaurs but was a key feature of sauropods. Presumably this tooth-to-tooth contact evolved because it enabled quick cropping of large mouthfuls of plant material.

Shunosaurus is one of the best known archaic sauropods. At about 10 m (30 ft) in length, it was far bigger than most earlier sauropodomorphs, and better able to support massive weight. Later sauropods became larger still.

Turiasaurs, mamenchisaurids and cetiosaurs

Shunosaurus-like ancestors gave rise to a large diversity of new sauropod groups that evolved in the Middle and Late Jurassic. Larger size, an increasingly complex set of air sacs extending through the bones of the skeleton and even longer necks all evolved in these animals. They spread to all continents and were by far the dominant group of large herbivores

Cetiosaurus is known from two partial skeletons and numerous fragmentary remains. It seemed to have been a generalized, 'average' sauropod that lacked the unusual features typical of later sauropod groups.

worldwide during Late Jurassic times. One of the most significant of these animals from a historical point of view is *Cetiosaurus*, discovered in the Middle Jurassic rocks of England and named by Richard Owen in 1841. Later discoveries from the USA were far more complete than *Cetiosaurus* but it remains an important animal in terms of our knowledge of sauropod evolution. It has 12 or 13 neck bones, and a neck and body shape which suggest that it was a generalist herbivore, able to feed from tall trees, from the ground and from levels in between.

Cetiosaurus is close to the ancestry of several other sauropod groups. Among these are the turiasaurs, a group of species that are so far entirely limited to western Europe. Large, spoon-shaped teeth with heart-shaped crowns are a distinctive feature of this group, and they also tend to have strongly built forelimbs. Some of them were enormous and among the biggest sauropods of all. *Turiasaurus*, named in 2006, was perhaps more than 25 m (82 ft) long and over 40 t.

A small group of mostly east Asian sauropods possess especially long necks formed of long and low vertebrae. These are the mamenchisaurids, named for *Mamenchisaurus* from the Late Jurassic of China. Mamenchisaurid limbs are often long and slender and they have a higher number of neck vertebrae than other sauropod groups (over 15, compared to the ancestral number of 12 or so). These features suggest that they were high-browsers, eating at heights well above those used by other sauropods and other dinosaurian herbivores. Again, some mamenchisaurids were

Mamenchisaurus is one the longest-necked sauropods of all. Some museum mounts (like this one) incorrectly give it a long, shallow, *Diplodocus*-like skull. Its skull actually had a far shorter, deeper snout.

enormous, exceeding 30 m (about 100 ft) and perhaps 75 t. In the largest species, the neck might have been an incredible 17 m (56 ft) long. Another peculiar feature of this group is the presence of a small tail club in several of the species. Again, the function of these clubs is unknown.

Diplodocoids and macronarians

The majority of sauropod species belong to one of two major groups, both of which evolved during the middle of the Jurassic and then persisted until the end (or close to the end) of the Cretaceous. These two groups are the diplodocoids and the macronarians. Diplodocoids contain several groups that generally have long, squared-off snouts, peg-like teeth and long, whip-like tail tips. They also have short, powerfully built forelimbs. *Diplodocus*, *Apatosaurus* and *Brontosaurus* – all of which are from the famous Upper Jurassic Morrison Formation of the USA – are diplodocoids and belong to a clade called Diplodocidae.

The relatively small, short-necked dicraeosaurids and the weird rebbachisaurids of the Cretaceous are also members of the diplodocoids. These two groups include some of the strangest sauropods of all. *Amargasaurus* – a dicraeosaurid from the Early Cretaceous of Argentina – has long, twinned spines growing upwards and backwards from its neck bones. *Nigersaurus* – a small rebbachisaurid from the Early Cretaceous of Niger – has a delicate skull where the tooth rows of the upper and lower jaws have both rotated so that they run along the leading edges of the jaws, not along their sides.

The long necks, unusual snouts and peg-like teeth of diplodocids like *Diplodocus* and *Apatasaurus* suggest that they were specialized for a distinctive lifestyle, since they really are very different from other sauropod groups. One idea is that they were high-browsers that reached up into the canopy and cropped leaves growing out of reach of other plant-eaters, perhaps regularly rearing up to stand in a two-legged posture. Another idea is that they reached down to feed on ground-hugging plants and were specialized low-browsers. We talk more about diplodocoid feeding strategies in Chapter 4.

In contrast to diplodocoids, macronarians typically have big, bony nostrils (this explains the name macronarian, which means 'big nose') and a more rounded snout. The Late Jurassic sauropods *Camarasaurus* and *Brachiosaurus* from the USA and *Giraffatitan* from Tanzania are macronarians, as are the titanosaurs, the

Diplodocoid skulls – like that of *Diplodocus* here – are unusual compared to those of other sauropods. The nostril openings are located high up on the forehead. However, the traces of blood vessels and other structures show that the fleshy nostrils were likely located closer to the edge of the mouth.

most diverse and longest-lived sauropod clade of all. It used to be thought that macronarians were especially unusual sauropods that had evolved a remarkably odd skull anatomy compared to early, ancestral sauropod species. Now that we know that early sauropods like *Shunosaurus* possessed blunt snouts and big nostrils, we understand that macronarian-like skulls were typical for sauropods, and that it's the low-snouted, small-nosed skulls of diplodocoids that are unusual.

A burst of newly discovered titanosaurs from the Americas, Europe, Africa, Madagascar and Asia has shown that this group evolved enormous diversity during its history. Some titanosaurs were gargantuan and among the biggest of sauropods, and hence the biggest ever land-living animals. *Argentinosaurus* from the Late Cretaceous of Argentina was perhaps 30 m (about 100 ft) long and exceeded 50 t. *Dreadnoughtus* – also from the Late Cretaceous of Argentina – was similar in length and perhaps approached 40 t. Many other titanosaurs were 'mid-sized' as sauropods go – say, 14 m (46 ft) long or less, and less than 15 t. Yet others, such as *Magyarosaurus* from Romania, were positively tiny in sauropod terms, and were only 8 m (26 ft) long or less, perhaps weighing just 1 t.

Titanosaurs were diverse in shape and proportion. Some, like *Saltasaurus* from the Late Cretaceous of Argentina, had short, stocky limbs and an unexceptional neck. Others were more slender and had an extremely long neck, like *Rapetosaurus* from the Late Cretaceous of Madagascar. As macronarians, it follows that titanosaurs began their history with broad, relatively short snouts and broad-crowned teeth, and at least some titanosaurs were like this. Others had long snouts and narrow-crowned teeth. Some of these long-snouted titanosaurs had an expanded, almost 'duckbilled' mouth. These features show that titanosaurs adapted to several feeding strategies during the Cretaceous, and perhaps filled some of the roles occupied by diplodocoids earlier on in the Mesozoic, another example of evolutionary convergence.

As recently as the 1990s it was thought that sauropods were a mostly Jurassic event and that they had largely disappeared by the Cretaceous. We now know that this view was completely inaccurate, and that sauropods were a major presence on many continents throughout much of the Cretaceous. And, rather than being stagnant or static in evolutionary terms, they were constantly evolving new anatomical features and new ways of cropping plants.

This *Camarasaurus* skull displays the features typical of macronarian sauropods – the jaws are short and heavily built and the bony nostril opening (the big hole at the front) is huge.

ORNITHISCHIANS: ARMOURED DINOSAURS, DUCKBILLS, HORNED DINOSAURS AND KIN

The final, third great dinosaurian group is Ornithischia, the mostly herbivorous clade that includes the armoured ankylosaurs, plated stegosaurs, the often crested, duckbilled hadrosaurs, and the horned ceratopsians. The most familiar ornithischians are large, quadrupedal species, most of which were similar in size to modern rhinos or elephants. But there were also numerous small, bipedal, lightly built species too. The very earliest ornithischians were like this. They were small, bipedal omnivores with grasping hands, similar to the earliest members of Theropoda and Sauropodomorpha.

Several key anatomical features allow even the earliest ornithischians to be distinguished from members of the two other dinosaur groups. One of the most obvious of these is the toothless predentary bone, located at the tip of the lower jaw. In life, this bone was sheathed in beak tissue. It formed a cutting structure that, together with the beak-covered tip of the upper jaw, was used to bite off leaves, twigs and other plant parts. We know that beak tissue was definitely present in ornithischian jaws because these beaks are preserved in place in some fossils. Ornithischians did not rely on their beaked jaw tips alone, of course. They also possessed teeth that were used to slice and mash plant food, and several groups (most notably hadrosaurs and ceratopsians) evolved tooth batteries containing hundreds of tightly packed teeth. We look more at tooth batteries and how they must have worked in Chapter 4.

Another key ornithischian feature concerns the hip girdle. In reptiles generally, the bone at the front of the hips (the pubic bone) is directed forwards and downwards, but that of ornithischians projects backwards and downwards. Why did this unusual configuration evolve? The usual explanation is that this allowed the guts to become larger and extend further back in the body cavity – an advantageous feature for animals that relied on plant food. There are some problems with this idea. One is that other herbivorous dinosaur groups (like sauropodomorphs) didn't evolve back-turned pubic bones when they would surely have been useful. Another is that back-turned pubic bones also evolved in maniraptoran theropods, a group of dinosaurs that almost certainly were

This simplified cladogram of Ornithischia shows how the group consists of three main clades: the armoured thyreophorans, the fairly plain ornithopods, and the horned and bone-headed marginocephalians.

not as dedicated to a diet of plants as were early ornithischians. For now, this aspect of ornithischian evolution remains mysterious and further research is needed.

The earliest ornithischians

The earliest ornithischians include *Pisanosaurus* from Argentina, *Laquintasaura* from Venezuela, and *Eocursor* and *Lesothosaurus* from South Africa and Lesotho. Most of these early animals are from the Early Jurassic but *Pisanosaurus* and *Eocursor* are from the Late Triassic. All come from the southern continents – another indication that early dinosaur evolution mostly happened in Gondwana. They don't appear to be as specialized for herbivory as later ornithischians and were probably omnivorous, eating insects and other small animals as well as the select parts of plants. Beyond this, we know little of their lifestyles or behaviour. Having said that, *Laquintasaura* is intriguing because a large number of individuals died together in the same place. This is suggestive of a social, herd-dwelling lifestyle like that present in the later, more advanced ornithischians of the Late Jurassic and Cretaceous. Maybe ornithischians were highly social animals right from the very start of their evolution.

Laquintasaura from Venezuela is one of the oldest known ornithischians. As is typical for the early members of all dinosaur groups, it was small – less than 1 m (3 ft) long – and with teeth and a body shape suggesting some degree of omnivory.

An especially unusual group termed the heterodontosaurids may be among the earliest of ornithischian groups to evolve. This is suggested by the fact that they have long, grasping hands, similar to those of theropods, and lack many of the advanced features of the teeth and jaws present in the majority of other ornithischian groups. But read on.

The name heterodontosaurid means 'different toothed lizard' and refers to the fact that the jaws of these dinosaurs combine incisor-like, fang-like and molar-like teeth. The cheek teeth look typical of those linked with a herbivorous diet in other ornithischian groups, but the fangs and grasping hands have led some experts to suggest that these dinosaurs might also have preyed on small animals. Heterodontosaurids were initially discovered in rocks dating to the Lower Jurassic but today we know that they survived well beyond this time, since there are also species from the Late Jurassic of China and Early Cretaceous of England. The Chinese heterodontosaurid – *Tianyulong* – is especially important because it preserves long, hair-like filaments on its body and tail. Heterodontosaurids are also interesting in mostly being small. *Fruitadens*, from the Late Jurassic of Colorado, USA, was 75 cm (30 in) long or less as an adult, making it one of the smallest ornithischians yet discovered.

As mentioned earlier, the majority of dinosaur experts favour the view that heterodontosaurids are primitive, 'archaic' members of Ornithischia that evolved early in the history of the group. But heterodontosaurids also possess features seen elsewhere in horned and boneheaded dinosaurs, including large, fang-like upper jaw teeth. The possibility therefore exists that heterodontosaurids are, instead, early members of this horned and boneheaded group, and not 'archaic' members of Ornithischia at all.

The majority of ornithischian species belong to one of three or four major clades, each of which evolved distinct body shapes and ways of life. The first of these is called Thyreophora. This is the armour-plated ornithischian group, best known for including the stegosaurs (or plated dinosaurs) and the ankylosaurs (or armoured dinosaurs). Both groups possess rows of bony plates – termed osteoderms – along the top of the neck, back and tail. The best-known early thyreophoran is *Scutellosaurus* from the Early Jurassic of the USA. This animal was a little over 1 m (3¼ ft)

The skull of *Heterodontosaurus* caused a sensation when discovered in South Africa during the early 1960s. A bony bar can be seen projecting into the eye socket. In life, soft tissue would have connected this bar to the top of the skull, overhanging the eyeball.

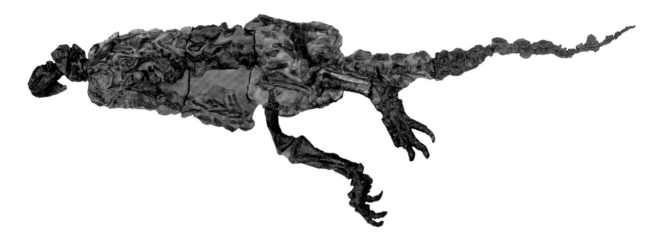

long and the anatomy and proportions of its arms and legs show that it was a biped. Its osteoderms were arranged in several parallel rows and are of simple shape, essentially being just rounded plates of bone with a raised central ridge on the upper surface.

Closely related to *Scutellosaurus* is the larger and more heavily built *Scelidosaurus* from the Early Jurassic of England. The limb proportions of this dinosaur suggest that it was quadrupedal, and it possesses a more extensive and elaborate amount of armour than *Scutellosaurus*. An intriguing thing about *Scelidosaurus* is that some specimens have far more armour than others do. Some possess horns on the skull, thorn-like osteoderms on the limbs, and rows of armour on the body, all of which are lacking from other individuals. Maybe this is evidence that the amount of armour varied between the sexes or that older individuals possessed far more armour than younger ones.

Ankylosaurs: walking fortresses

Over time, a group of *Scelidosaurus*-like thyreophorans evolved larger size, more heavily built limbs, and a larger and more elaborate covering of armour. These eventually gave rise to the ankylosaurs, a group first known from the fossil record of the Middle Jurassic and which persisted right to the end of the Cretaceous. Discussions of ankylosaur history usually focus on the remarkably diverse, extensive body armour evolved by these animals. Sheets of rectangular or oval osteoderms covered much of the neck, back and tail of many ankylosaurs, triangular plates projected sideways from the bodies and tails of some species, and large spines or cones grew upwards from the backs of others. Then there are the

The Early Jurassic thyreophoran *Scelidosaurus* from England is known from several well-preserved specimens. The one shown here was the first to be discovered in 1858. It represents a near-complete articulated skeleton, partially encased in a series of mudstone blocks.

collar-like armour rings present on the necks of some species, the giant, hammer-like bony tail clubs seen in some, and the thorn-like spines arranged along the arms and legs of others.

Ankylosaurs are among the most unusual of dinosaur groups in terms of anatomical structure. The large skull openings that are normally obvious in both saurischians and ornithischians are closed by newly formed bone, and thick, lumpy masses of bone are present across much of the upper surface of the skull. The nostrils are often positioned in peculiar places (sometimes facing forwards, rather than sideways), and the internal anatomy of the nose is surprisingly complicated. Ankylosaur hips are also weird. They're incredibly wide, formed mostly of the big, flat-topped, shelf-like bones called ilia. The dinosaur hip socket is normally an open hole. But in ankylosaurs the hip sockets are cup-like sockets, typically with a complete bony wall on the inner side. Vertebrae along at least part of the backbone are often fused together in ankylosaurs, presumably to provide stiffness to the body and help support the weight of the armour. Finally, ankylosaurian limb bones are often short and robustly built.

Several distinct ankylosaurian groups have been recognized, but the precise way in which they are related is the topic of some argument. Many familiar ankylosaurs belong to the clade Ankylosauridae. Members of this group have short, wide skulls with triangular horns at the skull's rear outer corners. Those ankylosaurs with tail clubs – such as *Ankylosaurus*

Armour of several different sorts covered the ankylosaur body. The different structures shown here all belong to the European Cretaceous ankylosaur *Polacanthus*. The small, clustered, scale-like features formed a pavement across part of the animal's back while the larger, more plate-like objects projected upwards and sideways from the body and tail.

and *Euoplocephalus* from the Late Cretaceous of North America – belong here. Members of a second group, termed Nodosauridae, typically have longer, narrower skulls that are plainer in appearance, though they do tend to have a big rounded lump above and behind each eye. Several nodosaurids have long, massive spines projecting from the neck and shoulder region. In some species, these spines projected outwards and backwards, but in others – like *Edmontonia rugosidens* from the Late Cretaceous of North America – they project outwards and forwards, and sometimes have forked tips.

An additional group – the polacanthids – are recognized by some experts for a group of ankylosaurs from the Early Cretaceous of western Europe and the USA. The best known of these is *Polacanthus* from England and Spain. These dinosaurs have a shield-like plate of armour covering the hip region, and their skulls possess a combination of ankylosaurid-like and nodosaurid-like features. It remains the topic of argument whether polacanthids are closer to nodosaurids or to ankylosaurids, and even whether the group deserves to be recognized at all. They might actually be early members of either one of the two main ankylosaurian groups.

The skull of *Stegosaurus* – the most famous and best known of all stegosaurs – is long and slender, and almost tubular in form. Note that the antorbital fenestra (see p. 32) is strongly reduced and almost closed.

Stegosaurs: plates and spines

Stegosaurs are famous for the namesake member – *Stegosaurus* – from the Late Jurassic of the USA, Portugal and possibly China. This iconic animal is best known for the diamond-shaped plates arranged along its back. Articulated *Stegosaurus* specimens show that the plates were arranged in an asymmetrical, staggered pattern – an odd configuration that contrasts with the more normal, symmetrically paired structures present in other stegosaurs and other thyreophorans. Why and how this asymmetrical plate pattern evolved has so far gone unstudied, and it's difficult to know exactly how it can be studied given that it presumably involved some weird genetic event.

In addition to the plates, *Stegosaurus* possesses a long, shallow skull with a narrow, beaked mouth. It has strongly built, muscular forelimbs, long hindlimbs, and a tail tipped with two pairs of long, conical spines. Studies of stegosaur tail flexibility and muscle strength show us how these tail spines might have been used. We revisit this subject in Chapter 3.

Stegosaurus is actually an unusual member of its group. Firstly, it is much larger than the majority of other stegosaurs. *Stegosaurus* can be as long as 9 m (30 ft), whereas other stegosaurs are more in the region of 4 to 7 m (13 to 23 ft). Secondly, those asymmetrically arranged plates are very different from the symmetrically arranged, far smaller plates or spines of other members of the group. Stegosaurs differ quite considerably with respect to their 'spikiness'. *Stegosaurus* and its relatives only have spines at the tail-tip, but in others – the classic example is *Kentrosaurus* from the Late Jurassic of Tanzania – spines run along the whole of the tail and part of the back too. Thirdly, *Stegosaurus* lacked shoulder spikes. These otherwise seem to be a fairly typical stegosaurian feature: long spines, sometimes with broad, rounded basal sections, projected outwards and backwards from the shoulders of many species. The Chinese stegosaur *Gigantspinosaurus* has enormous shoulder spines that curve outwards and backwards from its body. Each of these spines is similar in length to the animal's entire ribcage.

The ornithopods: *Iguanodon*, the duckbills and their relatives

Less spectacular and unusual than thyreophorans are the second major ornithischian group, the ornithopods. This group occurred worldwide from the Middle Jurassic to the end of the Cretaceous, its many species filling the role of small and mid-sized herbivore in numerous habitats. The biggest ornithopods – hadrosaurs like *Shantungosaurus* from the Late Cretaceous of China – were similar in size to sauropods, reaching 15 m (nearly 50ft) and perhaps 13 t. Ornithopod jaw joints and jaw edges are unlike those of other ornithischians. Over time, the number of teeth in the jaws increased (some members of the group had over a thousand teeth at any one time), and the teeth themselves became more complex in internal structure.

At the 'core' of Ornithopoda is the small, bipedal *Hypsilophodon* from the Early Cretaceous of England, the giant, heavily built Early Cretaceous European *Iguanodon*, and the many crested and crestless duckbilled dinosaurs, or hadrosaurs. Hadrosaurs evolved during the Early Cretaceous from an *Iguanodon*-like animal, most likely in Asia. From here they spread to all continents except Africa and Australasia. *Iguanodon*, the hadrosaurs and a large number of related groups differ from little *Hypsilophodon* in having a U-shaped (rather than V-shaped) predentary bone and a deeper lower jaw. These '*Iguanodon*-like' ornithopods are included within a clade called Iguanodontia.

For much of the 20th century it was thought that virtually all small, bipedal ornithischians were close relatives of *Hypsilophodon*, and all were united in a family called Hypsilophodontidae. Supposedly, this family included archaic ornithischians from the Early Jurassic (like *Lesothosaurus*) as well as large, iguanodontian-like animals like *Tenontosaurus* from the Early Cretaceous of the USA. Good anatomical features that might really demonstrate close links between these animals were never identified and it now seems that several of the ornithopods concerned are not close relatives of *Hypsilophodon* at all, but close relatives or members of Iguanodontia. The robust-bodied rhabdodontids of the European Late Cretaceous are also members of Iguanodontia, and so are the dryosaurids, a Jurassic and Early Cretaceous clade notable for their long, slender feet, short arms and short faces. Dryosaurids are known from England, Tanzania, Niger, the USA and elsewhere. Several ornithischian groups once included within Hypsilophodontidae now seem to be outside the clade that includes *Hypsilophodon* and Iguanodontia and may not even be ornithopods at all. These include the North American zephyrosaurs, thescelosaurs and orodromines, and the Chinese jeholosaurs. Nevertheless, the basic body

Much of ornithopod evolution involved small, swift-running bipeds less than 3 m (10 ft) long. However, during the Jurassic a new ornithopod clade termed Iguanodontia evolved. Iguanodontians eventually gave rise to giant, quadrupedal forms like *Iguanodon* and the hadrosaurs. Recent research indicates that several ornithischian groups previously regarded as ornithopods – including thescelosaurids – are actually outside of the group that includes marginocephalians and ornithopods.

The skulls of iguanodontians – this one (above) belongs to the western European form *Mantellisaurus* – are long-snouted and have a broadened, toothless region at the front. Giant size is a key feature of this group. This skull is 45 cm (18 in) long.

The teeth of *Iguanodon*, *Mantellisaurus* and similar iguanodontians have large, diamond-shaped crowns (above centre) with prominent ribs and coarsely serrated edges. Over time, these crowns were worn down at the tips, as is the case in the tooth on the above right.

Jeholosaurus from the Early Cretaceous of China is a fairly typical small bipedal ornithiscian. A primitive feature is the six teeth at the front of the upper jaw. Later, larger ornithopods lacked teeth in this part of the skull.

plan of all of these groups is similar – all are small bipedal herbivores. Rhabdodontids might have differed from this generalization, as the odd proportions of their limbs and hips hint at the possibility that they might have walked on all fours.

Dinosaurs like dryosaurids show that *Iguanodon* and its relatives, and hadrosaurs and their relatives, all descend from a mid-sized, bipedal herbivore that was a reasonably good runner and had relatively short arms and small hands. Iguanodontians of this new, larger-bodied sort increased in number and diversity during the Early Cretaceous, becoming an important plant-eating component – perhaps the most important plant-eating component – in animal communities across Europe, Asia and North America during the Cretaceous.

Hadrosaurs are the largest and most important of these groups. Equipped with tooth batteries, a broad toothless beak, and able to walk both quadrupedally and bipedally, they evolved a diversity of body sizes and skull shapes. It's often implied that hadrosaurs are all essentially alike, differing only in the shapes of their heads. After all, we know of hadrosaurs with long snouts and expanded, duck-like beaks (like *Edmontosaurus*), of others with deep, down-curving snouts and large nasal cavities (like *Maiasaura*), and of those with solid, spike-like crests (like *Saurolophus*), hollow, plate-like crests (like *Corythosaurus*), and hollow, tube-like crests (like *Parasaurolophus*). Quite why these dinosaurs evolved this array of diverse head crests is an interesting issue that we tackle further in Chapter 4.

The generalization that hadrosaurs 'are all essentially alike' isn't accurate, because the many lineages within the group differ substantially in body shape. Long, slender forelimbs are present in brachylophosaurs and gryposaurs, short and stocky limb proportions are present in parasaurolophines, and a tall bony ridge is present along the top of the back in the lambeosaurines, giving them a finned-backed or hump-backed appearance. Presumably, these differences relate to lifestyle and feeding behaviour.

Margin-headed dinosaurs: the boneheads and horned dinosaurs

Ornithopods share a set of anatomical features with two additional groups: the boneheads or dome-skulled dinosaurs – the pachycephalosaurs – and the ceratopsians, or horned dinosaurs. Ceratopsians are familiar due to the fame of giant, quadrupedal, Late Cretaceous members of the group like *Triceratops*. The majority of ceratopsians possess horns over the nose and eyes as well as a frill that projects upwards and backwards from the skull. Pachycephalosaurs are very different. All are bipedal, and many possess thick, often domed tops to their skulls.

While the best-known pachycephalosaurs and ceratopsians are highly distinct, this is not so when we look at their earliest species. Both groups share features that aren't seen in other ornithischians, the most obvious of which is a shelf of bone that projects backwards from the rear of the skull. Because of the presence of this feature, the two groups are united in the clade Marginocephalia, a name which means 'the margin-headed ones'. As discussed earlier, the possibility exists that heterodontosaurids might be close relatives of this group.

Pachycephalosaurs are one of the most enigmatic dinosaur groups, since the majority of species are known from fragmentary remains. Only one or two good skeletons have been discovered. These show that pachycephalosaurs had broad bodies and hips, short forelimbs, and a long, slender tail. The pachycephalosaur tail is unusual because, in addition to the usual complement of vertebrae, it contains numerous curved bony segments. These are stiffened, bony versions of the normally soft tendons that grow at the edges of the muscle blocks running along the tail. Such features are well known in some fishes (such as the teleosts, the huge group that includes catfishes, salmon, cod and so on), but are otherwise unknown in land-living vertebrates. Quite why pachycephalosaurs evolved these structures is a complete mystery.

A more familiar pachycephalosaurian feature is the flat-topped or domed skull, the edges and sides of

This *Stegoceras* skull from the Late Cretaceous of Canada displays the prominent shelf at the back of the skull typical of marginocephalians. Its small, leaf-shaped teeth look suited for shredding leaves.

The amazing dome-headed skull of *Pachycephalosaurus* from the Late Cretaceous of the USA combines a thick, rounded dome with knobs, lumps and hornlets. The whole animal was about 4.5 m (15½ ft) long.

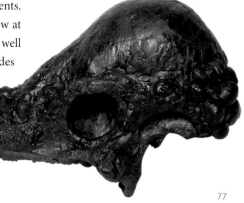

We know comparatively little about the pachycephalosaur body. So far as we can tell, all members of the group had short, slender forelimbs and were fast-running bipeds. The pachycephalosaur shown here is *Prenocephale* from Mongolia and the USA.

which are decorated with bony lumps and hornlets. In the most familiar species – the best example is *Pachycephalosaurus wyomingensis* from the Late Cretaceous of the USA – the domed skull roof is as much as 40 cm (16 in) thick. In others – such as *Homalocephale calathocercos* from the Late Cretaceous of Mongolia – the top of the skull is flat.

Views on how the different pachycephalosaur species might be related to one another are currently in a state of flux. Since the 1970s it has been thought that flat-skulled and dome-skulled pachycephalosaurs represent distinct groups that went their own separate ways after emerging from a common ancestor. But it has since been argued that some flat-skulled species are more closely related to the dome-skulled group than are other flat-skulled species, in which case 'flat-skulled pachycephalosaurs' are not a clade. More recently still, some experts have argued that flat-skulled boneheads are simply the juveniles of dome-skulled ones. We discuss this idea further in Chapter 4.

Ceratopsians are known mostly from the Cretaceous but a few fossils show that the group was also present during the Late Jurassic. The oldest members of the group include *Yinlong* and *Hualianceratops* from China, both of which are small, bipedal dinosaurs less than 2 m (6½ ft) long. Like other early ceratopsians, *Yinlong* lacks horns and a large frill. The back of its skull is deep, broad, has huge openings for the jaw-closing muscles, and possesses rough patches of bone on the cheeks and behind the eyes. Like all ceratopsians (and unlike all other ornithischians) *Yinlong* has a unique bone termed the rostral at the tip of its upper jaw. This hook-shaped bone might have helped strengthen or enlarge the hooked beak that was such an obvious and important part of the ceratopsian skull.

Virtually all early ceratopsians are small, ranging from cat-sized to sheep-sized. A few bipedal ornithischians that have been identified as possible early ceratopsians (like *Albalophosaurus* from the Early Cretaceous of Japan) are not especially different in appearance from bipedal ornithopods. Confidently identified early ceratopsians tend to have narrow beaks, bony lumps or horns on their cheeks, and a short, shelf-like frill. Some were bipedal: a classic example is *Psittacosaurus* from the Early Cretaceous of China, Mongolia and Siberia. Others were quadrupedal, like *Protoceratops* from the Late Cretaceous of China and Mongolia. Virtually all are from eastern Asia where they were a constant presence in dinosaur communities throughout the Cretaceous. They also persisted to the end of the Cretaceous in western North America and parts of Europe.

Around 90 million years ago, a *Protoceratops*-like, Asian or North American ceratopsian gave rise to a lineage of larger animals that started their history with long brow horns, an enlarged frill and a greater number of teeth. The majority of species in this group belong to the clade Ceratopsidae. This is the group that includes *Triceratops*, spiky-frilled *Styracosaurus*, and *Pachyrhinosaurus*, famous for the lump-shaped mass that decorates its snout in place of a horn. All ceratopsids were large – ranging from rhino-sized to elephant-sized – and all had bodies and limbs specialized for a quadrupedal lifestyle. Ceratopsids were abundant in many Late Cretaceous dinosaur communities of western North America. Over 30 different species inhabited the region during this time.

The amazing horns, frills, spines and bony bosses of ceratopsids almost certainly functioned as signalling devices of some sort, and as weapons. How they were used and which pressures led to their evolution in the first place has been controversial. This subject is highly relevant to our understanding of dinosaur behaviour and we return to it in Chapter 4.

Like virtually all ceratopsids, *Chasmosaurus* had a massive bony frill, a sharp beak and a large nose horn. Paired spines decorated the edges of its frill. The many ceratopsid species varied considerably in frill size and shape and in the configuration and number of their horns and spines.

3 ANATOMY

WHEN WE THINK OF DINOSAUR FOSSILS, we generally think of complete skeletons such as those displayed in museum halls across the world. Such specimens provide an enormous amount of information to palaeontologists. Firstly, they are the source of the evidence used to reconstruct the pattern of evolution (see Chapter 2) since they possess the anatomical features that are used to deduce the relationships between different dinosaur species. Secondly, the sizes, shapes and other features of bones (such as evidence of muscle attachments, or holes for nerves and blood vessels) can be used to work out how the animal functioned – for example, how it used its senses, fed, moved around and grew. But it should also be said that smaller parts of skeletons, and even individual bones or fragments of bones, provide useful insights too.

In this chapter, we look at what we understand about dinosaur anatomy (that branch of science dealing with the study of skeletons, organs and muscles), and what that anatomy tells us about non-bird dinosaurs as living animals. We begin by looking at what we know of dinosaur skeletons before moving on to look at our knowledge of dinosaur muscle anatomy, the respiratory system, the digestive system and, finally, the integument – the skin and other features that cover the outside of the body.

THE DINOSAUR SKELETON

Dinosaurs are vertebrates, and share a skeletal plan that is common to fish, amphibians and mammals, as well as to other reptiles. More specifically, they are tetrapods – part of the group of vertebrates that (unlike fishes) possess limbs and digits (fingers and toes) that are connected to shoulder and hip girdles. The fact that dinosaurs possess the tetrapod body plan means that they have a skeleton that is essentially similar to ours. So, if you know something about the human skeleton, you know a lot about the dinosaur skeleton too.

One of the key features of the vertebrate skeleton is the vertebral column or spine, a long structure made of numerous individual segments called vertebrae, and attached to the skull at its front end. The skull houses the brain and the main sense organs (eyes, ears, nose, tongue). A series of nerves emerge from the skull via special bony openings (called foramina) and connect the brain to the various regions of the body. A thick cable of nerve tissue called the spinal cord, attached at its front end to the brain, runs along the spine, sending off more nerves along its length.

All vertebrate animals share the same basic skeletal plan. To correctly assemble a dinosaur skeleton – this is a replica of the British theropod *Baryonyx* – a good knowledge of vertebrate anatomy is required.

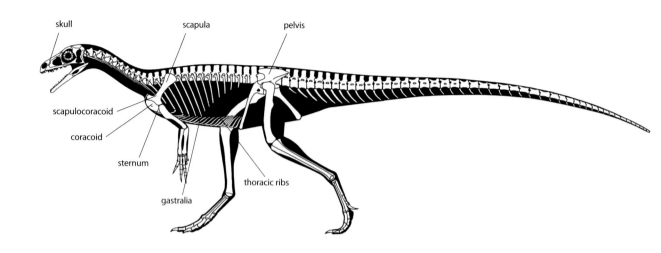

skull scapula pelvis

scapulocoracoid

coracoid

sternum

gastralia

thoracic ribs

Both articulated fossil skeletons and our knowledge of living animals allow us to reconstruct non-bird dinosaurs like this *Eoraptor* with some degree of accuracy. A basic knowledge of anatomy is obviously crucial when discussing the dinosaur skeleton.

The skull is complicated, and formed of numerous different bones. Teeth grow from the bones that line the jaws and are made up of two especially tough materials: dentine and enamel. Dinosaur teeth grew in distinct sockets within the jaw bones, as ours do. Most dinosaurs grew new teeth throughout their lives, with individual teeth being replaced after just a month or so of use. This system seems unusual to humans since we only produce two sets of teeth in a lifetime, but it's actually the normal, typical condition for vertebrates. We look at dinosaur tooth diversity later on in this book (see Chapter 4).

We tend to think that the only mobile parts of a skull are the jaw joints. These allow us to move the lower jaw relative to the rest of the skull while we chew, or talk. The tiny bones in our ears – a uniquely mammalian feature – are mobile too, and move in response to sound vibrations received via the eardrum. Most of our skull bones (and those of other mammals) are solidly joined and don't move relative to one another. Some dinosaurs may have been quite different from mammals in this respect, with possible zones of flexion in the face, lower jaw, roof of the mouth and snout perhaps allowing movement that was beneficial during feeding. This type of movement between skull bones is called cranial kinesis. Exactly how much cranial kinesis occurred among non-bird dinosaurs is controversial, as we'll see shortly.

Another obvious way in which dinosaur skulls differ from those of humans is that – in addition to the openings for the eyes and nostrils – most dinosaurs have large, window-like openings on the snout and at the back of the skull. The most obvious of these is called the antorbital fenestra, and is located on the side of the snout between the nostril and

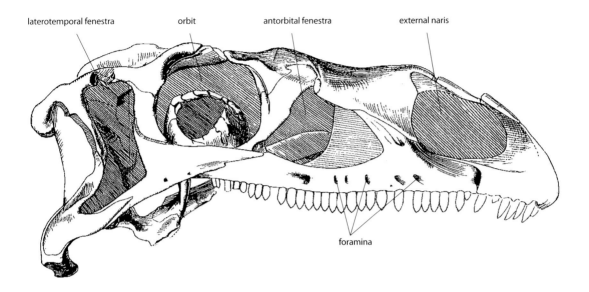

laterotemporal fenestra   orbit   antorbital fenestra   external naris

foramina

the eye. Then there are two more openings behind the eye, termed the temporal openings. The tall opening on the side is the laterotemporal opening (or fenestra), and the rounded one on the top of the skull is the supratemporal opening (or fenestra). Temporal openings are not unique to dinosaurs but are present throughout the larger group of reptiles that dinosaurs belong to, Diapsida (a name that means 'two openings'). This group also includes crocodylians, lizards and snakes. We saw in Chapter 1 that the antorbital fenestra is not unique to dinosaurs either. It's a normal feature of archosaurs, the diapsid sub-group that dinosaurs belong to, along with crocodylians and several extinct groups.

Why these extra openings appeared in the first place is a good question. They are partially filled by the muscles used in opening and closing the jaws, so the usual explanation for their presence has been that they provided attachment points for these jaw muscles. It has also been argued that they helped make the skull stronger and better able to withstand the stresses produced within the bones during biting. This explanation seems to be partly true. However, the giant antorbital fenestra perhaps wasn't as important in anchoring jaw muscles as we used to think, since new evidence suggests that it was filled mostly by a large air-filled sac, not by muscles. This sac was part of what's known as the pneumatic system, a feature of dinosaur anatomy that we discuss in more detail below. The skulls of many dinosaurs housed a surprising number of complex, air-filled structures.

Some dinosaur groups (like ankylosaurs) grew new bone over their skull openings. Others (like rebbachisaurid sauropods) enlarged the openings and developed lighter, more open-plan skulls. These

Dinosaurs ordinarily have a few skull openings that are not present in the human skull. The antorbital fenestra is present on the side of the snout, and the laterotemporal fenestra is a large, tall opening behind the eye socket. This is the skull of the Late Triassic sauropodomorph *Plateosaurus*.

evolutionary changes in skull design are related to the feeding styles used by these dinosaurs, and perhaps also to other things, like use of the skull in combat and noise-making.

Scientists tend to be especially interested in the skulls and teeth of dinosaurs, mostly because they provide so much information on diet, behaviour and lifestyle. Of course, the skull is only one part of the skeleton, and a small part at that. The majority of the skeleton is termed the postcranial skeleton – that is, everything other than the skull. As is typical for tetrapods, dinosaurs possess paired limbs and limb girdles on either side of the front and rear parts of the body. The front limb girdles are termed the scapulocoracoids or shoulder girdles. Each is formed of both a shoulder blade (the scapula) and a plate-like bone called the coracoid.

Along the centre of the chest, the coracoids contact the sternum, or breastbone. Additional bones – including the rod-like collarbones (or clavicles) – join with the leading edges of the shoulder girdle in some dinosaurs. Theropods possess a V-shaped wishbone, or furcula, a feature we know well thanks to its presence in birds. The furcula was once regarded as a unique feature of birds but was actually present throughout theropods, even in very early members of the group. A V-shaped bone formed from the clavicles is even present in the more distantly related sauropodomorph *Massospondylus*.

The dinosaur ribcage is formed of 13 or so pairs of large, curved thoracic ribs. As is the case in most tetrapods, dinosaur ribs are mobile,

The dinosaur ribcage – this one belongs to the thyreophoran *Stegosaurus* – includes long ribs that articulate with the vertebrae by way of mobile joints. The shorter ribs at the very front and back of the ribcage tend to be less mobile.

the two prongs at the top end of each rib allowing it to be moved by the muscles that are attached to it. Saurischian dinosaurs possess additional bony parts of the ribcage that are not found in mammals: a basket-like arrangement of flexible, rod-shaped and V-shaped bones arranged along the lower surface of the chest and belly. This set of 'belly ribs' is termed the gastral basket, and the individual bones that form it are termed abdominal ribs or gastralia. Like thoracic ribs, the gastralia were connected to each other by muscles and seem to have played a role in expanding the belly and chest during breathing. Today, gastralia are typical of crocodylians, and birds lack them. They're well preserved in many ancient birds of the Jurassic and Cretaceous and were obviously lost in later birds over time.

DINOSAUR ARMS, HANDS AND FINGERS

Dinosaur forelimb bones vary enormously in structure and shape. The main bones of the forelimb are the humerus (or upper arm bone), and radius and ulna (the two lower arm bones). Wrist bones – or carpals – allow for complex movements between the arm and hand. The hand itself is formed of three sets of bones. Metacarpals are the usually long, slender bones that form the palm, phalanges are the cylindrical bones that form the fingers, and unguals are the set of phalanges that form the tips of the fingers and are usually sheathed by the horny claws or hooves.

Long, column-shaped limb bones (sometimes with huge crests for muscle attachment) are typical of dinosaurs that walked on all fours, and members of these groups have hands specialized for weight-bearing too. We've already seen that sauropods evolved weird column-shaped hands where the metacarpals were arranged in a semi-circle and the phalanges were shortened or missing altogether. Stegosaurs, ankylosaurs, ceratopsians and some iguanodontians also evolved weight-bearing hands, but did so in different ways.

This *Tyrannosaurus* skeleton prominently displays the basket-like arrangement of belly ribs or gastralia beneath the ribcage. Note that these are lacking in the adjacent ornithischian skeleton.

Quadrupedal ornithischians of several groups evolved robust, pillar-like metacarpal bones and hoof-like unguals. These features are obvious in the hands of *Iguanodon* (left) and *Stegosaurus* (right).

Complete skeletons preserved with all of their bones in place suggest that stegosaurs and ankylosaurs possessed column-like hands, similar to those of sauropods, where the metacarpals were arranged as vertical pillars. This possibility receives support from the way in which individual bones fit together, and with evidence from fossilized trackways. Incidentally, this idea is not usually reflected in diagrams and museum specimens, since they often show stegosaurs and ankylosaurs with spreading fingers, the lower surfaces of which are shown as being in contact with the ground.

Ceratopsians evolved thickened, enlarged inner fingers that took most of the weight and were arranged in a semi-circle. Blunt, rounded hooves are present on those inner fingers while the two shorter outer ones seem to have lacked hooves.

Finally, iguanodontians evolved a weight-supporting hand by turning the three long inner digits into a thick, hoof-like structure. The thumb became a spike-like weapon, most familiar in *Iguanodon* where it was a giant and probably dangerous weapon, sometimes as much as 30 cm (12 in) long. For an unknown reason, the iguanodontian lineage leading to hadrosaurs lost the thumb entirely. Meanwhile, the fifth finger remained flexible and may have had a grasping function.

Theropods of some groups – megalosauroids and allosauroids among them – typically possess short arm bones, and have hands specialized for the grabbing of prey. Long, slender phalanges and curved, pointed unguals are typical of theropod forelimbs. Some theropod groups (maniraptorans in particular) evolved very long fingers while others (like abelisaurids) evolved very short ones. Like all dinosaurs, theropods started their history with five fingers but the outer two became smaller over time and are absent from many groups. Tyrannosaurids lost the third finger and ended up with a two-fingered hand, and alvarezsaurids and some birds did this too. A weird, toothless neoceratosaur from the Late Jurassic of China – *Limusaurus* – also possesses a strongly reduced hand where only the second and third fingers are present. Some alvarezsaurids and birds even ended up with one-fingered hands, and there are some birds that lack the hand, and even the entire arm, altogether (such as the now extinct giant, flightless moas that once lived in New Zealand).

Until recently, mounted museum skeletons and illustrations showed theropods posed with their palms facing the ground. But this view of theropod anatomy is contradicted by skeletons preserved with all of the bones in their original positions (otherwise known as 'articulated' skeletons). These have the palms facing inwards, not downwards. Several

Tyrannosaurids like this *Albertosaurus* have among the most unusual forelimbs to have ever evolved among dinosaurs. The arm bones are small and slim and the hands possess just two fingers. As is common in museum mounts, the bones of the shoulder girdle are way too far apart – they should be virtually touching along the midline of the chest.

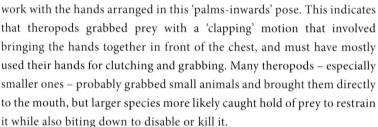

The forelimb joints of dinosaurs do not allow the hands to be rotated at the wrist, so the hands of bipedal species were permanently fixed in a 'palms-inwards' pose. These gigantic, three-fingered forelimbs belong to the giant Mongolian ornithomimosaur *Deinocheirus*.

Like the majority of maniraptoran theropods, this *Dromaeosaurus* has long, slender hands and the three fingers are tipped with strongly curved claws. The hands have been wrongly articulated in a 'palms down' pose.

palaeontologists have constructed models – both in real life and on the computer – to examine hand pose. Palaeontologist Phil Senter used three-dimensional models of theropod forelimb bones with realistic ranges of motion at their joints to show that theropod hands can only work with the hands arranged in this 'palms-inwards' pose. This indicates that theropods grabbed prey with a 'clapping' motion that involved bringing the hands together in front of the chest, and must have mostly used their hands for clutching and grabbing. Many theropods – especially smaller ones – probably grabbed small animals and brought them directly to the mouth, but larger species more likely caught hold of prey to restrain it while also biting down to disable or kill it.

Further support for this hand pose comes from fossil tracks made by a squatting theropod dinosaur of Early Jurassic age. These tracks show the theropod putting the upper surfaces of its fingers against the ground, not its palms or the undersides of its fingers. We should also say that bird hands – which are mostly completely hidden by feathers – are likewise arranged 'palms-inwards', so it seems that this is an aspect of anatomy that theropods kept throughout the whole of their history.

One further thing to say on hand pose concerns non-theropod dinosaurs. As we saw in Chapter 2, early members of all three main dinosaur groups were similar in overall shape – all were bipedal with grasping hands. The obvious question, then, is whether this 'palms-inwards' pose was present in bipedal sauropodomorphs and ornithischians too? The answer seems to be yes. Articulated skeletons of bipedal sauropodomorphs and ornithischians are preserved with palms-inwards hands, and modelling work (done both with real specimens, and using computer software) again shows that the hands only work when arranged in this way.

THE HIPS AND HINDLIMBS

Moving to the back of the dinosaur body, the key features of the dinosaur pelvis, and the main differences between saurischian hips and ornithischian hips, were discussed in Chapter 2. One of the most interesting things about dinosaur hips concerns the size of the ilium – the broad, plate-like bone at the top of the hip girdle. This is an attachment site for thigh muscles, and its broad surface is proof that virtually all dinosaurs had huge leg muscles. Dinosaurs vary considerably with respect to how wide their hips are. Some theropods were narrow-hipped, with the two halves of the pelvis almost touching at the top of the animal's back. But other theropods (the therizinosaurs), some sauropods, and thyreophorans were much wider-hipped, with the two halves of the hips separated by a considerable distance.

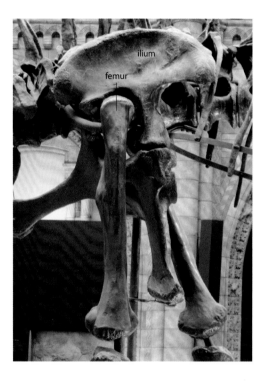

At the top of the dinosaur leg is the femur or thigh bone. This is typically the largest and most strongly built bone in the dinosaur skeleton, and its shape and length compared to the other parts of the limb can give us an idea on whether a dinosaur was a walker or a runner. In living animals, fast runners tend to have a relatively short femur, and this seems to apply to extinct dinosaurs too. A large muscle attachment point termed the fourth trochanter is present on the rear surface of the dinosaurian femur. In some groups, it's merely a raised, rough patch of bone whereas in others it's a large, projecting, finger-shaped spike. The fourth trochanter is important, since it formed the attachment point for one of the largest muscles in the dinosaur body, and changes in its shape and very presence tell us interesting things about the way dinosaurs were using their leg muscles. We discuss this subject further below.

No non-bird dinosaurs had kneecaps (as far as we know), but they did evolve in birds several times, including in the group of toothed Cretaceous diving birds that includes *Hesperornis*. In birds and mammals, the kneecap helps to improve the pull that the limb muscles have on the hindlimb bones. In view of this important role, its absence in non-bird dinosaurs is currently a mystery.

The next segment of the hindlimb is formed of the two shin bones, the large tibia (on the inner side of the leg) and the slim fibula (on the outside). Dinosaurs adapted for quick movement have long, slender shin bones, and we see these in lightly built theropods and ornithopods. At their lower ends, dinosaur shin bones are tightly connected to two large

A typical feature of the dinosaur hip girdle is an enormous, plate-like ilium – the big, flattened bone at the top of the hips. Hollow areas and bony crests on its side show where huge leg and tail muscles attached. This is the hip girdle of the sauropod *Diplodocus*.

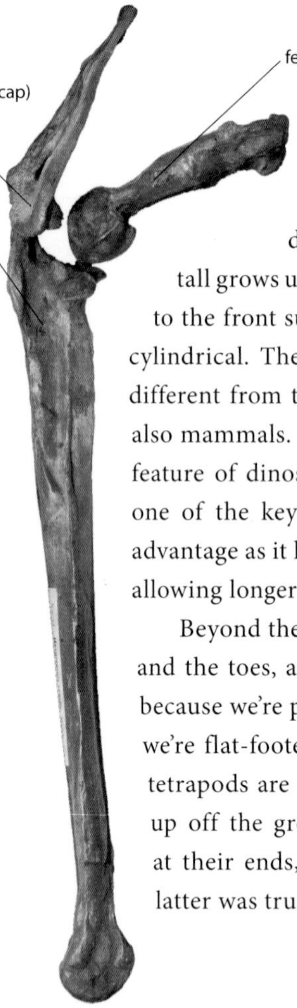

For reasons that remain unclear, non-bird dinosaurs lacked a kneecap, or patella. However, they did evolve in birds. The hindlimb of the Cretaceous North American swimming bird *Hesperornis*, shown here, has an enormous, spike-like patella almost as long as its femur.

ankle bones, termed the astragalus (on the inner side of the limb) and calcaneum (on the outer side). The dinosaur astragalus is very distinctive. A triangular flange that's often quite tall grows upwards from the astragalus and is firmly attached to the front surface of the tibia, while the bone's lower part is cylindrical. The result is a strong, hinge-like ankle joint, very different from the complex, flexible ankle of other reptiles and also mammals. This hinge-like, reinforced ankle is a distinctive feature of dinosaurs and their close relatives and was perhaps one of the keys to their success. Presumably, it provided an advantage as it helped stabilize the foot against twisting, thereby allowing longer and perhaps faster strides.

Beyond the ankle, the limb consists of the metatarsal bones and the toes, again formed of phalanges. Humans are unusual because we're plantigrade: our ankle is close to the ground, and we're flat-footed, walking on our metatarsals. The majority of tetrapods are digitigrade, meaning that the ankle is held well up off the ground, the metatarsals only contact the ground at their ends, and the animal walks mostly on its toes. The latter was true of dinosaurs – they were all digitigrade. Again,

The short, chunky metatarsals and block-like phalanges of dinosaurs like this *Edmontosaurus* are clear adaptations for weight-bearing. Like most animals, non-bird dinosaurs walked only on their toes and the metatarsals were normally held in a near-vertical pose.

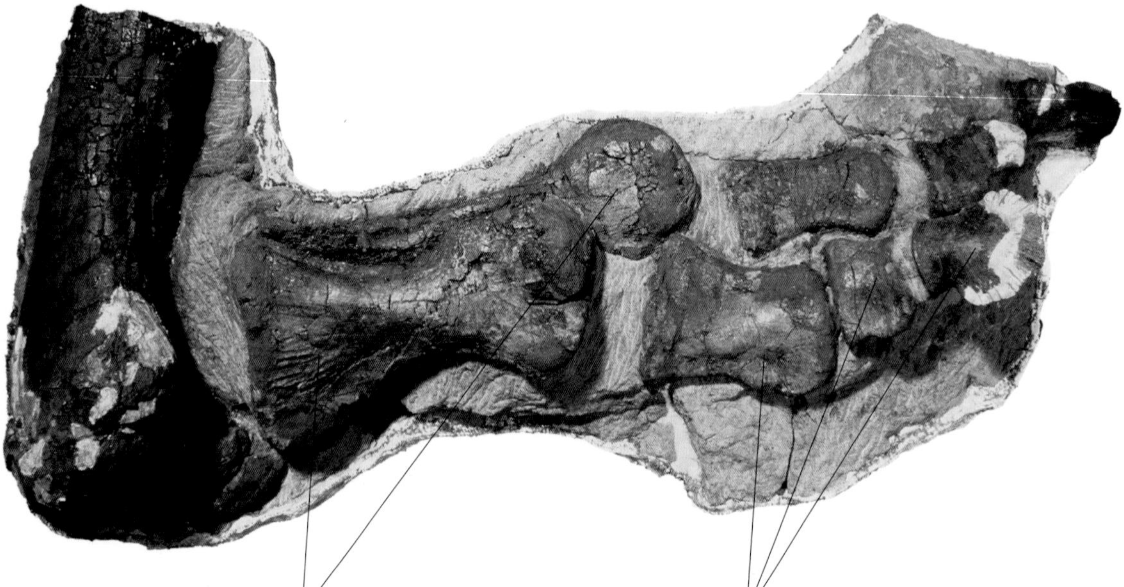

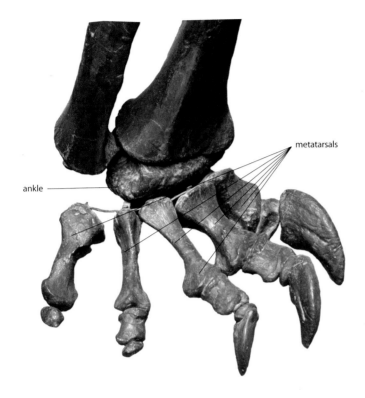

ankle

metatarsals

Sauropod hindfeet – this one belongs to *Diplodocus* – are strongly adapted for weight-bearing. A giant fatty pad formed the sole of the foot and kept the column-like metatarsals off the ground. The ankle is short and must have had limited flexibility.

In the longer, slender foot of tyrannosauroid theropods, like this *Albertosaurus*, the metatarsals are tightly locked together by special joints at their top ends. The result is a lightweight foot that's built for speed and good at transferring energy and supporting weight.

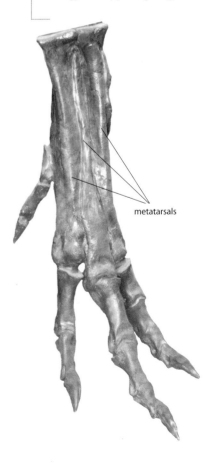

metatarsals

the metatarsals give us some clues to dinosaur lifestyle. Long, slender, metatarsals are typical of animals that move quickly, and metatarsals of this sort are seen in numerous theropods and ornithopods. The metatarsals of several theropod groups (including advanced ornithomimosaurs and tyrannosauroids) are tightly locked together, forming an especially strong, narrow foot.

Short, chunky metatarsals are present in thyreophorans, ceratopsians and sauropods. These are more in keeping with weight support and a lifestyle that involved slow walking. Sauropod metatarsals are so short that the ankle is quite close to the ground, in contrast to that of many other dinosaurs. But, as we've already seen, the foot was backed by an enormous fatty pad – similar to the one present in elephant feet. This meant that even sauropods were digitigrade too.

Finally, we come to the toes. Dinosaurs started their history with five toes but there was a tendency in their evolution for the toes on the inner and outer sides to be reduced in size. The outermost or fifth toe is missing in most dinosaur groups (often, only the short metatarsal remains), and the innermost or first toe (the hallux) is also small or even lacking in theropods and ornithopods. The majority of theropods and ornithopods walked only on the middle three toes of the foot. Some maniraptorans, like dromaeosaurids, modified the second toe into a raised weapon bearing an enlarged claw that was no longer used for walking. These dinosaurs therefore walked only on two toes.

The toe bones of dinosaurs vary in size and proportions. Sauropods, ankylosaurs and stegosaurs have short, block-like phalanges while dinosaurs with long, slim feet (like many theropods and small ornithischians) have long, slender ones. We therefore have dinosaurs with short, compact feet versus those with long, spreading feet. The proportions of the toe bones and the curvature of the claws on the ends of the toes can provide some indication to lifestyle, especially among birds and bird-like theropods. Many non-bird theropods have toe proportions showing that they were ground-dwelling runners or walkers. Some of these dinosaurs have features at least suggestive of an ability to climb on occasion. *Deinonychus* and *Microraptor* have been regarded as potential climbers by some experts, and debate continues over the perching and climbing abilities of *Archaeopteryx*, *Confuciusornis* and other birds and bird-like maniraptorans.

Small, bird-like maniraptorans like the pheasant-sized dromaeosaurid *Sinornithosaurus* had long, slender hindlimbs and long, slender arms and hands too. In the dromaeosaurid foot, the second toe was ordinarily raised up relative to the others, and the third and fourth toes alone were used for walking.

HOW DINOSAUR SKELETONS WORK

Bones provide us with a huge amount of information about how an animal's body works and also about the lifestyle it lived, the way it moved and the behaviours it was capable of. Articulated skeletons show not only how the bones fitted together in life, but also the ranges of movement that were possible between them, as well as the sorts of postures and poses dinosaurs might have adopted when alive. We saw earlier that this entire field – the sub-discipline of biology which uses the skeleton to reveal how the animal worked – is termed functional morphology.

It's important to remember that there is much more to anatomy than bones alone. Structures like cartilage pads between bones, muscles, and the rope-like ligaments that hold bones together all have an impact on the way bones move, and it remains a source of frustration to palaeontologists that virtually all of these features are missing from fossils. These structures are made of materials that usually rot away prior to fossilization and are often termed 'soft tissues', in contrast to the 'hard tissues' like bones and teeth. We can at least get some indication of what was possible in life by comparing the skeletons of fossil animals to those of living ones. Numerous techniques have been devised that allow us to account for those missing soft tissues and work out what impact they might have had on movement and flexibility.

The simplest and 'traditional' way of studying functional morphology in extinct animals is to move bones at their joints, and sometimes model them on paper or use mathematical calculations. This technique is not especially precise, and it doesn't usually account for the effects of the soft tissues mentioned above. It also requires direct access to the real fossil, which might be fragile or damaged. Technological advances have significantly improved the ways in which palaeontologists can study functional morphology. Digital models of skeletons, made by using photographs or scanners that capture the shapes of the bones in a computer, are now used on a regular basis. Using these computer models to examine how the bones could move is much easier than working with full-sized bones or copies of bones. Some of the results from digital modelling are exciting and confirm some controversial ideas about dinosaur behaviour. Let's look at areas of dinosaur anatomy that have been studied using both traditional and modern techniques.

Computer models and data from CT scans are typically used when studying functional morphology today. In the past, however, scientists often manipulated fossils themselves – or models of fossils – to see how the animals might have functioned when alive. Here, two experts manipulate a replica skull of *Allosaurus*.

For decades, dinosaur experts have examined the jaws of hadrosaurs and other iguanodontians in an effort to understand how these animals chewed. Many ideas were proposed, most of which do not explain how the distinctive wear patterns on the teeth could have been generated. A new idea was proposed by palaeontologists David Norman and David Weishampel during the 1980s. These scientists noticed a potentially flexible zone running across the side of the face in *Iguanodon*, *Mantellisaurus* and hadrosaurs. Based on the way the bones fit together around this zone, they argued that the maxilla – the big bone that forms most of the side of the face and contains the upper jaw teeth – could rotate inwards and outwards, resulting in a sideways grinding motion across the surfaces of the cheek teeth. Flexible regions in the other parts of the skull also seemed to allow this movement. According to this interpretation, iguanodontians possessed cranial kinesis (a term we met earlier on). This unique method of allowing

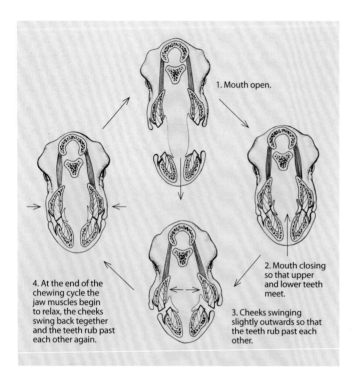

1. Mouth open.

2. Mouth closing so that upper and lower teeth meet.

3. Cheeks swinging slightly outwards so that the teeth rub past each other.

4. At the end of the chewing cycle the jaw muscles begin to relax, the cheeks swing back together and the teeth rub past each other again.

According to scientists David Norman and David Weishampel's model of pleurokinesis, ornithopods like *Edmontosaurus* evolved a unique way of grinding their upper jaw teeth against the lower jaw teeth. These diagrams show the sequence of movements involved, the animal's head being shown in cross-section.

the cheek teeth to meet and grind against each other is quite different from the system seen in any other animal, living or extinct.

Inspired by this proposal of cranial kinesis, other palaeontologists went on to suggest flexible skulls in many other non-bird dinosaurs. Allosauroids, tyrannosaurids, alvarezsaurids and others have all been suggested to have flexible zones in their skulls too. These ideas are controversial. In 2008, anatomists Casey Holliday and Larry Witmer argued that the skulls of all non-bird dinosaurs have interlocking bony projections that would have prevented any possibility of kinesis, and lacked the mobile, fluid-filled joints present in the skulls of living animals that have cranial kinesis, such as birds and lizards. If this is true, why do *Iguanodon* and other dinosaurs have features suggestive of at least some degree of kinesis? Maybe, Holliday and Witmer suggested, these are areas where new bone growth occurred, and not zones of flexibility. The debate continues.

Palaeontologists have also argued over where the shoulder girdle was placed on the side of the ribcage in sauropods and other quadrupedal dinosaurs, like ceratopsians. And a second area of argument concerns how the forelimbs were held in life – did they sprawl out to the side, like those of lizards or turtles, or were they held beneath the body in pillar-like fashion, as they are in big mammals like rhinos? The topics of shoulder girdle position and forelimb pose are connected, since the position of the shoulder girdle controls the position of the arm socket. This, in turn, affects the pose of the forelimb.

While different experts have different views on these issues, articulated skeletons show that the shoulder girdles are positioned low down in the skeletons of quadrupedal dinosaurs, so low that the coracoids were almost in contact across the chest. If we accept this as the real position for the shoulder girdle, it means that sauropod forelimbs were oriented in a vertical, column-like pose, but that the shoulder sockets were directed backwards, slightly outwards and slightly downwards in ceratopsians and other ornithischians. This means that ornithischian forelimbs didn't sprawl like those of lizards, but they weren't held directly beneath the body either. This particular forelimb pose results in a position and spacing for the hands that matches fossil trackways, suggesting that it's the correct one.

Another controversial area of dinosaur anatomy has been studied using both traditional and computer-assisted methods, and this is the sauropod neck. Over the years, palaeontologists have disagreed over how the sauropod neck was used, how it was held, and how flexible it was. Given the neck's extraordinary length, it might seem logical that it was used to reach high up into trees, allowing sauropods to take advantage of plant food beyond the reach of other plant-eaters. But is this view really supported by what we understand of sauropod anatomy?

By articulating the neck bones of the British sauropod *Cetiosaurus*, palaeontologist John Martin argued that the sauropod neck most likely worked as a beam that was held straight out in front of the animal's body and couldn't be raised high above the level of the back. Some experts have applied this idea to almost all sauropods, including the exceptionally long-necked brachiosaurs and mamenchisaurids. The same experts have argued that relatively little motion was possible between adjacent neck vertebrae, and that sauropods did the majority of their feeding at ground level or shoulder-height.

In order to investigate sauropod neck flexibility more thoroughly, computer scientist Kent Stevens and palaeontologist Mike Parrish constructed digital models of *Apatosaurus* and *Diplodocus*. The necks of these digital dinosaurs were thought to be capable of the same ranges of movement considered likely for the live animals. Stevens and Parrish's conclusions mostly matched those of Martin: the necks worked as horizontal beams, better able to reach sideways and downwards than upwards, with little movement at the neck's base.

This seems like a case where computer modelling confirms work done using traditional bone manipulation. This view of straight-necked sauropods is based mostly on the idea that only a small amount of motion

Experts have put forward several different ideas on how the scapulocoracoids and forelimbs of quadrupedal ornithischians may have been arranged in life. At the extreme ends of this argument are suggestions that these dinosaurs had either fully sprawling or fully erect forelimbs, as shown in these diagrams. The truth is probably somewhere in between.

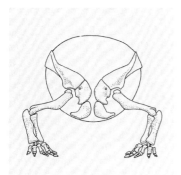
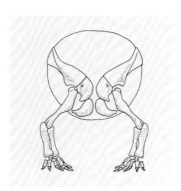
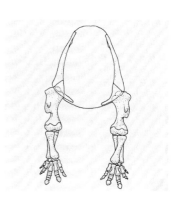

is possible at the joints between neck vertebrae. But, if we look at what we know about cartilage in the necks of living animals, we should assume that the joints between sauropod neck vertebrae were capable of a wide range of motion – enough to enable the neck to be bent far to the side, or up into the air and down to the ground. The point here is that some computer modelling studies, and some bone manipulation studies, might not produce accurate results because they fail to account for the soft tissues that are often lost from the fossils, but still have to be considered. These soft tissues mean that live animals might well be capable of performing acts that seem unlikely when we use the evidence provided by bones alone.

Digital studies of dinosaur skeletons have also been produced by other experts. German palaeontologist Heinrich Mallison has made and studied digital models of sauropodomorph forelimbs, stegosaur tails and other dinosaur body parts. His work on the arm and hand of the sauropodomorph *Plateosaurus* allowed the range of motion in the forelimb to be reconstructed. The fingers could be clenched substantially, the hands were fixed in a palms-inwards pose, and the wrist allowed the hand to be bent inwards, but not rotated. This anatomical arrangement should sound familiar, because it's the same as the arrangement we saw earlier in theropods.

Mallison's digital model of the spiky African stegosaur *Kentrosaurus* showed that the tail was flexible enough to be swung around to the side of the body and high up to the side. This degree of movement matches the

If we account for the cartilage discs located in between the neck vertebrae of sauropod dinosaurs, we find that the neck was highly flexible, and could easily be bent sharply upwards (and downwards). The upper diagram shows *Apatosaurus* and the lower one *Diplodocus*.

By working out how much motion was possible between the tail and vertebrae of the African stegosaur *Kentrosaurus*, experts have shown that *Kentrosaurus* could bend its tail far to the side of its body.

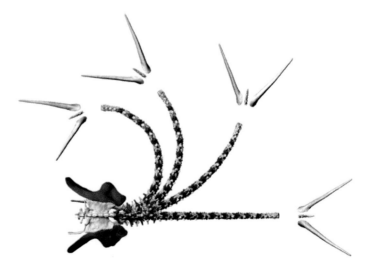

idea that the spines at the stegosaur tail tip were used as weapons, and that stegosaurs were able to move the tail far enough to defend themselves from large theropods. Digital studies that take proper account of the soft tissues between the vertebrae indicate that the necks and tails of non-bird dinosaurs were often quite flexible.

We're still in the early stages of understanding dinosaur functional morphology and a huge amount of work remains to be done. What's perhaps especially interesting is that increased interest in the functional morphology of non-bird dinosaurs has inspired many scientists to study the anatomy and functional morphology of living animals, since the anatomy of a great many of these has, perhaps surprisingly, never been studied in detail. As is clear from the arguments discussed here – those concerning cranial kinesis and sauropod neck flexibility and so on – new and developing techniques are helping palaeontologists to study many areas of dinosaur anatomy and functional morphology in greater depth and detail than was possible before.

DINOSAUR BONE UNDER THE MICROSCOPE

We tend to think of bones as objects that form the internal scaffolding of an animal's body. This is true, but bones are much more than this. Bone is a living, growing tissue that's in a constant state of change. It changes in thickness, size and shape according to the loads and pressures placed upon it; it's re-formed or grown according to the needs of its owner; and it records the growth, age, and even the health and life story of the animal. By studying thin slices of bone under the microscope, palaeontologists have learnt a huge amount about dinosaur biology.

The study of anatomy only visible at the microscopic scale is termed histology. For palaeontologists studying this subject, the main tools required are a bandsaw or drill (used to cut or remove the section of bone that will be studied), and a microscope.

The bones of non-bird dinosaurs are mostly formed of a kind of bone known as fibrolamellar bone. This contains a chaotic, tangled structure of bone fibres and blood-transporting tubes. We know from living animals that the continuous production of fibrolamellar bone is evidence of rapid bone growth, and of rapid growth overall.

By cutting bones into pieces – this is the sectioned rib of a *Tyrannosaurus* – we can see the bone's detailed internal structure. Growth lines, holes for blood vessels and distinct kinds of bone tissue can all be examined in this way.

At the outer edges of a non-bird dinosaur bone, we often see that the fibrolamellar bone contains fewer spaces for blood vessels. A number of growth lines might also be visible. These growth lines, which look rather like tree rings, are called lines of arrested growth, or LAGs. It's assumed that these are annual growth rings based on their similarity to growth lines seen in the bones of living animals. As a result, counting these growth lines can give an approximate minimum age of the animal when it died. What sorts of result do they show? Were non-bird dinosaurs (especially big ones) long-lived animals with a lifespan of many decades? The results obtained so far are fairly surprising, since they show that all dinosaurs were relatively short-lived, with even giant species rarely living beyond their 40th or 50th year.

At the very edges of a bone section, a distinct band of bone, termed the external fundamental system (or EFS), is sometimes present. This feature is found in mature, adult dinosaurs and features many closely spaced LAGs. It shows that non-bird dinosaurs did not continue growing throughout life, but stopped growing, or at least grew only very slowly, at maturity. If an EFS is missing from the bone, it shows that the dinosaur was still growing rapidly at its time of death, had not yet reached full adult size, and was thus either a young adult or a juvenile.

Most data on dinosaur bone histology shows that non-bird dinosaurs grew at rates much higher than those seen in reptiles like tortoises or lizards. As recently as the 1980s it was suggested that giant dinosaurs like sauropods required more than a century to reach adult size. Newer studies show that even the biggest sauropods reached full size in 40 years or less. This fast growth has implications for dinosaur biology as a whole, a subject that we'll return to in Chapter 4.

Ignoring growth rates for now, what else might dinosaur bone anatomy tell us about the biology of non-bird dinosaurs? Several dinosaur specimens preserve broken and healed bones, and some have unusual lumps, rough patches or areas of unusual bone texture. Broken and healed bones show that dinosaurs became injured in battles or even in falls or other accidents. There are horned dinosaurs missing parts of their horns or with gouge marks on their facial bones, a *Tyrannosaurus* with broken ribs, an injured arm and an infected shin bone, and *Allosaurus* hip and tail bones that preserve holes apparently caused by the tail spikes of stegosaurs.

Based on what happens to animals today, we assume that non-bird dinosaurs were sometimes afflicted with diseases and abnormal growth conditions. Some experts on bone anatomy argue that we can identify the medical causes of these abnormalities and have diagnosed cancer,

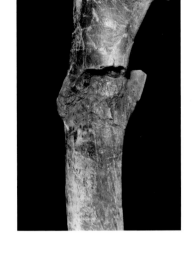

arthritis and other conditions. The majority of experts reject this view. At best, we can only make educated guesses about whatever it was that caused these problems – sadly, we cannot subject these bones to the sorts of tests needed to work out the disease processes that might have been at work.

It's perhaps surprising that we can gain information on a dinosaur's sex and reproductive status from its microscopic bone anatomy. It's been known for decades that female birds possess a unique type of bone called medullary bone, which forms at the same time as they are growing eggs. Medullary bone grows inside the inner cavity (the medulla) of the leg bones, appearing as a kind of spongy mass, and its only function is to act as a store for the chemical element calcium, used by the birds to form eggshells. Scientists who work on animal remains discovered at archaeological sites have been using the presence of medullary bone to identify the sex of ancient birds since the early 1980s, and several palaeontologists suggested during the 1990s that it might eventually be discovered in non-bird dinosaurs, perhaps in a theropod found sat on top of its nest. This prediction came true in 2005 when medullary bone was discovered in the leg bone of a *Tyrannosaurus*. Yet another supposedly 'avian' piece of biology was not unique to birds at all. It actually evolved substantially earlier, deep within the theropod family tree.

Since 2005, medullary bone has been discovered in other non-bird theropods (*Allosaurus*) and in ornithischians (the iguanodontian *Tenontosaurus*). What looks like medullary bone has also been discovered in the sauropodomorph *Mussaurus*. This distribution suggests that medullary bone was produced by members of all dinosaur lineages and

An unusual, raised, roughened collar of bone on this *Iguanodon* toe bone above left (the third of the four toe bones shown here) represents abnormal growth of some sort. It might show that this dinosaur suffered from arthritis in its toe.

The break in this pelvic bone above – again belonging to an *Iguanodon* – healed, but did so with the two segments of the bone out of alignment. How the animal broke this bone remains unknown, but the break obviously healed during the animal's lifetime.

was inherited from the common ancestor that all dinosaurs descended from. It has to be remembered that although the presence of medullary bone can be used to positively identify an egg-laying female dinosaur its absence doesn't necessarily mean an animal was male. Lack of this bone type might indicate that an individual was a male, but alternatively it might have been a female that wasn't laying eggs. Medullary bone is a useful guide for sexing a dinosaur, but it isn't a fool-proof technique. We'll come back to this subject and what it means for dinosaur nesting behaviour in Chapter 4.

The mere presence of medullary bone is really interesting, because it allows us to identify the sex of at least some Mesozoic dinosaur specimens. But what makes it especially exciting is what it tells us about dinosaur biology. Any animal that grows medullary bone is obviously sexually mature. In other words, the individual concerned had reached an age where it was able to grow eggs, and was able to mate. We might predict, then, that medullary bone will only ever be found in full-sized dinosaurs. But this is not the case. The *Allosaurus* and *Tenontosaurus* individuals that possess it are youngsters, half the size of full-grown specimens. This means that non-bird dinosaurs of some species (perhaps many species) were reproducing long before they had reached adult size, and long before they had stopped growing. They were teenage parents. Maybe non-bird dinosaurs of many kinds were courting, mating and raising babies long before reaching full adult size – a possibility that affects the way we imagine the look of dinosaur nesting colonies and the sorts of interactions that must have occurred during breeding seasons.

HOW HEAVY WERE NON-BIRD DINOSAURS?

Scientists and lay-people alike have long been interested in the size – in particular the weight or mass – of non-bird dinosaurs. After all, many of them are much bigger than living rhinos, hippos and elephants, and the biggest sauropods appear to be on par with whales, making them the largest land-going animals ever to have evolved.

Working out the size of a fossil animal is more than a fun exercise. Size is a key aspect of biology, and knowing it can help us develop ideas on the role a species played in an ecosystem, its food requirements, its athletic abilities and other aspects of its biology. Ideally, complete remains are needed if we want to work out an animal's mass, enough for us to get a firm idea of the animal's length and shape. When parts of a skeleton are missing, we can make sensible guesses about the missing parts by looking at related species.

When a complete or near-complete skeleton is available, one old-fashioned technique used to estimate body mass is to make a scale model of the complete living animal that includes all the reconstructed soft tissues (its muscles, skin and organs). This model can then be dunked in water (or sand) to see how much it displaces, and the mass of the water (or sand) displaced by the model can then be scaled up to obtain the mass of the full-sized creature. While described as 'old-fashioned', this technique is probably fairly reliable if performed correctly. However, it's difficult to be confident that the models used are as accurate as they need to be. Has the model-maker attached the right amount of muscle, for example? Has the model-maker accounted for the large quantities of air that the live animal would have contained? As we discuss below, the bodies of saurischians contained a large number of air-filled sacs, in addition to the air within the dinosaur's lungs and gut.

The technique just described relies on information from the whole animal. Work on living animals has shown how an animal's body mass can often be worked out from a single measurement taken from just one bone. In birds, there seems to be a reliable relationship between 'whole body mass' and the circumference of the femur. Working out a fossil bird's mass – even a fossil bird known only from a few bones – is therefore possible. But this technique only works because ornithologists have collected data from hundreds of individuals of numerous species where the body mass has been measured precisely from living animals.

Mass estimates for extinct dinosaurs like *Stegosaurus* have varied a great deal from one study to the next. This is partly because some methods used to estimate mass are more reliable than others, but it might also be because members of a species can vary a great deal according to how well nourished and how muscular they are.

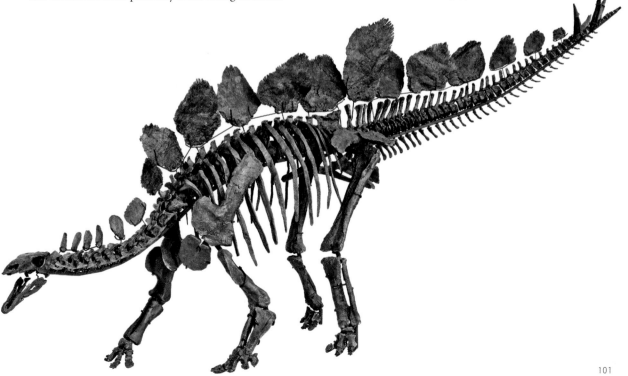

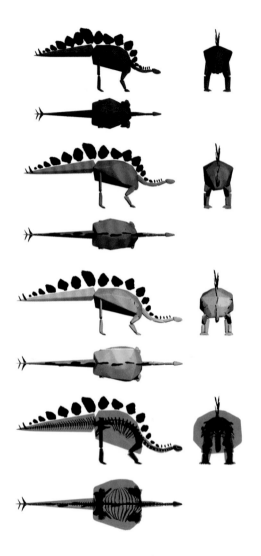

A digital modelling technique called convex hulling allows the soft tissue outline of an animal to be estimated. The problem is that knowing exactly how much soft tissue an animal possessed when alive is often not possible. These different convex hull models of *Stegosaurus* show the dinosaur with a small amount of soft tissue, an intermediate amount and a large amount.

Digital modelling techniques also allow palaeontologists to work out the volume and mass of dinosaurs. By photographing mounted skeletons from many angles and combining these photos in the computer, experts can create accurate three-dimensional models. A similar technique involves the use of lasers. By scanning the surface of a structure like a dinosaur skeleton, a laser scanner can build up a digital model of the whole thing. When assembled in the computer this can, again, be used to create a three-dimensional model of the object. These digital copies are far easier to work with than the real objects (especially if we're talking about entire skeletons). Because the models are three-dimensional, they can be used to work out the volume, and therefore the mass, of the animal.

Another digital technique – termed convex hulling – involves the creation of polygonal shapes around a scanned skeleton – shapes that try to approximate the amount of soft tissue present on the animal when it was alive. One problem with this technique is that it almost certainly underestimates the quantity of soft tissue that must sometimes have been present, since it doesn't take account of areas where large muscles extended well beyond the limits of the bones (as they did in some dinosaurs). When convex hulling has been applied to the skeletons of living animals, the masses that have been discovered are very similar to the actual masses already known for the animals concerned. This shows that the technique is quite accurate when properly applied. Convex hulling has been used on several dinosaur skeletons, including the *Stegosaurus* in the Natural History Museum, London. The specimen is ideal for this method since it's a complete, articulated individual.

With several techniques available for estimating mass, is any one better than the others? Different results are often found when different techniques are applied. Mass estimates for big specimens of *Tyrannosaurus* have ranged from 4 t to an incredible 18 t, while estimates for the giant South American sauropod *Dreadnoughtus* have ranged from about 40 t to almost 60 t. These are considerable differences. Maybe they show that some of these techniques are more reliable than others.

In 2015, Charlotte Brassey and colleagues compared different mass estimation techniques. Using convex hulling, they estimated a mass of

1.5 t for the *Stegosaurus* specimen. This figure is lower than the estimates (up to 3.7 t) gained using limb bone circumference data from other *Stegosaurus* specimens. Why the difference? The reason for this discrepancy is not that one of the methods is flawed, but that the London specimen was still growing at the time of death and hadn't reached full size, whereas the other specimens that gave the larger body mass were fully grown adults. While the use of limb bone measurements works best on adult dinosaurs, convex hulling can be used on dinosaurs of any size.

The more methods we have to estimate the mass of extinct dinosaurs, the better we can be at cross-checking the results, and the more likely it is that we can discover results that are close to reality. But, in some cases, maybe the variation we see in dinosaur mass estimates reflects the actual variation that must really have existed within dinosaur populations. Some *Tyrannosaurus* specimens, for example, may well have been far more muscular than others, and hence far heavier. We'll come back to this idea in a moment.

MUSCLES AND THEIR FUNCTION

Like all vertebrates, non-bird dinosaurs had a complex system of muscles. Many muscles are attached to bones. When activated via nerve impulses from the brain and spinal cord, they exert a pulling action on the bones and so allow animals to move their bones at various hinges and joints. Other muscles are attached to organs enclosed by the skeleton. There are, for example, muscles that enable the intestines to contract and move food through the digestive system, muscles that form the heart and keep it pumping, and muscles that allow eyelids and nostrils to be moved.

Virtually all of our ideas about the muscular anatomy of non-bird dinosaurs come from the bracketing technique discussed on p.19. In other words, we look at the muscles of living crocodylians and birds, and reconstruct the muscles of non-bird dinosaurs based on those present in the living animals that bracket them. These extrapolations receive support from information found directly on dinosaur skeletons, since ridges and mounds, rough patches (termed 'scars') and projecting wings and finger-like prongs of bone can often give us a good idea of where muscles were originally attached in life. Obvious ridges on bones, called intermuscular lines, also help us to work out the position of muscle attachment points.

We should say that the muscles of living animals do not always match the scars, bumps and other structures seen on skeletons, meaning that at least some of the ideas we have about muscle anatomy in non-bird dinosaurs are still up for debate. This is not really a problem for

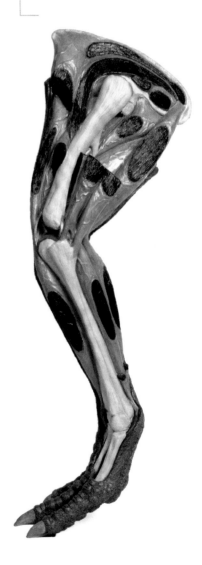

Information from living animals, combined with scars and bony lumps on fossil bones, allows palaeontologists to work out how the muscles of non-bird dinosaurs were arranged and how big they were. This reconstruction shows the hindlimb musculature of the ornithopod *Hypsilophodon*.

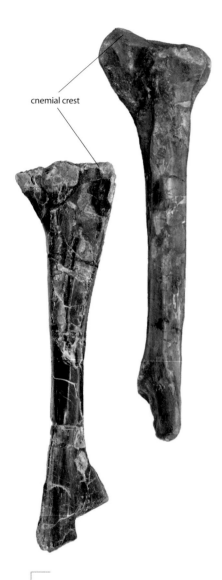

cnemial crest

The tibia or shin bone of virtually all dinosaurs possesses a prominent triangular projection termed the cnemial crest. This formed the main attachment site for a large, bulging muscle that would have covered the front surface of the shin. The tibia on the left belongs to the ornithopod *Mantellisaurus,* and the one on the right to the theropod *Megalosaurus.*

the majority of muscles, since we can be confident about their position in extinct animals on the basis of bracketing. This goes for jaw muscles, chest and arm muscles, and for the muscles present along the length of the neck, back and tail, and those that connect the ribs.

Non-bird dinosaurs resemble modern birds in the muscles of their lower legs, since large bony crests on the tibia – in particular the large, forward-projecting cnemial crest at the top of the bone's front surface – show that a massive, bulging muscle was present here. A similar bulging muscle was present on the rear surface of the tibia. Virtually all the dinosaurs of the Mesozoic must have had 'drumstick'-shaped shins, as birds do today.

One of the biggest and most interesting of muscles in the non-bird dinosaur body is called the caudofemoralis longus. This long, thick muscle attaches at one end to the fourth trochanter – the crest or finger-like bony structure on the back of the femur – and at the other end to the bony prongs that grow sideways from the tail vertebrae. This muscle is present today in lizards and crocodylians and is one of the most important muscles in walking. It pulls backwards on the femur, propelling the animal forwards during its walking or running cycle.

The fact that this muscle is attached to an obvious bony feature (the fourth trochanter) means that changes in the size, shape and position of the trochanter tell us interesting things about changes in dinosaur muscle anatomy. Ornithischians have a wide range of different trochanter shapes. Some have simple, ridge-shaped fourth trochanters while others have fourth trochanters that project downwards from the back edge of the femur, forming a spike- or finger-like growth. These different shapes match with the different walking and running styles used by the different ornithischian groups. Ridge-shaped fourth trochanters are typical of quadrupeds and spike-like fourth trochanters are typical of bipeds. We know from living animals that muscle activity has a major influence on the shape of trochanters, so these differences show that the caudofemoral muscle anatomy of quadrupedal ornithischians was quite different from that of bipedal ones.

Another important trend in the evolution of the fourth trochanter is seen in coelurosaurs. Over time, the fourth trochanter became smaller and smaller, changing from a thick, obvious ridge to a low scar, eventually disappearing altogether (most modern birds lack it entirely). What seems to have happened is that these dinosaurs switched from using their caudofemoral muscles in walking to using muscles that were attached to the hips instead. As the caudofemoral muscles became smaller and weaker, the fourth trochanter reduced in size. With the caudofemoral muscles no longer so important, the tail could become smaller, slimmer and shorter. In contrast to virtually all other dinosaur groups, maniraptorans reduced the bulk and length of the tail considerably, resulting in groups with drastically shortened tails, like therizinosaurs, oviraptorosaurs and birds.

Deep, robust, sideways-pointing bony wings project from the vertebrae at the base of the tail in many sauropods, ankylosaurs and other dinosaurs and show that the muscles here must have been enormous. Exactly how enormous is difficult to say, and little work has been done so far on how big these muscles were and on how they might have worked. Initial investigations indicate that the huge, broad muscles attached to the tail-base in the whip-tailed diplodocoids, club-tailed ankylosaurs and spiky-tailed stegosaurs were strong enough to allow these tails to be pulled hard to the side with enough force to allow the weaponized tail-tip to be used as a whip, a club or a mace. A computer-assisted study of tail muscles in club-tailed ankylosaurs by ankylosaur specialist Victoria Arbour showed that the tail had enough muscular force, and a strong enough club, to break bone.

The tail vertebrae of the North American sauropod *Diplodocus* have tall spines that project from their upper surfaces (termed neural spines) and rod-like bones that project from their lower surfaces (termed chevrons or haemal spines). In addition, long, wing-shaped bony prongs called transverse processes project sideways from each vertebra as well. In this image, the animal's body is on the right.

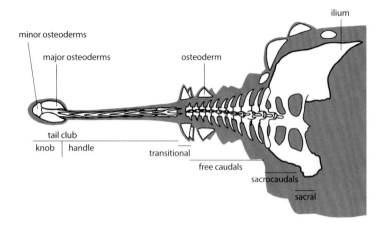

minor osteoderms

major osteoderms

osteoderm

ilium

tail club

knob | handle

transitional

free caudals

sacrocaudals

sacral

There are indications that we might have underestimated the amount of muscle present in some non-bird dinosaurs. If we look at the tail vertebrae in front or rear view, for example, the tendency among palaeontologists and artists has been to apply a thin layer of muscles over them that barely extends beyond the outer edges of the various body spines and wings that project from the top and sides of the vertebrae. But if we look at the tails of living lizards, crocodylians and even birds, we see that their tail vertebrae are deeply submerged in soft tissue, and surrounded on all sides by massive, thick muscles that extend well beyond the edges of these bones.

When reconstructed this way, the tails of dinosaurs like hadrosaurs and tyrannosaurs are broader, deeper and chunkier than shown in many reconstructions. It's possible that this view of heavier-tailed dinosaurs will have an impact on what we think about the athletic abilities of dinosaurs and on how weight was distributed across their bodies.

While we can be reasonably confident about the positions of muscles present in non-bird dinosaurs, one thing that we often cannot determine is exactly how big those muscles were. Living animals show that individuals of the same species can vary a huge amount in terms of muscle sizes. This variation is partly genetic, but also depends on the history of the individual, with factors like health and the quality of the animal's diet being important. This variation might make quite some difference as regards the life appearance of the animal concerned and, again, might also make a difference when it comes to our efforts to reconstruct an extinct animal's

Some North American ankylosaurids possessed a stiffened, handle-like end section to the tail, tipped with a bony club. Bony spines projected from the sides of the tail's flexible base. The pelvis in these animals was incredibly wide, as was the body as a whole.

Huge muscle attachment sites are present on the rear part of the ankylosaurid pelvis. These muscles were also attached to the tail and would have made it an incredibly powerful organ. These images show the pelvis as if the animal was facing away from the reader in three-quarters view.

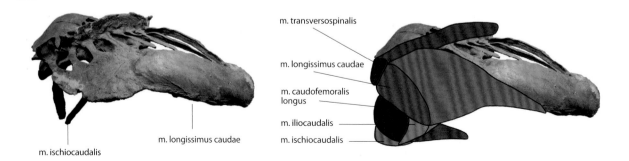

m. transversospinalis

m. longissimus caudae

m. caudofemoralis longus

m. iliocaudalis

m. ischiocaudalis

m. ischiocaudalis

m. longissimus caudae

athletic abilities. An animal with huge hindlimb muscles, for example, might be able to run much faster than one with undersized muscles.

This topic was explored in a digital modelling project published by John Hutchinson and colleagues. Hutchinson constructed a digital *Tyrannosaurus* and showed how the same individual animal could have had slim, lightweight muscles or much larger, thicker, heavier muscles – or any number of intermediates between these two – depending on its health, diet and lifestyle. The resulting models – all of which are equally plausible – emphasise the fact that even a single individual dinosaur might have varied a great deal in mass and also in life appearance.

RESPIRATION AND THE AIR-SAC SYSTEM

The idea that the bones of non-bird dinosaurs were unusual compared to those of both mammals and reptiles such as lizards emerged as long ago as the 1850s. Even fragmentary dinosaur bones discovered in England during the 19th century showed that some non-bird dinosaurs had pneumatic skeletons (where some or many of their bones contained air-filled sacs, connected to the lungs by tubes called diverticula). We can identify this pneumaticity by finding large open holes (pneumatic foramina) on the outsides of bones. These holes lead into large internal chambers. This pneumatic system is a familiar and normal feature of the bird skeleton, and today we know that it was widespread in non-bird saurischians too. Virtually all extinct theropods were pneumatic, and the majority of sauropodomorphs possessed these air sacs too.

Elsewhere in the dinosaur family tree, ornithischians lack any pneumaticity in the skeleton. Furthermore, pneumaticity is only very poorly developed in the oldest sauropodomorphs and theropods. In the species concerned, only two or three of their vertebrae possess pneumatic features, and several early members of both groups lack pneumaticity altogether. The picture is further complicated by the fact that pterosaurs – distant cousins of dinosaurs within bird-line archosaurs – have pneumatic bones too.

We don't yet fully understand what happened in the evolution of pneumaticity in early dinosaurs and their close relatives. It might be that pneumaticity evolved independently on two or more separate occasions in early saurischians, or it might be that pneumaticity was present in the

As shown by this simplified archosaur cladogram, skeletal pneumaticity was shared by both pterosaurs and saurischians, yet it remains unknown from ornithischians and from early dinosauromorphs like *Marasuchus*. Maybe it evolved several times.

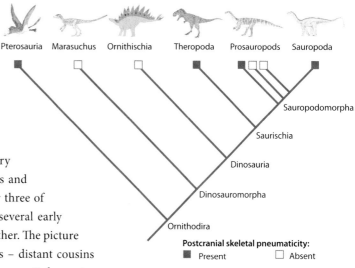

Pterosauria   Marasuchus   Ornithischia   Theropoda   Prosauropods   Sauropoda

Sauropodomorpha

Saurischia

Dinosauria

Dinosauromorpha

Ornithodira

Postcranial skeletal pneumaticity:
■ Present   ☐ Absent

dinosaur common ancestor and then lost two or more times in different dinosaur lineages. This is another case where more fossils will help provide the answers.

In birds, the air sacs inside the bones are not the only ones present. There are also a series of large air sacs located within the body's main cavity, including a pair on either side of the neck, a large one close to the furcula, and three pairs in the chest and abdomen. Each of these sacs sends off diverticula which contact the bones nearby and cause them to become pneumatic too. The air sacs within the neck vertebrae are connected to the air sacs on either side of the neck, and vertebrae and other bones further back in the skeleton are air-filled because diverticula from the chest and abdominal air sacs have invaded these bones and caused the growth of new air sacs in these bones as well.

Living birds possess a series of large air-filled sacs throughout the body, all of which are connected to the lungs. Strong evidence indicates that air sacs of this sort were also present in several groups of non-bird dinosaurs.

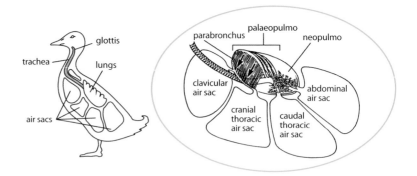

What this means is that the presence and distribution of any pneumatic openings in the non-bird dinosaur skeleton can reveal the presence of the various air-sac groups seen in living birds. We can say that the air sacs present on either side of the neck evolved very early on in the history of saurischian dinosaurs, as most of them have pneumatic openings in their neck vertebrae that would have been connected to these air sacs. We also know that chest and abdominal air sacs were widespread across theropods and sauropods for most of their evolutionary history, as other parts of their skeletons contain the tell-tale openings associated with these particular air sacs. Evidence that the so-called interclavicular air-sac was present in some non-bird dinosaurs comes from the pneumatized furculas and shoulder girdles seen in several theropods, diplodocoids and titanosaurs. It's abundantly clear from all this evidence that saurischian dinosaurs of many sorts possessed an air-sac system very similar to that present in birds today.

The presence of these complex air-sac systems has several implications for dinosaur biology. For one thing, these dinosaurs must have been lighter than previously thought. If a substantial portion of their internal volume was occupied by air – rather than by tissue or fluid – then they were less dense compared to non-pneumatic animals. Mathew Wedel, a sauropod expert with a special interest in pneumaticity, has calculated that the pneumatic system of *Diplodocus* made it approximately 10% lighter than it would be without air sacs.

Skeletal pneumaticity literally changed the body shape of at least some of the dinosaurs that possessed it. The vertebrae of sauropods, for example, are proportionally huge relative to those of other big animals. It seems that this is because the vertebrae expanded outwards during evolution as they developed larger, more complex air-filled chambers. Exactly why sauropods expanded their vertebrae in this way is uncertain. Perhaps it increased the size of muscle attachment sites on the vertebrae and so allowed for bigger, stronger muscles, or perhaps these expanded vertebrae had a protective function for the more vulnerable parts of the spinal column.

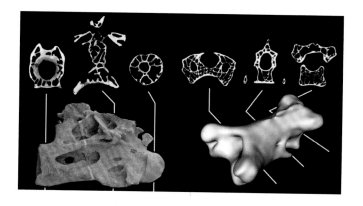

Whatever the force driving this trend, the fact that the vertebrae contained so much air means that they were extremely light for their size. Wedel's calculations show that the entire neck skeleton of a big sauropod was similar in mass to just one of its arm bones. The fact that sauropods (and other saurischians) could evolve such lightweight neck skeletons probably helps explain why they were so good at evolving incredibly long necks. In other animals that lack air spaces in their bones (like mammals) a neck skeleton the same size as a sauropod neck would have been considerably heavier.

The fact that huge quantities of air were continually being pushed around much of the body's interior, as well as the skeleton, also means that these dinosaurs were probably able to flush unwanted heat out of the body via this internal pneumatic system. The gigantic muscles and enormous guts of big sauropodomorphs – filled much (or all) of the time with fermenting plant material – almost certainly generated vast amounts of heat. Some experts have suggested that these heat levels could have been dangerously high, so much so that specialized heat-loss mechanisms or behaviours might have been required. Maybe the pneumatic system was a key solution to this problem.

The cross-sections of the *Apatosaurus* neck vertebra shown on the left are very similar to the cross-sections of the modern swan neck vertebra shown on the right. The black spaces represent air within the bones. Both bones are substantially air-filled.

The presence of these air-filled sacs and bones also mean that saurischians were buoyant should they choose to go swimming. By accounting for pneumaticity in digitally modelled sauropods, palaeontologist Donald Henderson showed that sauropods would have floated high in the water like gigantic corks and would also have been unstable and prone to tipping.

The air-sac system might also have contributed to dinosaurian vocal abilities. Studies of living birds show that their long windpipes, large air sacs and air-filled chest bones enhance their abilities to make louder, deeper calls than might otherwise be possible. Sauropods and the larger theropods were big animals that would very probably have made loud noises and sent vocal signals over great distances, so it's tempting to speculate that they would have used air sacs in similar ways. For now this idea is speculative but we hope to see it tested in the future.

DIGESTION

There's no doubt that non-bird dinosaurs possessed a digestive system. Working out exactly what that system was like is almost impossible, given that stomachs, guts and other organs are virtually – but not completely, as we'll see – unknown as fossils. Nevertheless, many clues from the fossil record allow us to make educated guesses, and phylogenetic bracketing can help us too.

We can say with confidence that fossil dinosaurs of all sorts would have had an oesophagus that connected the mouth to an expanded, bag-like stomach, and an intestine that would have ended with a chamber and its exit, the cloaca. However, the bracketing technique provides us with

2m

Sauropods were so air-filled that they must have floated higher in the water than previously thought, and been highly unstable when in deep water. Perhaps they avoided swimming and restricted their aquatic activities to wading.

The crocodylian digestive system is essentially like that of a bird, but a crop is never present, and the anatomy of the stomach is different. Were non-bird dinosaurs crocodylian-like in anatomy, or bird-like? Or were some crocodylian-like and others bird-like?

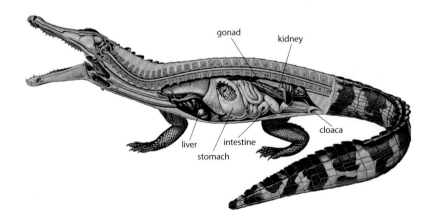

gonad

kidney

cloaca

liver

intestine

stomach

ambiguous answers if we try to understand things in more detail, since modern birds and modern crocodylians have digestive systems that differ in several ways.

Crocodylians have a large stomach at the end of the oesophagus, which is divided into two compartments – one called the cardiac sac at the front, and another called the pyloric region at the back. The bird stomach also consists of two sections: a tubular part at the front called the proventriculus – it has a ridged internal surface and is the place where mucus and acid is produced – and a more muscular gizzard section behind, which often has roughened structures that are used to mash up hard food items. Many birds further differ from crocodylians in having a widened section along the oesophagus. This structure is termed the crop and is used in storing food. We know from amazing fossils found in China that all of these structures – a crop and a two-part stomach with a distinct gizzard – were present in birds that lived during the Early Cretaceous, about 120 million years ago.

The fact that crocodylians and birds differ in anatomy here means that we can't be entirely confident about the condition in non-bird dinosaurs. They might have had the sort of anatomy we see in crocodylians, or they might have shared crops and gizzards with birds. What seems likely is that non-bird dinosaurs possessed a range of digestive features, perhaps with the more bird-like theropods possessing those features seen in birds while other dinosaur groups were more crocodylian-like. This possibility receives some support from fossils, since stomach stones, called gastroliths, which are used to mash up food within the muscular gizzards of birds, are also known in ornithomimosaurs and oviraptorosaurs among non-bird theropods.

Within saurischians, crops are unknown other than in birds. A peculiar swelling in the neck region that's been termed a crop is preserved in a mummified specimen of the hadrosaur *Brachylophosaurus*. If this really is a crop, it shows that at least some ornithischians evolved a crop independently of the one seen in birds – a reminder that bracketing is only a rough guide to the anatomy of extinct groups. And for all our predictions from bracketing, the possibility exists that other dinosaur groups evolved their own crops or crop-like structures, or their own gizzard-like organs.

We're not entirely restricted to bracketing when it comes to the anatomy of dinosaur guts – one exceptional fossil has its gut preserved

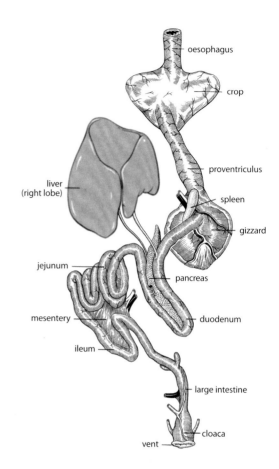

The digestive system of modern birds consists of a tube – the oesophagus – that connects the mouth to the stomach, and a far longer intestine that connects the stomach to the cloaca. An expanded region termed the crop is often present along the oesophagus. Part of the stomach is occupied by a muscular gizzard.

Guts and muscle fibres are present in this only known specimen of *Scipionyx*, but none of the external covering of its body is present. Its large teeth and big hand claws suggest that it was able to look after itself, despite being very young.

in place. This is *Scipionyx* from the Lower Cretaceous rocks of Italy, a juvenile theropod that's just 23 cm (9 in) long. The fossil of *Scipionyx* is almost entirely complete and fully articulated, lacking only its feet and the end of its tail. Remarkably, *Scipionyx* preserves a near-complete, looping section of intestine, preserved in place between the chest and the base of the tail. As expected, the cloaca is located just beneath the start of the tail.

A small segment of oesophagus is also present, as are parallel lines near the tail-base that appear to be bundles of muscle fibres. There's no direct evidence for a stomach, presumably because the strong acid it once contained dissolved it away before fossilization began. Scales and bone fragments inside the guts show that *Scipionyx* had eaten fishes and lizards.

We can also make educated guesses about the anatomy of the non-bird dinosaur digestive system by applying our knowledge of modern animals that are not close relatives of dinosaurs, but are similar in lifestyle or diet. Sauropods and other large herbivorous dinosaurs, for example, were herbivores that swallowed and digested huge quantities of low-quality plant material. Among living animals, a similar strategy is practised by herbivores like hippos, cattle and elephants, but also by animals more closely related to sauropods, including iguanas, geese, grouse and ostriches. All use a system called hindgut fermentation, where the food spends relatively little time in the stomach and most of the digestion takes place in the intestines. The intestines in these animals are enormous, and digestion is relatively inefficient, resulting in droppings that contain a significant quantity of poorly digested plant material. It's likely that sauropods were hindgut fermenters too, broadly similar in digestive anatomy to their modern equivalents.

The amazingly well fossilized intestine of the tiny theropod *Scipionyx* is preserved in a looping arrangement that was almost certainly present in life. The tiny folds on the walls of the intestine can be seen, as can microscopically fine anatomical details.

DINOSAUR LIFE APPEARANCE

Our knowledge of dinosaur skeletons, of the positions and shapes of their muscles, and of such things as their digestive and pneumatic systems means that we have good insights into most aspects of non-bird dinosaur anatomy. As a result, we can make confident statements about the overall shape and size of those non-bird dinosaurs known from good remains. These areas of information tell us what non-bird dinosaurs looked like on the inside, but what about their external anatomy? How did they appear in life?

In decades past, non-bird dinosaurs were shown as flabby, thick-bodied creatures with small, slender muscles. This changed during and after the Dinosaur Renaissance. Non-bird dinosaurs (and Mesozoic birds too) were now depicted as lightly built, skinny creatures with bulging, muscular limbs but slim necks, bodies and tails. This view of lightly built, 'streamlined' dinosaurs is partly correct in view of what we know, but it also seems that scientists and artists sometimes went too far. They gave their dinosaurs big leg muscles, but fat and loose skin tissue were removed, tails became too narrow and bony, and just a thin veneer of skin was left across the face. The result was reconstructions that made dinosaurs look undernourished or even zombie-like. The reconstructions sometimes lacked soft tissue structures that were definitely present during life, like the big intestines and plump bellies of herbivores, and the broad tail muscles that must have been present in those dinosaurs with a long, powerful tail. This artistic phenomenon has been called shrink-wrapping.

In recent years, a new generation of artists and palaeontologists who pay better attention to the anatomy of living animals has arisen. The new scientific approaches mentioned earlier in this book – involving technological advances like CT-scanning and digital modelling as well as new approaches to the study of extinct organisms, like phylogenetic bracketing – mean that palaeontologists interested in anatomy have been better able to show what the soft tissues of extinct dinosaurs were like. Also important is the fact that new fossils have been found, some of which provide exciting or surprising data on life appearance.

One area of debate and uncertainty concerns the appearance of the non-bird dinosaur face. Based on bracketing, it doesn't seem likely

Non-bird dinosaurs are usually shown with the fleshy nostril opening positioned at the back of the nostril region. But maybe this is wrong. Some experts argue that the fleshy nostril was more likely located far forwards, close to the mouth. Note also the competing ideas on whether non-bird dinosaurs had lips.

Bony nostril

Traditional caudal fleshy nostril

New hypothesis: rostral fleshy nostril

that non-bird dinosaurs had muscles across the face or cheek, so they should be reconstructed with faces that aren't too different in shape from the underlying skull bones. However, the jaw edges of many non-bird dinosaurs possess features that some scientists have interpreted as evidence for fleshy lips and cheeks. Among these are lines of small holes (foramina) and ridge-like structures that extend along the sides of the face and lower jaw, parallel to the tooth rows. It makes sense to imagine that some dinosaurs had lip-like structures similar to those of lizards or snakes. These would have kept their gums moist and sealed the mouth when the jaws were closed. It also makes sense to think that dinosaurs that sliced or mashed up plant material might have possessed cheek-like structures to help keep food inside the mouth. And while cheeks are not typical of living reptiles, there are birds (including flamingos, condors and parrots) that possess sheets of skin that form structures of this sort.

While these ideas seem logical, 'logical' is not the same thing as 'well supported by evidence'. In recent years a team of anatomists led by Larry Witmer have studied non-bird dinosaur skulls with the aim of testing these possibilities. Some of their conclusions run counter to many of those previously proposed by other palaeontologists, and they suggest some surprising new ideas regarding non-bird dinosaur appearance. Based on nostril position in living turtles, crocodiles and birds, and on the pattern of bony holes and grooves associated with blood vessels, Witmer has argued that the fleshy nostrils of certain fossil dinosaurs were not positioned far back within the bony opening as usually shown, but right at the front, close to the edge of the upper jaw. Witmer has argued that this was true even of sauropods, a group where the bony nostril openings are frequently positioned way up on the forehead.

Witmer and colleagues have also argued that cheek- and lip-like structures were probably not present, but that non-bird dinosaurs either had a crocodile-like arrangement of tightly fitting facial skin and near-exposed teeth, or hardened skin that formed beak-like edges to the jaw margins. We know for sure that ornithischians had beak tissue sheathing the edges of the upper and lower jaws, since this is preserved in place in some specimens. The idea that beak-like tissue might have continued along the rest of the jaw edges would certainly make ornithischians look odd compared to more familiar reconstructions that show the presence of cheeks.

What was the body covering of non-bird dinosaurs like overall? The scaly skin recorded in many fossil dinosaur species is not thick and wrinkled as sometimes shown by artists but covered

We know that ornithischians had beak tissue covering the tips of their upper and lower jaws. But did they also have fleshy cheeks further back, or did tough beak tissue line the edges of their jaws, as shown in the ceratopsian *Leptoceratops*?

Complete, articulated skeletons like this *Edmontosaurus* from Alberta, Canada, are sometimes preserved with skin patches (or the impressions left by skin patches) in place.

This fossilized patch of skin from an *Edmontosaurus* shows the small, rounded, non-overlapping scales typical of big, scaly-skinned dinosaurs. Unusual dry conditions are required for skin to be preserved in this way.

by scales arranged in chainmail- or honeycomb-like arrangements, sometimes interspersed with larger, pyramid-like scales. Most of these scales are small and densely arranged, meaning that the skin would have had a smooth appearance when viewed from a few metres away. Many excellent examples of non-bird dinosaur skin are known, providing a great deal of detailed information on the skin surface. Among the most famous examples are the several mummified hadrosaur specimens from the Late Cretaceous of Canada.

Artists have often drawn spines, frills and spikes projecting from the necks, back and tails of non-bird dinosaurs, an idea based on similar features seen in modern lizards. Today we know that some non-bird dinosaurs really did possess these features. Low, bony nodules are present along the backbone of the theropod *Ceratosaurus*, while tall, triangular spines have been discovered in association with the tail of a *Diplodocus*-like sauropod from Wyoming. How widespread these nodules and spines were remains unknown. Was *Ceratosaurus* a uniquely flamboyant theropod, or did many related theropods have ornaments like this? Similarly, were those dorsal spines unique to *Diplodocus*, or were they present across all sauropods or sauropodomorphs? Future finds will shed light on these questions.

The mummified hadrosaurs also reveal that crests and frills were present in some non-bird dinosaur groups. Serrated frills and frills resembling picket fences are known for several hadrosaur species. These frills attach to the rear edge of the bony head crests in crested species, suggesting that bony crests were continuous with the back frills in these dinosaurs.

Several tantalizing but poorly preserved fossil impressions hint at the existence of other soft tissue structures in some dinosaurs. One specimen of the Asian tyrannosaurid *Tarbosaurus* has a dewlap or throat-pouch preserved beneath its lower jaw. A similar feature is also present in the ornithomimosaur *Pelecanimimus*. And one specimen of the giant ceratopsian *Triceratops* has short spikes projecting from the centres of some of the scales across its flanks and back.

The most exciting news about non-bird dinosaur appearance concerns the many species now preserved with feathers, filaments and similar structures. Palaeontologists have thought for decades that bird-like theropods – perhaps all maniraptorans or even all coelurosaurs – were very probably feathered. Confirmation of this idea arrived during the late 1990s. Thanks to spectacular fossils from the Lower Cretaceous rocks of Liaoning in China, we now know for sure that oviraptorosaurs, dromaeosaurids, troodontids and members of related maniraptoran groups were feathered. Long feathers grew from their hands and lower

Small maniraptoran theropods preserved with their feathers in place show that a thick plumage covered the body. Bushy head crests and long hand, arm, leg, foot and tail feathers are preserved in some species. This is *Jinfengopteryx* from the Early Cretaceous of China.

arms, the end part of the tail, and sometimes from the hindlimbs as well. Much of the face and snout was covered in fuzz, not scales. Short feathers covered the body, and the feet and toes were also fuzzy or feathery in at least some of these dinosaurs.

One of the most famous fossil maniraptorans – *Velociraptor* – comes from rock layers laid down in a Late Cretaceous desert, an environment in which feathers and other soft structures are rarely preserved. But it turns out that the bones of this dinosaur reveal evidence of the feathers that once covered its body. Small, regularly spaced bony lumps present along the ulna in the arm of *Velociraptor* are extremely similar to the quill knobs of living birds that help anchor the tips of the feather shafts. The fact that quill knobs are present in *Velociraptor* means that there are some non-bird dinosaurs where the presence of feathers can be demonstrated, even though the feathers themselves aren't preserved.

The members of several non-maniraptoran coelurosaur groups were not clothed in true, complex feathers. Instead, they had coverings of simpler, hair-like filaments. Fossils from Liaoning show that this was true of compsognathids and tyrannosauroids. Masses of long filaments are preserved on *Yutyrannus*, a tyrannosauroid from Liaoning, which reached up to 9 m (30 ft) in length. Filaments of this sort are not unique to Chinese theropods. Two small theropods from the Late Jurassic of Germany – *Sciurimimus* and *Juravenator* – possess filaments on their bodies and tails, as do ornithomimosaur fossils from the Late Cretaceous of Canada.

One ornithomimosaur has dark stripes on its lower arm bones that show it had long feathers or feather-like structures growing from its arms. Interestingly, these are not present in a juvenile specimen of the same species, indicating that only adults possessed these longer arm structures. This hints at a role in sexual display.

The fuzzy and feathery coats of these theropods show that coelurosaurs of several sorts possessed both simple, filament-like structures as well as complex feathers, with the latter perhaps being unique to maniraptorans. At the moment, it seems

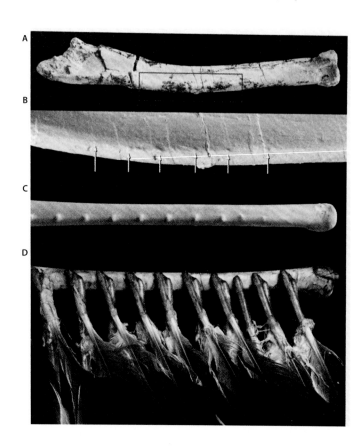

The lower arm bones of the Mongolian theropod *Velociraptor* possess widely spaced knobs (shown here in A and B). These are very similar to the quill knobs present in living birds (shown in C). In birds, these knobs are the attachment sites for the large wing feathers (D).

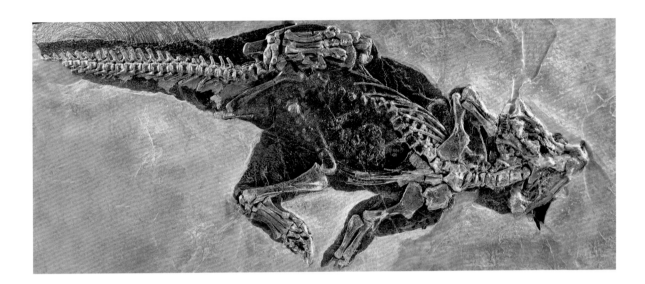

likely that the filaments we see in various non-birds were 'ancestral' to feathers proper. We'll return to this subject later, in Chapter 5.

Rather more surprising is the fact that hair-like filaments are known for several ornithischians. One specimen of the ceratopsian *Psittacosaurus* has long, hair-like filaments sprouting from the upper surface of its tail. The Late Jurassic heterodontosaurid *Tianyulong* also has long filaments on much of its body and tail, and the small, bipedal ornithischian *Kulindadromeus* from the Middle or Late Jurassic of Siberia has filaments across much of its body as well as longer, ribbon-like structures in a few places too. In addition, *Kulindadromeus* has small, plate-like structures that have thin filaments growing from the plate's rear edge. Small scales are present on its hands and feet and paired, rectangular plates cover the upper surface of its tail.

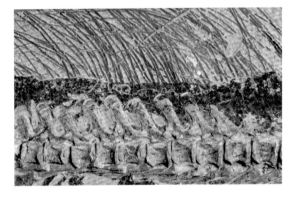

The fact that theropods and ornithischians both possess filaments raises the possibility that structures like this were present in the dinosaurian common ancestor, and therefore inherited by the early members of all dinosaur groups. Possible support for this view comes from the fact that pterosaurs, which are close relatives of dinosaurs within the archosaur family tree, possess filaments too. The possibility also exists that these structures evolved independently on several occasions – a plausible model in view of how diverse dinosaurs were and how many evolutionary possibilities might have been available to them. In addition, the vast majority of ornithischians, all sauropodomorphs and many early theropods only show

This complete specimen of the Chinese ceratopsian *Psittacosaurus* has much of its body outline preserved, and scaly skin patches are present too. Surprisingly, long, curved filaments sprout from the upper surface of its tail.

Viewed up-close, the filaments on the tail of a *Psittacosaurus* specimen are flat, but they might have originally been cylindrical and perhaps tubular. They're also deeply embedded in the skin.

A patch of skin from the base of the tail of the Chinese theropod *Sinosauropteryx* (marked with an arrow in A) possesses filaments filled with microscopically tiny, rounded melanosomes (B) of the sort associated with reds and browns.

The filaments of the Chinese maniraptoran theropod *Sinornithosaurus* (C) are also filled with melanosomes. Again, there are rounded ones of the sort associated with reds and browns, while oval, aligned ones shown in (D) are associated with blacks and greys.

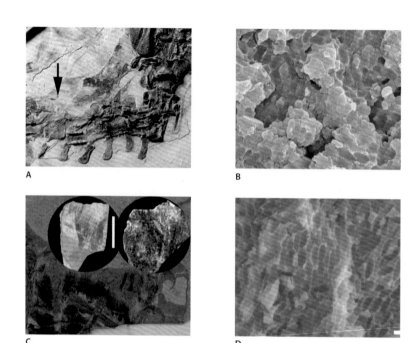

A

B

C

D

evidence for scaly skin, making it more likely that the filaments seen rarely in ornithischians are unrelated to those present in bird-like theropods.

One of the most frequently asked questions about dinosaur life appearance is how you know what colour it was. Until very recently, the response to this question was that colour is unknowable and that the decisions made by artists mostly represent guesswork and whimsy. This changed in 2010 when microscopic structures called melanosomes were reported from the filaments of the small Cretaceous theropod *Sinosauropteryx*. Melanosomes are microscopic grain-like structures that contain the pigments responsible for giving animals their colours. Different shapes of melanosomes are linked to different colours. In modern birds, rounded melanosomes contain red and brown pigments, and long, rod-shaped melanosomes contain pigments that give grey or black colouration. Those of *Sinosauropteryx* indicate that this dinosaur was mostly brown, with brown and white striping along its tail. Since 2010, melanosomes of different sorts have been reported from other non-bird theropods, including *Sinornithosaurus* and *Microraptor*, and in early birds too, including *Anchiornis*, *Archaeopteryx* and *Confuciusornis*.

So far, all of the melanosomes reported from these animals suggest dull colorations involving greys, blacks and browns, though a reddish head crest has been described for *Anchiornis*. The melanosome data for *Archaeopteryx* comes from the famous single feather of this animal, discovered in 1860 or 1861. It seems to show that this one feather (which comes from the upper surface of the wing) was black, but we can't say for sure that the whole of the wing's upper surface was black, that the whole wing was black, or that the whole of *Archaeopteryx* was black!

Perhaps the most remarkable of these claims is that the melanosomes preserved on the feathers of *Microraptor* are of a shape unique to black, iridescent feathers. If these observations are valid, *Microraptor* was a black, glossy dinosaur. Based on the size of the ring-like arrangement of plate-like bones in its eye sockets, some experts have proposed that *Microraptor* was active at night. But a problem here is that modern birds with iridescent plumage are always day-active and don't routinely forage in low-light conditions, so maybe this view of a night-active *Microraptor* is incorrect. Hold that thought.

There's also a possibility that these structures might not be true melanosomes at all, but fossil bacteria instead. This suggestion has been considered at length, and most palaeontologists currently accept that the features are true melanosomes. It does seem, however, that the shapes of at least some of the fossil melanosomes might have been modified during the fossilization process. As a result, it may be misleading to use their shape to work out the original colours. In experiments, modern-day bird feathers of all sorts of colours have been buried and heated up, thereby mimicking some aspects of the fossilization process. The melanosomes of the feathers used in these experiments always end up looking like those melanosomes associated with greys and browns. This makes it possible that a wider range of colours was originally present in these fossil feathers, but the modifications to the feathers that happened over millions of years may be hiding their true, original appearance. If this is correct, maybe it's the evidence from the melanosomes, and not the eye sockets, that's giving us misleading information on the biology of *Microraptor*.

The isolated *Archaeopteryx* wing feather, discovered in 1860 or 1861, preserves melanosomes across its surface. These show that the feather was almost certainly black. The feather is just 58 mm (2 in) long and from the upper surface of the wing. It seems to be an upper primary covert.

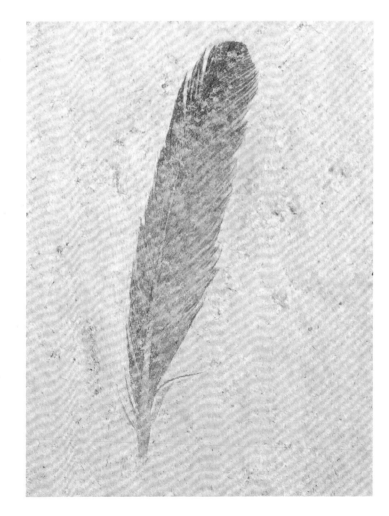

BIOLOGY, ECOLOGY AND BEHAVIOUR

IN PREVIOUS CHAPTERS we've looked at dinosaur diversity and evolution (Chapter 2), and at dinosaur anatomy and appearance (Chapter 3). In this chapter, we show how numerous different pieces of evidence and scientific techniques have been combined to allow scientists to paint a detailed picture of dinosaur biology – to examine how non-bird dinosaurs hunted and ate, how they moved, what sort of metabolism they had, how they reproduced, grew and matured, and how they interacted with the species that they lived with.

DINOSAUR DIET AND FEEDING BEHAVIOUR

One area of dinosaur biology that remains a constant topic of research is diet and feeding behaviour. Partly this is because understanding an extinct animal's diet gives us an easy-to-interpret insight into its life and behaviour, and partly because jaws and teeth are easy to analyse and study. It's easy to make a number of basic observations on the overall shape and general features of dinosaur teeth and jaws, and to link these ideas to diet and lifestyle. These ideas, based on basic anatomy and comparisons with living animals, have also been supported by additional work, such as that involving microscopic wear on the surfaces of teeth and computer modelling of tooth and skull function, as well

The skull of a dinosaur like this *Allosaurus* from the Late Jurassic of the USA is deep and narrow, has a jaw joint suited for rapid opening and closing, and features rows of recurved, serrated teeth. These clues all give us insights on the animal's lifestyle and behaviour.

as discoveries like fossilized stomach contents and droppings, all of which we'll look at later. Teeth that are curved backward (or 'recurved') towards their tips, narrow from side to side and are finely serrated are referred to as 'ziphodont' (meaning 'sword-toothed'). Such teeth are found in living predatory lizards and sharks and are obvious indicators of a predatory lifestyle that involves the attacking and eating of animals. Among dinosaurs, they're typical of big theropods like *Ceratosaurus*, megalosaurids and allosauroids. Ziphodont teeth are usually found in combination with a deep, narrow snout and evidence at the back of the skull and lower jaw for large jaw muscles used in rapid, powerful closing of the mouth.

These dinosaurs also have jaw joints which show that the jaws opened and closed in simple, scissor-like fashion, there being no possibility of complex movements involving sideways, forwards or backwards movement at the joint. This tooth and skull anatomy suggests that rapid, slashing bites were used to weaken and kill prey animals, and that up and down movements of the jaws were used to slice up food items into manageable pieces.

This *Troodon* tooth from Alberta in Canada – just a few centimetres tall – has fine serrations along its leading margin but massive, hooked denticles along its rear margin. This is a tooth that could have been used for eating both flesh and plants.

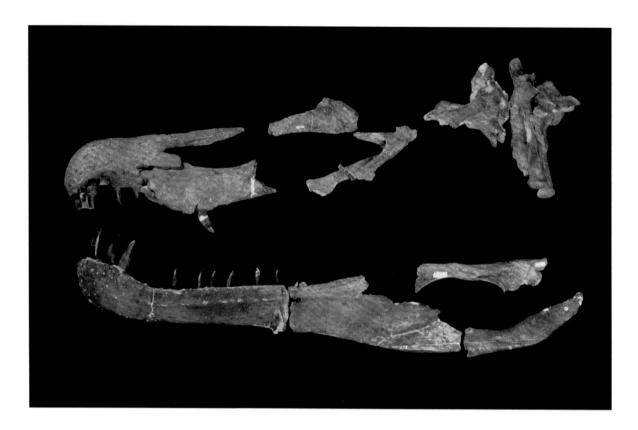

The long, shallow snouts and sinuous jaw margins of spinosaurids like *Baryonyx* (above) from Europe are similar to those of living crocodiles and suggest that these dinosaurs caught fish. Spinosaurid teeth are unusual compared to those of other theropods – they either possess extremely fine micro-serrations or lack serrations entirely.

Evidence from anatomy, stomach contents, and where its remains were preserved, indicate that *Baryonyx* hunted in lakes and rivers for large fish, grabbing them with its long jaws and perhaps its massive hand claws (opposite).

Theropods that fed in this way can be considered typical members of the group, but not all theropods were like this. Long, narrow snouts and jaws and cone-shaped, unserrated teeth are present in spinosaurids. These features resemble what we see in living crocodiles. For these reasons, we interpret spinosaurids as fish-grabbing dinosaurs, and additional data on spinosaurid lifestyle and behaviour confirms this idea. A few other non-bird theropod groups also have especially long, slender snouts and might have preyed on fish too, including the coelophysoids of the Late Triassic and Early Jurassic and a group of Cretaceous maniraptorans called the unenlagiines. Nevertheless, fish eating was fairly rare among predatory dinosaurs.

In strong contrast, broad snouts and jaws, thickened skull bones, evidence for truly enormous jaw-closing muscles, and thick, blunt-tipped teeth are present in some tyrannosaurids, most notably *Tyrannosaurus*. These features suggest a predatory lifestyle that involved bone-crushing bites and perhaps even an ability to eat bone. Other pieces of information support this view of tyrannosaurid behaviour, like stomach contents and fossil droppings (see later). *Tyrannosaurus* and similar tyrannosaurids almost certainly took crippling, fatal bites from the dinosaurs they preyed

The serrated, spike-like teeth of *Tyrannosaurus* are unusually thick and massive compared to those of most other theropods. They appear to have been better at breaking through bone that those of other theropods. Tooth length is highly variable in the jaws, the shortest being present at the front and rear.

upon, and they would have been able to break open carcasses and crunch up bones as well. This style of killing and feeding would have been very different from the behaviour of theropods with narrow ziphodont teeth, since their slender teeth and more lightweight skulls cannot have been strong enough to withstand the huge forces needed to bite through bone.

Peg-shaped, leaf-shaped and grinding teeth are associated with plant eating in living mammals and reptiles, as are batteries of closely packed teeth that form rasping surfaces or long, blade-like edges, so these are good indicators of herbivorous diets in dinosaurs. Many herbivore teeth get heavily worn as they grind against each other to pulp vegetation, in contrast to carnivore teeth, which rarely come into contact with each other directly. A great diversity of tooth shapes are present in herbivorous non-bird dinosaurs. Slender, narrow, cylindrical teeth are present in some sauropods, like diplodocoids, where they're arranged in rake-like fashion. These look like teeth used in stripping foliage from branches or from ground-covering plants like ferns. Broader-crowned, almost spoon-shaped teeth are present in other sauropod groups and look more suited for a function in chopping. Tooth crowns shaped like arrowheads or leaves, with coarsely serrated edges, are present in many sauropodomorphs and ornithischians. These resemble the teeth of modern herbivorous lizards and look suited for the fine chopping of leaves and other plant parts. Thyreophorans inherited teeth of this sort, but some lineages evolved basin-like structures and thick, lip-like ridges (cingula) on the sides of their tooth crowns. These features presumably enabled them to better mash up plant food while chewing.

Iguanodontian ornithopods also started their history with leaf-shaped, serrated teeth, but evolved larger, more closely packed teeth over time. In the most extreme members of the group – hadrosaurs – the diamond-shaped crowns fit snugly together, forming a giant battery of hundreds of teeth. There might be 60 tooth positions in each battery, with as many as five replacement teeth being stacked up beneath the one in use. The sides of the battery form a rough, rasp-like surface, while the lower edge of the battery in the upper jaw, and the upper edge of the battery in the lower jaw have strongly worn crowns that form long, flattened surfaces. These flattened surfaces were used in crushing, grinding and slicing, as proved by wear marks on their surfaces. Hadrosaur teeth are incredibly complex structures, formed from six different materials that functioned in resisting wear, in preventing the formation of cavities, and in keeping the teeth firmly in place. They're perhaps the most complex teeth that have ever evolved.

Tooth batteries also evolved in ceratopsians, but this time the teeth are stacked vertically and don't form the wide, rasp-like side surfaces present in hadrosaurs. The teeth at the edges of ceratopsian tooth batteries formed sharp, strongly angled shearing surfaces that must have been used to slice up plant tissue, and the way the upper and lower tooth batteries

In hadrosaurs like the North American *Edmontosaurus* shown here, hundreds of diamond-shaped teeth are packed together to form tooth batteries. The battery is long and deep and could have been used as a rasp on its inner surface and as a crushing or slicing structure on its upper surface.

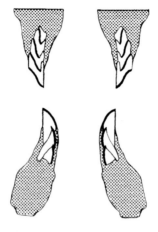

Seen in cross section, the tooth batteries of the giant ceratopsian *Triceratops* look like sets of shearing blades. Several generations of teeth were stacked on top of each other and sharp slicing edges formed at the jaw edges.

met together resulted in the creation of complex basins and sharp rims. Again, these teeth are highly complex, and formed of five different tissues that helped reduce wear and keep the teeth cemented together.

The broad, squared-off muzzles and lower jaws of some sauropods and ornithischians surely allowed for the cropping of large mouthfuls of vegetation, and we imagine the feeding behaviour of these dinosaurs to have been similar to that seen in broad-mouthed herbivorous animals today, like white rhinos and hippos. Such herbivores are called bulk feeders. Narrow, pointed snouts and jaws are typical of so-called selective feeders – species that select the choice parts of plants, like new shoots, buds and fruits. Stegosaurs look like selective feeders, as do various long-snouted, narrow-beaked ornithopods. A number of ornithischians cannot be tidily assigned to either a bulk feeder or selective feeder skull shape and are somewhere in the middle. This suggests that they were what we call 'mixed feeders': herbivores that do a bit of everything.

Herbivorous non-bird dinosaur species differ in other ways, some of which seem to be important as regards working out their feeding behaviour. The width of the back of the skull provides an indication of how much muscle was attached to the rear of the head, and hence how good the animal was at controlling its head movements. In living animals, those that graze need to have finer control over their head movements than those that browse, with browsers relying less on fine head movements and more on the actions of the mouth alone.

Some herbivorous dinosaurs had wide mouths suited for cropping plant material from ground level. A similar mouth shape is present in some living grazers, like the white rhino. This is a young one.

Herbivorous non-bird dinosaurs also vary a great deal in terms of the sorts of movement possible at their jaw joints. Some sauropodomorphs and ornithischians were limited to scissor-like jaw actions like those present in theropods, but many groups evolved jaw joints that allowed back-and-forth sliding or side-to-side rotation of the lower jaw. Such jaw movements allow tooth crowns to be drawn across one another, meaning that plant food can be broken down into fine pieces.

Herbivorous dinosaurs also differ in skull depth, jaw shape and in other ways which show how strong their bites

were, and they also differ considerably in feeding height. The short legs and necks of ankylosaurs, for example, show that they were feeding at or close to ground level. In contrast, the longer legs, necks and skulls of hadrosaurs show that they could feed higher up when they wanted to, and an ability to stand bipedally means that they could potentially feed several metres above ground level. These sorts of differences mean that contemporary dinosaurian herbivores were able to exploit different plant foods without competing with each other for the same resources – a topic that we discuss further below in the section on dinosaur communities.

So far, we've looked at features related to a carnivorous or herbivorous way of life. But there are some non-bird dinosaur groups which combine features of both lifestyles. These animals were omnivores: generalists that made a living by snacking on leaves, fruits and seeds while also

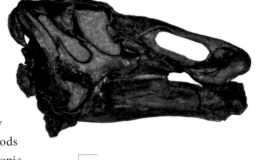

The broad, duck-like toothless beak of the North American hadrosaur *Edmontosaurus* might have allowed cropping at ground-level. But this dinosaur's height, flexible neck and tall, narrow skull shape are more consistent with browsing at height. It's probable that hadrosaurs were generalists, able to feed at many different levels on many different plant types.

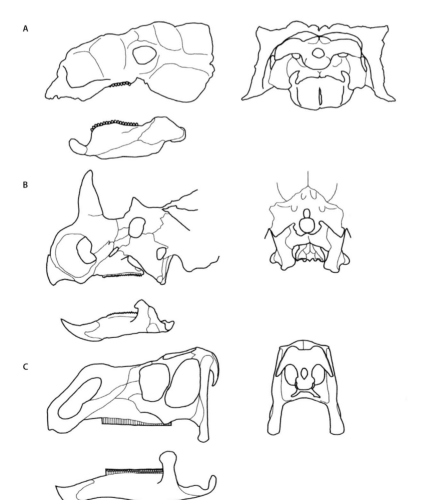

A

B

C

These diagrams show how contemporaneous herbivorous dinosaurs from the Late Cretaceous of North America differed in skull shape, height and width, and how big their jaw muscles were. These differences related to the different feeding styles used by these different groups. These diagrams show the skulls of (A) an ankylosaurid, (B) a ceratopsid and (C) a hadrosaurid.

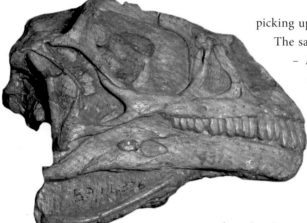

Early sauropodomorphs like *Massospondylus* from southern Africa have both leaf-shaped, serrated teeth and conical, fang-like ones. They were probably omnivores, though with the bulk of their diet being leaves and other plant parts.

picking up small animals and perhaps nibbling on carcasses too. The sauropodomorphs of the Late Triassic and Early Jurassic – *Massospondylus*, *Plateosaurus* and their relatives – combine leaf-like teeth suited for leaf-shredding with pointed, cone-like teeth and inwards-facing, clawed hands that could well have been used in grabbing small animals. The bodies of these dinosaurs are not as specialized for a plant-based diet as those of undoubted herbivores like sauropods and large ornithischians.

Not all theropods were predatory. Leaf-shaped, peg-shaped and incisor-like teeth are present in several groups and resemble those of living animals that eat plants, or eat plants as well as small animals. Ornithomimosaurs, therizinosaurs and oviraptorosaurs are among these omnivorous or herbivorous theropods. These 'weird-toothed' groups tended to lose their teeth completely over time, and to give rise to toothless descendants that were even more committed to plant-eating lifestyles. The toothless species in these groups had beak tissue lining their jaws, giving their faces an especially bird-like appearance. The shapes of their bodies and claws are also in keeping with omnivorous or herbivorous lifestyles – therizinosaurs have broad hips indicating the presence of large guts, for example, and ornithomimosaurs have relatively straight claws on their hands and feet that are unlikely to have been useful in capturing or killing animals. Oviraptorosaurs and ornithomimosaurs are also preserved with masses of small stones (gastroliths) in the stomach. In modern birds, gastroliths are typical of plant-eating species.

TOOTH MICROWEAR

So far, we've looked only at very basic techniques for working out a fossil animal's diet, many of which involve simple comparisons with living animals. But several sophisticated, precise techniques have also been applied to dinosaur jaws and teeth in an effort to better understand diet and feeding style.

For several decades now, biologists interested in the feeding habits of animals have used high-powered microscopes to study wear marks left on teeth. These marks provide clues on the sorts of food the animal was eating, and detailed information on how it was moving its jaws. Some animals simply open and close their mouths, producing vertical scratches and wear marks on their tooth crowns, while others move their jaws from side to side, from front to back or even in a rotary motion and so leave more complex patterns of wear on the tooth surfaces. The study of this microscopic wear – called microwear – was first used on the teeth of fossil primates during the 1970s. The technique proved so useful that experts were soon studying the teeth of numerous other fossil animals, especially mammals. The technique was not applied to dinosaurs until the late 1990s.

Dinosaur teeth do not preserve microwear as well as mammal teeth do. Partly this is because they were eating plants that belong to different groups from those consumed by mammals, but it's also partly because dinosaurs were constantly replacing their teeth. Dinosaur teeth were only used for a short time before falling out and being replaced, whereas mammals retain their teeth for many years, allowing much more time for wear patterns to develop. Growth lines observed in the teeth of sauropods and other dinosaurs show that they only kept a tooth for about a month before it was pushed out of its socket by a new one.

Despite these limitations, a great deal has still been learnt about dinosaur tooth microwear. Studies on microwear in thyreophorans show that the Late Cretaceous ankylosaurid *Euoplocephalus* might have used complex movements of its lower jaw when chewing. The microwear seems to show that the lower jaw slid backwards and forwards during the chewing stroke, a style of jaw movement termed propaliny (this kind of jaw movement is not used by humans, but it is practised by other living animals such as elephants and rabbits). The shape of the jaw joint, which allows this sliding back and forth, and the overall shape of obvious, visible tooth wear provide further support for this view of complex jaw movements in *Euoplocephalus*. Other studies of tooth wear in thyreophorans, such as the Early Jurassic *Scelidosaurus*, show how certain species mostly used simple, vertical slicing movements while chewing. Microwear on hadrosaur teeth consists of numerous fine scratches. This suggests a diet dominated by conifer leaves and also suggests that they had complex jaw motions that involved some degree of propaliny.

Microwear studies have yet to be done on a great many dinosaur species – stegosaurs have not been studied in this way, for example. Even without such studies, it's already obvious that stegosaurs have relatively little tooth wear, with only a few individuals of some species possessing small vertical wear facets that have been caused by contact between tooth tips, or contact between tooth tips and plant food. The low amount of

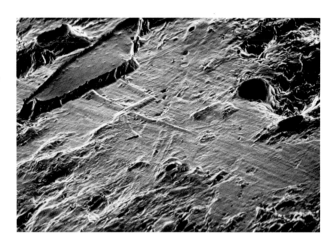

This image shows the microscopic wear present on a tooth tip of the sauropod *Diplodocus*. Fine, parallel scratches can be observed. These run parallel to the long axis of the tooth crown and must have formed as food was drawn across the tooth tips.

wear seen on stegosaur teeth, and the fact that the wear they do have is at the tooth tips alone, indicates that these dinosaurs did not chew their food extensively, nor did they feed on tough foodstuffs.

The microwear we see on dinosaur teeth generally matches previous ideas about dinosaur feeding based on evidence from the shapes of the teeth and jaws. There are a few dinosaur groups in which this is not the case, and where tooth microwear data seems to contradict some of the other information we have.

Several studies have looked at microwear in diplodocoid sauropods. Numerous, fine, parallel scratches are typical of diplodocoid teeth, and studies published during the 1990s found these teeth to be lacking the microscopic pits typical of herbivores that eat close to ground level. These pits are caused by tiny grit particles that get stuck to plants that grow on or close to the ground. These studies were therefore thought to provide evidence for a high browsing style of feeding for these dinosaurs – it matched the view, already predicted by the great neck length and bipedal abilities of these particular sauropods, that they mostly fed from branches high in tree canopies.

More recently, this idea has been challenged by studies that have reported numerous pits on rebbachisaurid and diplodocid teeth. These are the pits caused by the accidental eating of grit, and their presence suggests that these dinosaurs were mostly feeding at ground level, cropping a

Diplodocoid sauropods like *Diplodocus* had unusual jaw joints that allowed the lower jaw to slide backwards as the jaws were closed. This style of jaw movement is called propaliny and it allows plant eaters to perform a shearing action on objects in the mouth.

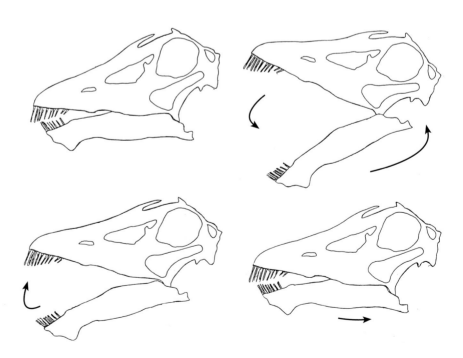

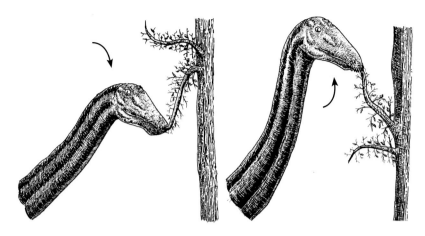

Unusual wear patterns on the long, slender teeth of *Diplodocus* suggest to some experts that this dinosaur sometimes fed by grabbing branches and then pulling sharply either downwards or upwards to strip off the leaves.

variety of different plant foods in unselective fashion. A ground-level feeding style for diplodocoids is also supported by the broad mouths of some of these dinosaurs. This is not the 'last word' on diplodocoid feeding behaviour though. A large amount of unusual wear is present at the tooth tips of these dinosaurs, and it also seems that the diplodocoid skull was strong, and good at withstanding high bite forces. Neither this kind of wear, nor this kind of jaw strength, seems to be explained by a diet that simply involves cropping plants at ground level. Instead, these features seem more to do with the stripping of leaves from branches.

These results paint a confusing – even contradictory – picture. But this is because interpreting the diet, behaviour and lifestyle of a long-extinct animal is difficult, with numerous different pieces of evidence sometimes producing different results or pointing in different directions. We also know from the behaviour of living species that animals are often not restricted to a single way of behaving or feeding, but that they can be adaptable, opportunistic, and able to switch what they do according to the resources that are available. Maybe some diplodocoids were generalists, feeding at ground level on some occasions and from the canopies of trees on others.

THEROPOD HANDS AND FEET

We saw above how theropod tooth and jaw anatomy gives a good indication of the way these dinosaurs attacked, killed and dismembered their prey. But of course theropods did not rely on their jaws and teeth as their sole weapons – their hands and feet were important weapons too. Non-bird theropods of most groups possessed three-fingered, inwards-facing hands with enlarged, strongly curved claws and large ligament and muscle attachment sites. These hands were (as we saw earlier) almost certainly specialized for the grabbing of prey animals – smaller non-bird theropods probably caught mammals, lizards, baby dinosaurs and other prey this way. The inwards-facing orientation of the hands means that prey could be clasped between both hands before being passed to the mouth. Note that the hands can still be used in this grabbing, predatory fashion even when long feathers grow from the fingers and hands – these feathers are obviously not on the palms or on the undersides of the fingers, so don't interfere with the grabbing function.

The fact that most giant theropods possessed hands of this sort strongly suggests that they used their hands in the same way, the much larger size of these animals meaning, of course, that their prey were much larger too. A big theropod, say, 7 m (23 ft) long, perhaps mostly preyed on dinosaurs 2 to 3 m (6½ to 10 ft) long, in which case grabbing would have happened at the same time as the theropod attacked the prey animal with its jaws and teeth. Additional support for this grab-and-bite killing style comes from the fact that the finger joints of big theropods seem to have been very flexible: the fingers could clench tightly, digging the claws into a prey animal's body, but they could also withstand being bent backwards to a remarkable degree. This flexibility makes sense given that a grabbed prey animal would struggle and resist its capture.

The enlarged and strongly curved second toe claw of maniraptorans like *Deinonychus* was certainly a formidable weapon. But how was it used? Many experts have suggested that it was a disembowelling weapon. This now looks unlikely.

This technique of grab-and-bite was abandoned several times during theropod history. Tyrannosauroids started their history with long, slender, maniraptoran-like hands but switched to relying on an increasingly powerful bite, the end result being giant species with short, reduced arms and super-strong jaws and teeth. Non-bird maniraptorans retained long, grabbing hands throughout their evolution, but several groups especially closely related to birds came to rely on the use of their feet in subduing prey. It's been clear ever since *Deinonychus* was described in the 1960s that dromaeosaurids and troodontids possess feet where the second toe was held in a peculiar posture, its enlarged, sickle-shaped claw kept raised up above the ground. Flexible joints mean that the whole toe could be swept in an arc that extended from high above the foot to well below it.

How were these so-called sickle-clawed toes used? A popular idea has been that the claws had a slicing function, and that they were used as disembowelling weapons, deployed against the bellies or flanks of prey animals. This proposed function now looks extremely unlikely. Tests done with replica claws and robot

legs show that the sickle-claws perform poorly at slicing. In any case, there are few parts of a prey animal's body where slicing is possible or easily achieved. If we look at living animals, similar enlarged second toe claws are present in falcons and hawks. These birds don't use the claws in slashing or disembowelling, but in pinning a prey animal down to the ground. The prey is killed with the mouth, not the foot claws. Perhaps this gives us a more realistic view of predatory behaviour in these dinosaurs – maybe they leapt onto prey, kept them pinned down with their weight, and then attacked with the mouth. It may not be coincidental that these theropods also had large, fully feathered arms and hands – presumably, they needed to keep their balance on top of their struggling prey, and wing-like forelimbs would very likely have helped with this.

Deinonychus and similar maniraptorans may well have killed using similar techniques to those employed by hawks and falcons today. Prey is restrained with the powerful clawed feet, and the predator keeps its balance via movements of its feathered forelimbs and tail. The prey is eaten alive.

COMPUTER MODELLING AND THE STUDY OF DINOSAUR FEEDING BEHAVIOUR

We've seen on several occasions that new, computer-assisted techniques allow palaeontologists to test possibilities relevant to the way dinosaurs functioned and behaved. One of the most noteworthy of these techniques is called finite element analysis, or FEA, a computer-based method originally designed to test how objects like buildings and aircraft perform when subjected to strong forces, such as high winds or vibrations from large engines. FEA works by turning a three-dimensional shape into a mesh of tiny interconnected shapes called polygons. As force or pressure is applied across the mesh, a computer programme works out how this pressure is distributed and where the zones of greatest strength and weakness are. These zones are shown using a colour-coded system, often with red showing areas of high stress and blue showing areas of low stress.

FEA has become an extremely popular technique in the study of feeding behaviour and bite strength and members of most dinosaur groups have now been examined in FEA studies. The first modern study was performed by a team led by Emily Rayfield, who used a complete skull of *Allosaurus* as an FEA subject. The results indicated that the *Allosaurus* skull was very good at resisting stress, apparently far better than it needed to be given the strength of its bite. This discovery may provide support for the idea that *Allosaurus* used the whole skull as a hatchet-like weapon that was repeatedly slammed into the body of a prey animal to make slashing wounds.

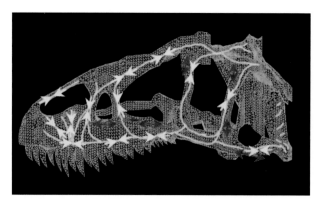

By building a three-dimensional digital model of the skull of *Allosaurus*, Emily Rayfield and colleagues were able to show which parts of the skull were under compression and tension during biting. The yellow arrows show compression and the red arrows show tension.

FEA was later applied to other non-bird theropods, including *Coelophysis*, *Carnotaurus*, *Baryonyx* and *Tyrannosaurus*, and to sauropods including *Diplodocus* and *Camarasaurus*. The results so far have matched other ideas about the feeding behaviour of these dinosaurs. The main advantage provided by FEA is that it reveals far greater detail on skull function than was previously available from examinations of the overall shape and build of the skull. For example, the way the stresses are conducted along the long, slender snout of the spinosaurid *Baryonyx* matches the stress patterns that we see in the skulls of crocodylians like the fish-eating gharial, and so supports the idea that the spinosaurid skull was used in a similar way. FEA therefore substantially improves our ability to study skulls as 'feeding machines'.

Rayfield's FEA study of *Tyrannosaurus* showed how the skull of this animal was well able to withstand the enormous stresses that must have built up when the animal bit through bone – a behaviour we know it performed due both to *Tyrannosaurus* bite marks left on other dinosaurs and an enormous bone-filled coprolite that we discuss later (see p.141). Rayfield's FEA study also showed how many of the stresses sent through the *Tyrannosaurus* skull were conducted through the nasal bones along the top of the snout. This presumably explains why *Tyrannosaurus* (and other tyrannosaurids) possessed such thick, gnarly, fused-up nasal bones – they had a crucial role in withstanding these stresses.

It is typical in FEA studies to use different colours to show how stresses are distributed across an object when it's placed under load. In this model of a *Tyrannosaurus* skull, the areas under greatest stress are shown in red, while the blue areas are under the least amount of stress.

The use of FEA has gone hand-in-hand with efforts to better understand how skulls and skeletons worked when their owners were alive, and has also happened at a time when palaeontologists have worked hard to use more precise, more mathematically rigorous techniques when studying extinct animal behaviour and anatomy.

The more we've learnt, the more it seems that FEA might only provide part of the picture when it comes to understanding the way a skull or other body part might have worked. After all, animals are not made of bone alone. Muscles, ligaments and other soft structures play a key role in how a skull or other part of the body works. In fact, they play such an important role in biting and feeding that it's misleading to rely on bones alone. There are even studies of living animals which show that the parts of the head most affected by the stresses and strains of biting don't match at all with those parts of the skull predicted by FEA to be the ones most affected!

FEA also only gives good results when the object being studied is accurately modelled. It's not enough just to know the shape of the structure – its internal, three-dimensional shape has to be understood too. While FEA is definitely a useful tool, it shouldn't be used in isolation, as it's easy to misinterpret the results it can provide, and it can only be used properly when a huge amount of information has been collected.

The good news is that our ability to deal with these problems – to account for soft tissues and internal structure – are increasing rapidly all the time. Modern computer models of skulls and other parts of dinosaur skeletons are far more complicated that they were 10 years ago, and our ability to understand and model bones, skulls and skeletons three-dimensionally are improving at an incredible rate.

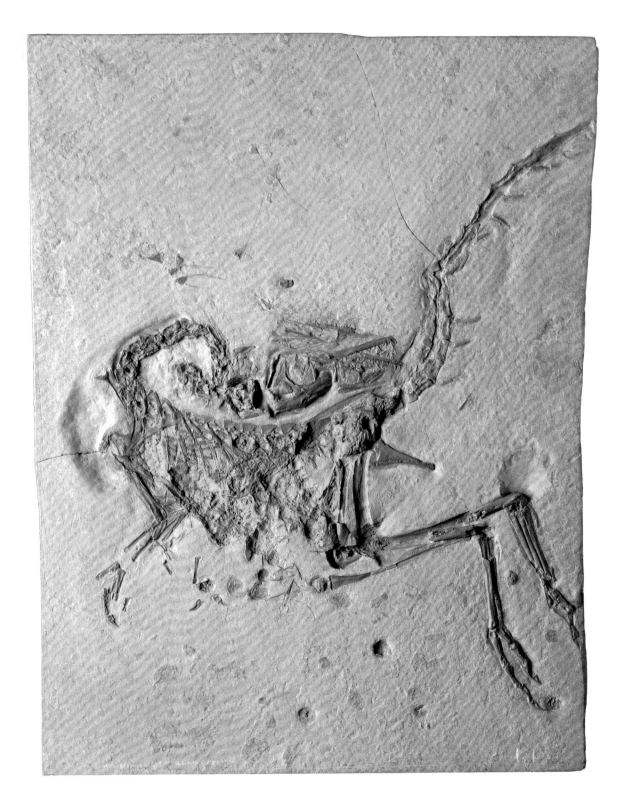

GUT AND STOMACH CONTENTS, AND COPROLITES

Animals that are buried rapidly and incorporated swiftly into the rock record – those that are buried in volcanic ash or mudflows, for example – are sometimes preserved with the contents of their last meals still inside their stomachs and guts. Such fossils are rare, but those that have been discovered are extremely significant in providing us with direct information on diet.

Most of the stomach remains reported so far come from non-bird theropods. As expected, they demonstrate that these dinosaurs were predators, sometimes of other dinosaurs. Perhaps the most famous dinosaur with stomach contents preserved is the Late Triassic theropod *Coelophysis*, two specimens of which have the remains of small archosaurs preserved within their bellies. For years, it was claimed that these were *Coelophysis* babies and that they demonstrated cannibalism in this dinosaur. Cannibalism is common in predatory animals today, so such a discovery wasn't particularly surprising. Alas, it turns out that the stomach contents were misidentified. They're not baby *Coelophysis* at all, but the remains of small crocodile-line archosaurs.

A tyrannosaurid from the Late Cretaceous of Montana has hadrosaur bones preserved as stomach contents and the British spinosaurid *Baryonyx* is preserved with fish scales and juvenile iguanodontian bones that almost certainly represent stomach contents. We also know of a *Compsognathus* specimen from the Late Jurassic of Germany that has a lizard in its stomach, a *Sinosauropteryx* from Liaoning that has mammal bones preserved as stomach contents, and specimens of *Sinocalliopteryx* (a large relative of *Sinosauropteryx*, also from Liaoning) that have the remains of birds and other theropods inside their bodies.

A specimen of yet another theropod from Liaoning – the famous 'four-winged' dromaeosaurid *Microraptor* – has a fish preserved in its body. This find is especially interesting since it shows that *Microraptor* – often imagined as a climbing, gliding dinosaur – was not just hunting prey among branches and on tree trunks. It was also foraging on the ground, including at the water's edge. Another *Microraptor* specimen has a partial bird skeleton preserved in its belly, so it seems that *Microraptor* was a generalist, feeding on a range of prey. A few non-bird coelurosaurs, sometimes suggested to have been herbivores, have stomach contents

This German specimen (opposite) of the small, long-tailed theropod *Compsognathus* has the skeleton of a lizard preserved in its stomach region. This is consistent with our expectations – we assume that this small, fast-running predator ate lizards and similar animals.

This *Sinosauropteryx* specimen (above) from China has the jaw bones of a small mammal (left) preserved within its stomach. Small, shrew-sized and mouse-sized mammals must have been common prey for small predatory dinosaurs.

The small gliding dromaeosaurid *Microraptor* consumed a fish at the edge of a Chinese lake. We don't know whether the *Microraptor* would have caught the fish itself or scavenged one that was already dead.

showing that they ate small animals on occasion. These include *Oviraptor* (one specimen has a lizard preserved within it) and the giant ornithomimosaur *Deinocheirus* (one specimen of which contains a fish). The stomach contents mentioned here match anatomical evidence suggesting that these dinosaurs were omnivores.

Stomach contents in sauropodomorphs and ornithischians are rare. An Early Jurassic sauropodomorph from Canada, provisionally identified as *Ammosaurus*, has the remains of a small lizard-like reptile preserved inside its body. This adds support to the idea that early sauropodomorphs were omnivores, not strict herbivores. Among ornithischians, chopped plant fragments, seeds and fruit-like objects have been discovered in the stomach of a small Australian ankylosaur and finely chopped leaf segments have been discovered in a specimen of the hadrosaur *Brachylophosaurus*.

Additional evidence for extinct dinosaur diet comes from fossil droppings, or coprolites. Because droppings are soft and tend to be rapidly broken down by insects, fungi and bacteria, they rarely get preserved as fossils. Despite this, enough droppings were buried by mud or sand and

incorporated into the fossil record to give us a good idea of the full range of droppings that dinosaurs produced. Most are shaped like fat curved sausages or segments of thick rope, the average length being about 8 cm (3 in). Some non-bird dinosaur coprolites are much smaller though. A mass of small, pellet-like coprolites – each less than 1 cm across – seem to have been produced by a small ornithischian. At the other end of the scale one of the biggest dinosaur coprolites yet discovered is a huge example from the Late Cretaceous of Saskatchewan, Canada. This object – 64 cm (25 in) long and filled with small chunks of bone – must have been produced by *Tyrannosaurus*, the only giant carnivore that inhabited Late Cretaceous Saskatchewan. The idea that *Tyrannosaurus* might have crunched up and swallowed bone is consistent with studies of its jaw and tooth anatomy. A coprolite this long is big, but it's likely that giant sauropods and other large herbivores produced even bigger droppings – they almost certainly generated great piles of excrement similar to those made by elephants, horses and also ostriches and other giant birds.

Some theropod coprolites even preserve the remains of undigested muscle tissue. These finds mean that we have additional fossil fragments of non-bird dinosaur muscle tissue (you might remember the earlier mention of muscle tissue preserved in the theropod *Scipionyx*). They also show that food passed through the theropod digestive system quite quickly, an observation suggestive of fast metabolism.

Coprolites that mostly contain plant remains are identified as those of herbivorous non-bird dinosaurs. These coprolites can't usually be assigned with confidence to particular species, but they clearly show that the dinosaurs concerned were eating such plants as horsetails, ferns, cycads, conifers and flowering trees. A few specimens have revealed surprising insights into dinosaur diet. Several herbivorous dinosaur coprolites from the Late Jurassic and Late Cretaceous contain wood fragments. Huge quantities

This small, well preserved Australian ankylosaur, often incorrectly referred to as *Minmi*, but now known as *Kunbarrasaurus*, is so complete that it even has the contents of its guts preserved.

Many dinosaur coprolites are sausage-shaped blocks, and identifying them to a particular species can be impossible. These coprolites were produced by a herbivore, perhaps a sauropod.

of woody material are preserved inside Late Cretaceous coprolites thought to have been produced by the hadrosaur *Maiasaura*. These dinosaurs were almost certainly eating wood, and were presumably able to digest and extract nutrients from this unusual food source.

Coprolites from the Late Cretaceous of India, thought to have been produced by titanosaurs, are also interesting because they contain microscopic mineral grains thought to be unique to grasses. These coprolites preserve the remains of several different grass species that belong to different branches of the grass family tree. Not only do they show that grasses of several sorts had appeared by Late Cretaceous times, they also reveal that the titanosaurs that produced the coprolites ate grass, at least some of the time. As grasses did not become important until after the end-Cretaceous extinction, it was generally assumed prior to this discovery that non-bird dinosaurs never ate grass. Again, we wouldn't know about this particular feeding behaviour were it not for this rare line of evidence.

LOCOMOTION 1: WALKING AND RUNNING

There's no doubt that non-bird dinosaurs and archaic birds walked and ran while going about their lives. Their bones – and the muscles that existed in life – show that virtually all species were built for a life that involved a substantial amount of walking. Long, slender leg bones indicate that many non-bird dinosaurs were speedy runners. Indeed, the idea has long been popular that such dinosaurs as ornithomimosaurs were able to run as fast as modern ostriches or horses. Sticking for a moment with the basic technique of comparing non-bird dinosaurs and archaic birds with modern animals, it has been commonplace in dinosaur books to note that ornithomimosaurs are built something like ostriches, that ceratopsians are vaguely like rhinos, and that sauropods have similar proportions to elephants. As a result, people have tended to ascribe the running abilities of those modern animals to the extinct dinosaurs. Many books, for example, give ornithomimosaurs a running speed of 72 km/h (45 mph), sauropods a supposedly elephant-like speed of 40 km/h (25 mph), and so on.

It's important to note that there are major problems with claims of this sort. Firstly, and perhaps surprisingly, we know too little about the running speeds and athletic abilities of living animals.

Computer models of the bones and muscles of non-bird dinosaurs – like the *Tyrannosaurus* at far right – can be compared with models of living animals like ostriches (far left) and elephants (centre). The results indicate that big dinosaurs were fast movers, albeit not as fast as suggested by some.

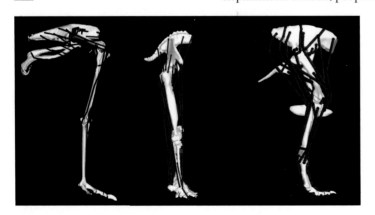

Many 'facts' repeated in books have proved unreliable, or rely on poorly recorded accounts. Claims about the running speeds of elephants, for example, never make it clear where this specific information comes from. Recent studies on elephant locomotion actually reveal a top speed of 6.8 m/s, equivalent to 24 km/h or 15 mph. The good news is that a rapidly growing number of studies devoted to the walking and running abilities of mammals, lizards, crocodylians, birds and other animals mean that the state of our knowledge is rapidly improving. Much of this work, incidentally, has been inspired by questions initially asked about non-bird dinosaurs.

Another issue is that the above-mentioned superficial similarities are simply not good enough, or anywhere near precise enough, when it comes to gaining a reliable idea of what an extinct animal could do. A sauropod might be something like an elephant, but it isn't really like an elephant at all – elephants have a small, shallow pelvic girdle and a small, skinny tail whereas sauropods have an enormous, deep pelvis and a gargantuan tail, the biggest muscles of which (the giant caudofemoralis longus muscle we saw in Chapter 3) were attached to the back of the thigh. Non-bird dinosaurs are not really built like any living animals, meaning that we cannot rely on simple, superficial comparisons for meaningful results. So, what to do?

Digital modelling has helped make work on the walking and running abilities of extinct dinosaurs a scientifically rigorous activity. Functional morphologist John Hutchinson has produced a digital model of *Tyrannosaurus* with its reconstructed leg muscles placed in their anatomically correct positions (opposite). *Tyrannosaurus* is an attractive subject for studies of this sort because, as one of the largest bipeds to have ever evolved, it represents an extreme that shows how animals have experimented with the physical limits of life on land. Indeed, a long-running debate has surrounded this animal's abilities, with some experts arguing that it was a non-runner, only capable of slow walking, others proposing that it was a fleet-footed sprinter able to maintain racehorse-like speeds, and still others supporting every possibility in between. Hutchinson's results indicate that *Tyrannosaurus* could run at about 8 m/s, equivalent to 29 km/h or 18 mph. That's not bad for an animal as big as an elephant, but it's substantially slower than a racehorse.

When it comes to other non-bird dinosaurs, studies are currently in their infancy. Some experts argue that the caudofemoral muscles were

Studies indicate that the enormous, powerfully muscled dinosaurian tail probably allowed these animals – theropods especially – to be very good at making sharp, swift turns when running. The tail was probably held well above the ground, though whether it was raised as high as shown here remains unknown.

Dinosaur trackways can show how fast a dinosaur was moving. These enormous tracks from Plagne in France are part of a trackway that's more than 150 m (492 ft) long. They were made by an enormous sauropod that might have been more than 30 m (98 m) long and over 50 t.

so big and so important in the majority of non-bird dinosaurs that they may have enabled even the very biggest dinosaurs (including sauropods) to move their limbs faster, and more powerfully, than assumed before. If so, these animals may have been capable of achieving higher speeds than usually thought, though speeds greater than those calculated for *Tyrannosaurus* don't look likely.

So far, we've only considered the locomotory abilities of non-bird dinosaurs by discussing what we can learn by looking at bones and muscles. More direct evidence for the walking and running abilities of these animals exists in the form of fossil tracks. Dinosaur tracks are not rare or hard to find, but plentiful and obvious, existing in their millions worldwide. A whole community of specialized palaeontologists study dinosaur tracks, and use them to inform us about dinosaur behaviour.

Tracks provide two key pieces of information on terrestrial locomotion. One concerns the hand and foot posture adopted by the trackmakers. Suggestions that various dinosaurs kept their hands and feet wide apart when walking or running, or that they moved by walking, running, striding, leaping or even hopping can all be tested by examining tracks. The second key piece of information concerns the speed at which these animals moved. So long as we have some idea of limb length in the dinosaur concerned, we can compare it with stride length and hence estimate speed.

Several generalizations have emerged from our studies of non-bird dinosaur tracks. For the most part, tracks show non-bird dinosaurs walking at sedate speeds similar to those typical for living birds and mammals. Non-bird dinosaurs did not plod along slowly at rates comparable to those of giant tortoises or Komodo dragons, but at walking speeds similar to those seen in modern birds, mammals and active lizards. A few unusual ideas suggested by some palaeontologists – that *Velociraptor*-type theropods moved by bounding, or that ceratopsians walked with fully sprawling front limbs, for example – can also be tested directly thanks to the trackways produced by these animals. In both of these cases, the tracks do not provide support for these unusual views.

Again, digital technology is revolutionizing the study of dinosaur tracks. By scanning tracks with lasers or photographing them from many angles and merging the images in the computer, palaeontologists can study and measure tracks in digital space. This means that the complex, three-dimensional shape of a track is now stored (and can be shared and copied) without there being a need to visit it in person or remove it from its discovery site.

The existence of a digital version of the track also makes it easier to perform studies that look at the interaction between the foot and the sediment in which the track was made. Tracks are formed in dynamic ways and vary hugely depending on the condition of the sediment (whether it was sandy, muddy, wet or dry, for example) and the speed, mass and posture of the trackmaker. Thanks to digital modelling, we are becoming better at working out which of these factors are most important, and better at understanding the variation that fossil tracks preserve.

LOCOMOTION 2: WADING AND SWIMMING

Non-bird dinosaurs were predominantly land animals. But dinosaurs of many sorts were probably capable waders and a few might have been swimmers. Members of some species probably routinely crossed bodies of water, perhaps during migration events or as part of their regular foraging behaviour. As discussed in Chapter 2, there are now some reasons for thinking that the giant theropod *Spinosaurus* hunted and foraged in rivers and estuaries, and the possibility remains that a few other non-bird dinosaur species did likewise.

The deep, flexible tail of the horned theropod *Ceratosaurus* has led Robert Bakker (see p. 21) to suggest that this was another swimming dinosaur, and the fact that *Ceratosaurus* teeth are abundant in rock layers where the remains of giant lungfish are also abundant has been used as complementary supporting evidence. Amphibious and/or aquatic habits have also been suggested for ceratopsians like *Psittacosaurus* and *Protoceratops*, and big ceratopsids like *Anchiceratops* have been imagined as hippo-like, amphibious creatures by some experts. These claims are controversial, and can be seen as classic examples of cases where focusing on a single feature of a dinosaur can create an impression that isn't supported by the bulk of information available. Yes, *Ceratosaurus* may well have been a good swimmer, and yes it may well have shed its teeth after feeding on lungfish on occasion, but it lacks other features of the skeleton suited for life in water. Similarly, the complete skeletons of *Psittacosaurus*, *Protoceratops* and *Anchiceratops* also suggest that these dinosaurs were largely land based.

One of the great enigmas of the dinosaur footprint record comes from a rare number of odd tracks made by sauropods that consist only

A

B

C

D

Even the tracks made by a single individual can vary according to how it places its feet, and on how soft or firm the sediment is. This series of digital reconstructions depicts the several stages that occurred as a theropod placed its foot in soft mud (A, B), sank into the mud (C) and then extracted its foot (D) to leave a long, weird, slit-like track.

Even dinosaurs strongly adapted for life on land could probably swim or wade. Tracks that consist of sauropod handprints alone have been found in the USA, Korea, Portugal and elsewhere and have always been a bit of a mystery. Is this how they were made?

of hand prints – prints of the hindfeet are absent. One explanation for these tracks is that they were produced by floating sauropods that were pulling themselves along with their forelimbs alone. An alternative, more complicated explanation is that they were made by sauropods that carried more of their weight on their forelimbs than hindlimbs, and that perhaps the tracks are not tracks in the strict sense, but 'undertracks' (impressions of tracks that had been pushed down through several layers of deep sediment). This idea seems unlikely given that all sauropods, as far as we know, carried the majority of their weight over their hindlimbs. And given Henderson's conclusions on how buoyant sauropods would have been when in water (see Chapter 3), the original suggestion of floating, hand-walking sauropods looks quite plausible.

The rare fossil tracks that seem to have been produced by swimming theropods and ornithopods are less controversial. These are parallel groups of triple grooves that appear to have been made by dinosaur toe-tips as they contacted the river bed or lake floor. Tracks of this sort are known from the Early Jurassic of Utah (USA), the Early Cretaceous of Spain and elsewhere. They were clearly made by small and large dinosaurs alike, the largest belonging to an animal that left grooves 60 cm (about 24 in) long on the riverbed.

We would predict that non-bird dinosaurs of most sorts would have been competent swimmers. Many theropods and bipedal ornithischians are bird-like in shape, and modern large flightless birds are excellent swimmers. Many quadrupedal ornithischians – iguanodontians and stegosaurs, for example – have deep bodies and powerful limbs and a neck that would easily allow the head to be kept well clear of the water's surface. Elephants are surprisingly strong swimmers and it is possible to imagine at least some quadrupedal dinosaurs crossing rivers in the same way. Also important is that many non-bird dinosaurs had large, powerfully muscled tails that could presumably provide thrust during swimming. And at least some of these groups – many theropods and bipedal ornithischians among them – had long, spreading toes that would have enabled them to walk on soft muds and sands without becoming stuck. With these features in mind, it seems reasonable to imagine that most non-bird dinosaurs were quite able to cross bodies of water when needed, and to forage and feed in marshes, lakes and rivers. It's also possible that some of these dinosaurs were more aquatic than we usually think, and that there might have been species within these groups that regularly swam. It is, of course, difficult to estimate the amount of time an extinct dinosaur might have spent in or out of the water.

These generalizations don't apply to all non-bird dinosaurs. The large, heavy heads and short necks of ceratopsians suggest poor swimming abilities. Donald Henderson created digital models of ceratopsians and then simulated their behaviour in water (using the same techniques as those applied to sauropods and discussed on p. 110).

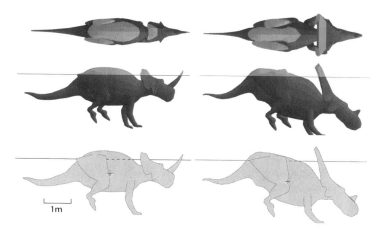

1m

Ceratopsian body shape, lung position and head and neck anatomy all make these animals poorly adapted for floating and swimming. Perhaps this explains why we find some deposits stuffed full of ceratopsian bones where they seem to have drowned in large numbers when attempting to cross flooded rivers.

LOCOMOTION 3: FLYING AND GLIDING

Some non-bird dinosaurs, at least some of the small, feathered maniraptoran theropods, seem capable of aerial behaviour – of gliding, parachuting or flying. An enormous amount of argument has surrounded the flight abilities of *Archaeopteryx*, the famous Late Jurassic maniraptoran usually described as the oldest bird (or, one of the oldest), and most discussions of flight in non-bird dinosaurs and archaic birds have been devoted to this one animal.

The body shapes, short necks and giant skulls and head frills of ceratopsians have led some experts to argue that they would have struggled to keep their heads above water when swimming. These computer reconstructions depict the possible floating poses that ceratopsians have adapted. Clearly none are ideal!

Archaeopteryx has large wings and we can make guesses about the size of its chest and arm muscles on the basis of several well-preserved skeletons. Its wing feathers have often been described as having a shape typical of birds that fly. On the basis of these features, some experts have considered *Archaeopteryx* a good flapping flier, similar in abilities to gulls or crows. But more recent research has questioned this view. It turns out that the long forelimb feathers of *Archaeopteryx* are most similar in shape to those of flightless birds, not flying ones. The shoulder socket in *Archaeopteryx* and other early birds is different from that of modern flying species and suggests that they weren't able to perform a proper flapping flight stroke, though gliding remains a distinct possibility.

We don't see clear flapping flight adaptations until later in bird history (see Chapter 5). But did flight of a sort also evolve elsewhere in maniraptorans? The possibility that *Microraptor* – famous for its long forelimb and hindlimb feathers – might have been a 'four-winged glider' has been popular ever since this dinosaur was described in 2000. *Microraptor* is not a member of the bird lineage. It is, rather, a dromaeosaurid, and thus part of the same maniraptoran group as *Velociraptor* and *Deinonychus*.

Archaeopteryx had large wings formed of long feathers, and it's mostly for this reason that it's been regarded as a capable flier. However, many assumptions about *Archaeopteryx* may be incorrect. Its wings and wing feathers do not definitely support the idea that it was a competent flier after all.

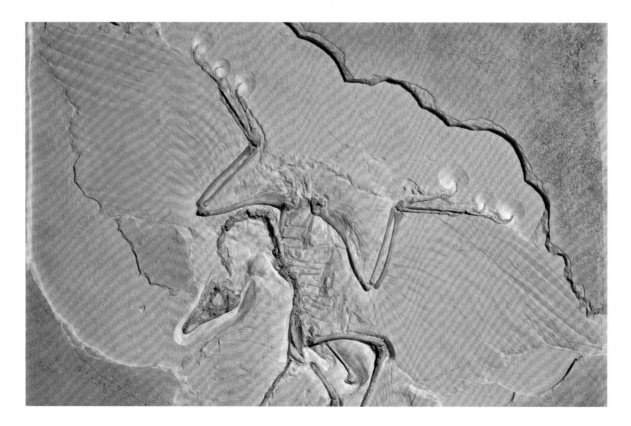

Numerous studies have been published on *Microraptor*'s possible flight behaviour. Some studies have involved the creation of life-sized models that were thrown through the air, others have involved computer modelling, and others have used accurately feathered models placed inside wind tunnels. These studies differ in what they conclude about *Microraptor*'s aerial abilities, and part of the reason for this is that they imagine different configurations for *Microraptor*'s arms and legs. Several of these studies reconstruct *Microraptor* with sprawling hindlimbs that stick out sideways from its hips – a configuration which looks somewhat logical given the large, wing-

like arrangements of leg and foot feathers. But this configuration doesn't match what we understand of dromaeosaurid hip sockets, since the shape of the pelvis and thigh bone better indicate that the hindlegs must have been directed downwards, with only a small amount of outward orientation being possible.

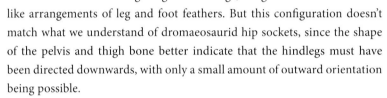

By placing this life-sized model of *Microraptor* – equipped with moveable legs and real feathers – in a wind tunnel, experts have shown that *Microraptor* performed best when its legs were directed downwards, and not when sprawling sideways as shown here.

Wind tunnel experiments performed by Gareth Dyke and colleagues in 2013 showed that *Microraptor* was capable of gliding but that it was inefficient, suffering from a large amount of drag that made the gliding distances quite short. These studies also showed that it performed better during flight when posed with the legs angled downwards and only slightly outwards – a configuration that matches what we think is possible based on the bones alone. While *Microraptor* may well have been capable of gliding, climbing and hunting prey among the branches, it was seemingly enough of a generalist that it could also hunt and forage on the ground.

It seems likely that gliding, and perhaps flapping, behaviour was practised by the members of several bird-like maniraptoran groups, and by early birds themselves. Uncertainty and argument surrounds the exact abilities of these animals and much work remains to be done – work that will involve computer modelling, wind tunnel studies, and the microscopic examination of fossil feathers and bones. It's also currently unclear whether gliding and flying evolved once in a maniraptoran that was ancestral to dromaeosaurids, birds and other groups, or whether these abilities evolved on two or more occasions.

If anything is clear, it's that we can no longer assume that good flight abilities were normal for those non-bird dinosaurs and archaic birds with large, long, complex feathers on their limbs. And it's also clear that the evolution of gliding and flight in maniraptorans was more complicated than we imagined just a few years ago.

THE GREAT PHYSIOLOGY DEBATE

Living animals use many different strategies to generate power, stay warm, avoid overheating, and convert the food they eat into energy and body tissue. All animals digest food and use the energy they get from it to power their muscles or organs. Many animals also collect heat from the sun or the ground, and many store heat internally. Animals that rely on external sources of heat are traditionally termed 'ectothermic' or 'cold-blooded', while those that generate and store heat internally are traditionally 'endothermic' or 'warm-blooded'. The process describing how animals function internally – for example how they digest food, generate power, maintain temperature or regulate water – is termed physiology and the type of physiology non-bird dinosaurs (and archaic birds) possessed has been one of the greatest sources of argument and disagreement in the entire field of dinosaur research.

Living birds and mammals are (mostly) endothermic. Endotherms store heat internally (frequently using insulation to keep it within the body), and use it to keep the organs at a high temperature. Keeping warm like this is beneficial since it means that organs operate at a faster rate, food can be digested more rapidly, and eggs (or babies) can be grown more quickly. Endothermy also means that an animal need not be limited by external temperature: it can live in a cold environment or do much or even all of its activity during the cool of the night.

Meanwhile, ectothermic animals have lower energy demands than endotherms and mostly rely on collecting heat from the sun. Because ectotherms rely on the temperature of the environment to warm up, they tend to be small, and they also tend to have smaller, less power-hungry organs than endotherms.

Because humans and the majority of other large living animals are endotherms, we often think that endothermy is superior to or more advanced than other types of physiology. But this is a very biased point of view that isn't particularly accurate. The fact that amphibians, reptiles and insects are so vastly abundant in so many habitats shows that ectothermy has to be considered a highly successful strategy for many animal groups.

Over the past few decades, a huge number of discoveries have shown that efforts to regard animals as either ectotherms or endotherms are horrendously misleading. Many animals which

We tend to think of endotherms like mammals as maintaining a high and constant internal body temperature. But this is not true for all species. Australasian echidnas like this short-beaked echidna have a temperature that fluctuates by several degrees even during normal conditions.

belong to groups conventionally regarded as ectothermic are capable of generating internal heat. There are insects, sharks and bony fishes with special heat-generating organs in their eyes, brains and bodies, and there are lizards that generate and retain heat internally too. We also know of animals conventionally regarded as endothermic that are poor at generating heat and rely instead on external sources of heat, or allow their body temperature to fluctuate according to the temperature of the environment. This is true for some mammals, like echidnas and some burrowing rodents.

In reality, the whole idea of a neat split between ectothermic and endothermic animals is so misleading that it should be avoided. How does this affect our view of non-bird dinosaur physiology? Over the years, views on the physiology of non-bird dinosaurs have varied an extraordinary amount, with some researchers arguing for ectothermic non-bird dinosaurs that relied entirely on the environment as a way of controlling their temperature, and others arguing for endothermic non-bird dinosaurs, fully as capable of generating and retaining heat as modern mammals and birds, and able to remain active in cool and even freezing conditions. The concept of fully endothermic non-bird dinosaurs came to the fore during the Dinosaur Renaissance of the 1960s and 1970s, a time when some researchers and writers wrote evocatively of 'hot-blooded dinosaurs' (see Chapter 1).

The generation of internal heat is far from unique to mammals and birds. Many other animals are able to create internal heat and maintain high body temperatures too. This is true of many fast-swimming fish, including the tuna shown here.

Non-bird dinosaurs are so diverse in size and shape that there was almost certainly no 'one physiology fits all' rule that applied across the group. But, as a generalization, extinct dinosaurs were active animals with large, power-hungry muscles and organs, and many must have lived lives where they were exposed to hot, cold, windy and rainy conditions. Also relevant is that virtually all extinct saurischian dinosaurs possessed a pneumatic system similar to that of modern birds, and so were able to circulate huge volumes of air around the body and fuel fast-working muscles and organs with large quantities of oxygen. The blood vessels of non-bird dinosaurs were similar in size to those of modern birds and mammals, as is revealed by holes on their bones (termed foramina) that received blood vessels during life.

Growth rings in bone also show that fossil dinosaurs grew quickly, perhaps at rates similar to those of living birds and mammals. Experts

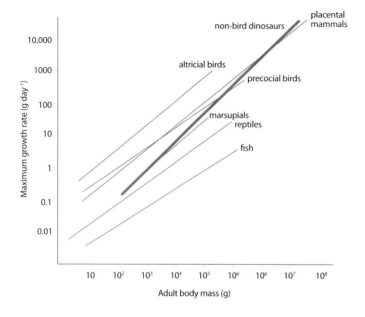

who support this view of rapidly growing non-bird dinosaurs have said that the production of bone tissue we see in these animals could only occur if the metabolic rate was consistently high. In other words, these rapid growth rates seem to be evidence for an endothermic physiology.

These factors all seem to make it likely that non-bird dinosaurs (and early birds too) were endothermic, and more similar in physiology to mammals and modern birds than to the majority of lizards and crocodylians.

Growth studies don't universally conclude that non-bird dinosaurs grew at those super-fast rates. Some experts argue that the results show non-bird dinosaurs growing at rates more similar to those seen in animals like tunas, sharks, echidnas and leatherback turtles. These animals all share a kind of 'intermediate' physiology where endothermic heat production does occur, but does not control overall body temperature as much as it does in fully endothermic mammals and birds. This strategy has been called mesothermy.

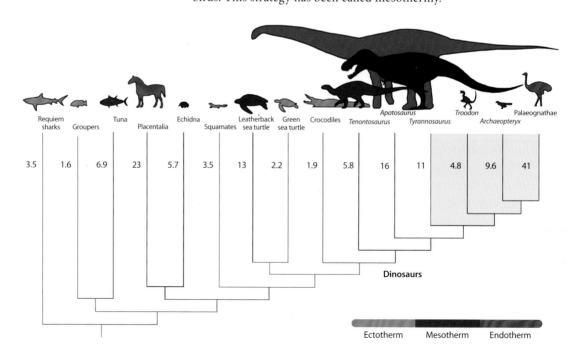

We may well never determine the true metabolic status of fossil dinosaurs with confidence, nor should we assume that all non-bird dinosaurs were alike in terms of how their bodies worked. But we do have enough data to show that non-bird dinosaurs didn't grow at rates expected for the majority of lizards and turtles, nor grow at the super-fast rates expected for some modern mammals or birds. Variable growth rates and an intermediate, 'mesothermic' strategy of heat production and growth may well have been the case for some or many non-bird dinosaurs, while more elevated, bird-like strategies may have been present in others.

REPRODUCTION AND THE
SEX LIVES OF DINOSAURS

Like all animals, non-bird dinosaurs needed to reproduce. Males and females mated, females laid eggs, and babies hatched from those eggs and grew into adults. Many guesses we might make about reproduction in extinct dinosaurs – that they practised internal fertilization, built nests, laid eggs – are based on the same bracketing technique we apply to other areas of extinct dinosaur biology. But we don't need to rely on guesswork alone, since we have substantial direct fossil evidence on the nesting and egg-laying behaviour of non-bird dinosaurs, and on the life histories and growth of these animals.

For obvious reasons, we know nothing concrete about the mating habits of extinct dinosaurs. The best we can do is to examine the behaviour of living animals and make some sensible guesses. Dinosaur experts have not exactly shied away from these questions. This subject is made all the more fascinating by the amazing body shapes and sizes of some dinosaur species. Some sauropods were so large that standing on their back legs for mating must have been difficult or dangerous, and the large plates and spines present on the backs and tails of stegosaurs makes it difficult to imagine how they got close enough to each other to mate.

People have tended to assume that giant dinosaurs behaved in a similar fashion to modern giant mammals, some of which spend hours copulating. In part this is because the mating behaviours of mammals are better documented than those of birds, crocodylians and large lizards. It is also because people have imagined non-bird dinosaurs to be behaviourally similar to mammals like elephants and rhinos, simply due to their shared large size. This view is probably partly accurate, but our knowledge of phylogeny and non-bird dinosaur anatomy means that we should rely more on the living animals that are the closest relatives of non-bird dinosaurs – crocodylians and large birds in particular.

Studies of growth rates (opposite) in non-bird dinosaurs show that they grew quickly – faster than most animals, though not necessarily as quickly as modern birds or the majority of mammals. Altricial birds refers to those species that spend the first part of their lives nest-bound and unable to walk. Precocial birds refers to those species able to walk and run soon after hatching.

This family tree diagram (opposite) shows how mesothermy evolved several times among fish, mammal and reptile groups that live today. Perhaps this metabolic strategy was typical of non-bird dinosaurs and archaic birds too.

153

Mating in crocodylians is the final act in a courtship process that involves noisy and visual display as well as touching and caressing. During this process the female sometimes climbs on to the male's back.

Mammals frequently practise long-term parental care where mothers put substantial time and energy into the raising of their babies. For giant mammals like whales, this results in a very slow rate of reproductive turnover.

If non-bird dinosaurs mated in a similar way to these living animals, a female might signal her readiness to mate by crouching and either raising her pelvic region or lifting or moving her tail aside. The male would then position himself behind or on top of her and, by manoeuvring his tail and pelvic region, aim to penetrate her cloaca with his everted penis. Mating is brief in crocodylians and many birds, so perhaps it was in non-bird dinosaurs too.

Once mating and fertilization had occurred, what happened next? What sort of particular reproductive strategy did non-bird dinosaurs practise? One of the first things to consider is whether these animals practised K-selection or r-selection. These two terms come from equations used to work out how populations of animals change in numbers according to the growth rates of the animals in those populations. K-selected animals produce a small number of babies at any one time, invest a lot of energy into the growth and care of those babies, and produce a low number of babies in their lifetime. Big mammals (including humans) practise the K-selection style of reproduction, but so do animals like sharks, and some lizards and turtles. In contrast, r-selected animals produce a large number of babies that have low chances of survival and require little investment from the parent.

In reality, the idea that these two strategies are distinct and that animals group neatly into one or other category fell apart decades ago, as numerous animals mix and match traits of both systems. Despite this, the terms are still useful. What we know of non-bird dinosaurs indicates that they were mostly r-strategists, producing large clutches of eggs and large numbers of babies, relatively few of which survived to adulthood. Non-bird dinosaurs of many kinds might have produced so many babies that the majority of the population at any one time would have consisted mostly of juveniles.

Support for this view comes from footprints, since there are rock layers where the majority of dinosaur tracks seem to have been made by juveniles, not adults. More support comes from the fact that a great many of the Mesozoic dinosaur skeletons we've discovered were not fully grown at the time of death, and from the fact that dinosaurs as a whole grew quickly –

overall, many seemingly practised a 'live fast, die young' strategy.

This has some interesting ramifications for dinosaur evolution as a whole. Small, juvenile dinosaurs of many species seem to have lived separately from adults, and almost certainly behaved as distinct 'species', living in different places and exploiting different food items from their parents. This means that one non-bird dinosaur species would potentially have occupied ecological spaces in its community otherwise occupied by several different species of different body sizes. We'll come back to this idea shortly, since it receives support from the fact that the juveniles of some dinosaur species looked very different from the adults.

Also of interest is that a dinosaur population consisting mostly of juveniles might perhaps mean that dinosaurs as a group were hard to kill off. An event capable of killing off adults (like a major climate shift, or a global disaster like an asteroid impact) would still have left a large surviving crop of small babies. And, indeed, we know that dinosaurs survived through many tough times during the course of the Mesozoic – while we often think of non-bird dinosaurs as animals that failed to survive a mass extinction event, it's important to remember that they had previously survived two or three other earlier extinctions.

Baby mammals are typically completely dependent on their mothers when born, even in very fast-growing mammals like rodents. This system works well, but requires major and timely investment from the mother.

EGGS, NESTS AND BABIES

Even if we completely lacked any fossils of eggs, nests or baby non-bird dinosaurs, bracketing would still lead us to conclude that non-bird dinosaurs produced hard-shelled eggs, that they laid these eggs in a nest, and that parents of one or both sexes probably practised parental care. Living crocodylians practise these behaviours, constructing mound-like nests of vegetation or sediment that they then guard until hatching time (some crocodylians dig burrows that they use as nest sites). Once the eggs hatch, the mother sometimes assists the babies in escaping from the nest and transports them to the water. These sorts of behaviours represent what's known as post-hatching parental care. The mother crocodylian then stays with the babies and guards them from predators.

In some cases, crocodylian parental behaviour is even more complicated. Co-operation between adults has been reported in crocodylians, females

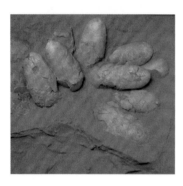

The unusual mound-nesting birds or megapodes – this is the Australian malleefowl (top) – construct huge piles of sediment and vegetation for use as incubators for their eggs. Similar strategies were used by many non-bird dinosaurs.

These elongate Cretaceous dinosaur eggs (above) were discovered in the Mongolian Gobi Desert during the 1920s. They were clearly laid together, and then deliberately arranged into a circular pattern.

sometimes nest in close proximity to each other, and some crocodylians adopt babies from other clutches, in cases resulting in crèches of a hundred babies or more. Parental care is not exclusively a female event, since males in some species assist in moving babies to the water and will also come to their defence. A handful of observations also suggest that crocodylians sometimes feed their babies and there are also cases where the care of babies is a long-term thing, sometimes lasting for as long as 3 years.

The fact that birds construct nests, brood their eggs and care for their babies is well known. Many modern birds nest in trees but if we look at the most ancient living bird groups we see that ground-nesting is more typical. In some ground-nesting birds, the nests are merely shallow depressions or low platforms, but in others they are great piles of vegetation or sediment. There are also birds that dig burrows or tunnels for nesting.

With this knowledge on living archosaurs as essential background information, let's look at what we know about non-bird dinosaurs. Thousands of non-bird dinosaur eggs are known, the vast majority of which are from the Late Cretaceous. While many egg fossils are mere fragments of shell, complete eggs are fairly common, and entire egg-filled nests are known too. It's sometimes been said that the first non-bird dinosaur eggs to be scientifically recognized were those found by a team from the American Museum of Natural History in Mongolia during the 1920s. This team – led by zoologist-explorer Roy Chapman Andrews – discovered a nest of oval eggs, each about 23 cm (9 in) long, that were originally thought to belong to the early ceratopsian *Protoceratops*. That proposed identification proved incorrect, as we'll see.

Actually, non-bird dinosaur eggs have been known to scientists since the 1800s and we even know from archaeological sites that people were finding and keeping fossil eggshell fragments thousands of years ago. Non-bird dinosaur eggs are extremely diverse in size and shape. Some are stretched ovals, others are not shaped that differently from chicken eggs, and others are near-perfectly spherical. The eggs found so far vary in size from less than 10 cm (4 in) to over 30 cm (12 in) in length.

Of course, the great mystery surrounding individual non-bird dinosaur eggs concerns their identity: what dinosaur species did they belong to? In most cases this simply cannot be established and we can only make educated guesses, suggesting that a given egg belonged to a dinosaur species discovered in the same region and rock layer, for example.

In one or two cases, complete eggs have been discovered inside the body of the mother. This is the case in an oviraptorosaur from the Late Cretaceous of China. This animal has two eggs inside its pelvis, both of which were due to be laid within hours or even minutes of the animal's death. The presence of two eggs shows that both reproductive canals – or oviducts – were operational in this dinosaur, something already suspected from the fact that the eggs of non-bird dinosaurs were laid in pairs. This is different from the condition in modern birds where only one oviduct (the left one) is functional. Obviously, theropods switched from using two oviducts to one alone at some point, presumably early in the history of birds.

Dinosaur eggshell varies a great deal in microscopic structure. The surface texture is variable, the number, density and size of the tiny pores in the eggshell is variable, and the number of mineral layers that form the eggshell is variable too. Some of these details are useful when it comes to working out the nesting behaviour of the dinosaur concerned. Especially big pores, for example, show that an egg incubated in a humid environment, for example beneath vegetation or buried in sediment (in these conditions larger pores are needed to get enough oxygen into the shell). Palaeontologists who specialize in the study of dinosaur eggshell have identified over 40 distinct eggshell types. But, again, how do we match these to specific dinosaur groups?

In some cases, embryos are preserved inside the eggs. Rounded eggs from the Late Cretaceous of Argentina have titanosaur embryos preserved within them while eggs from elsewhere have the bones of early sauropodomorphs, hadrosaurs, therizinosaurs and other dinosaurs preserved inside. Those '*Protoceratops* eggs' found in the 1920s proved not to be from *Protoceratops* at all, but from the parrot-headed, bird-like oviraptorosaurs. This is ironic, since oviraptorosaurs were originally regarded as egg stealers and wrongly accused of thieving *Protoceratops* eggs. Indeed, the name 'oviraptorosaur' means 'egg thief lizards'.

The microscopic surface texture of dinosaur eggshell is frequently both bumpy and porous – raised mounds and pores in the eggshell are both visible here. These features allow different eggshell types to be identified, but they had biological functions when the egg contained life.

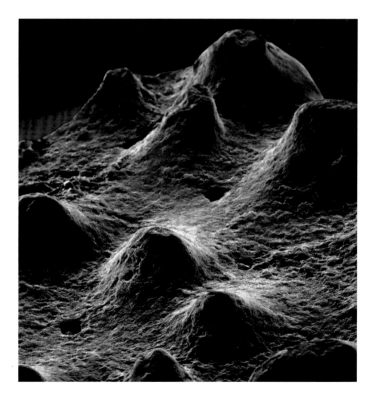

Eggshell fragments like these examples from the Gobi Desert – often centimetres or millimetres across – are abundant in many places. In regions once used as dinosaur nesting grounds there may be literally millions of eggshells and eggshell fragments.

Many eggs have been discovered in clutches or nests. These are also diverse and suggest different styles of laying behaviour. The commonest kinds of non-bird dinosaur egg clutches are circular, but some (thought to have been made by sauropods) are preserved in lines or arcs. We presume that non-bird dinosaurs of many species built nests of piled vegetation. After all, modern crocodylians and some birds do this, and many non-bird dinosaurs were too big to sit on their eggs to protect or warm them. The fossil record hasn't yet provided us with a case where a mass of leaves and twigs is preserved on top of an egg clutch. This isn't surprising, since piles of vegetation have a low preservation potential. Even post-Cretaceous bird nests formed of vegetation are virtually unknown from the fossil record – only two or three examples have been found, all made by waterbirds like ducks or relatives of flamingos.

The parental behaviour of non-bird dinosaurs is a popular area of discussion, and has been ever since the North American hadrosaur *Maiasaura* was announced to the world in 1979. The fossils of this dinosaur include the remains of adults as well as nests, the bones of babies and fossil eggshells. The palaeontologists who discovered this dinosaur – Jack Horner and Bob Makela – discovered an entire nesting ground where several layers of *Maiasaura* nests were preserved, one on top of the other. Not only did this discovery show that *Maiasaura* (and presumably other hadrosaurs too) nested in colonies but the successive layers of nests preserved showed that the dinosaurs nested in the same area year after year.

Maiasaura was a big animal – 7 m (23 ft) long and 2.5 t or so in mass. Assuming it stayed with its nest during the incubation period, we have to conclude (because of its size) that it didn't sit on its nest. We do know that Cretaceous maniraptoran theropods sat on their nests. We now have examples of oviraptorosaurs preserved sat on top of their egg-filled nests, and there are specimens of the troodontid *Troodon* and the dromaeosaurid *Deinonychus* preserved with folded legs and their bellies pressed against their eggs as well. These fossils demonstrate that nest-sitting, like that seen in birds today, was a widespread behaviour of non-bird maniraptorans.

It's assumed that these maniraptoran parents were brooding, that is, keeping their eggs at the right temperature. Animals do this by using their

body heat to keep their eggs warm, but they also provide shade, and move and reposition nest material to keep the eggs at incubation temperature. It's likely that these dinosaurs were guarding their nests as well. Non-bird dinosaurs lived alongside mammals, lizards and other animals that would have eaten dinosaur eggs or babies if they could. Direct evidence that baby dinosaurs were in danger comes from Cretaceous snakes discovered inside dinosaur nests, and a fossil mammal – the badger-sized *Repenomamus* from the Early Cretaceous of China – has the remains of young specimens of *Psittacosaurus* preserved as stomach contents.

It was once assumed that the maniraptorans discovered sat on top of their nests were females. But egg-sitting is not a female-only behaviour in many living birds. In some cases, both parents contribute to egg care. In others, males perform the majority of egg care or even all of it. This is the case in emus, cassowaries, rheas and kiwis. Thanks to the discovery of medullary bone in the skeletons of female non-bird dinosaurs (see Chapter 3), we're now sometimes able to sex fossil dinosaurs. The bones of females don't contain medullary bone all the time, but the production and use of this tissue means that the inner layers of their leg bones show evidence of remodelling, even when the medullary bone is no longer there.

Hadrosaurs, like *Maiasaura* shown here, nested in colonies where the nests were spread apart by a reasonable distance. Parents guarded their nests and probably brought food to their nestlings. Predators like small theropods and large lizards hunted for unguarded eggs and babies.

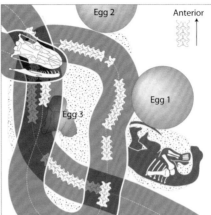

Egg 2

Anterior

Egg 1

Egg 3

We would predict that big Cretaceous snakes would have eaten baby dinosaurs. In 2010, this remarkable fossil was described from the Upper Cretaceous rocks of India. A large snake called *Sanajeh* was discovered inside the nest of a titanosaurian sauropod, right next to the eggs and babies.

'Remodelling' means that the bone layers concerned preserve evidence of having recently changed in shape and structure. The same layers of a male's bones, in contrast, lack evidence of remodelling. With this in mind, dinosaur reproduction expert David Varricchio and colleagues examined the bone microstructure of a nesting *Troodon* specimen and a nesting oviraptorosaur called *Citipati*. Both specimens lack bone remodelling. They seem to be males.

Varricchio and colleagues made another surprising suggestion about these nesting maniraptorans. The numbers of eggs found in non-bird maniraptoran nests is high (at 22–24), and the eggs themselves are large compared to adults. Perhaps this means that these nests don't represent the output of a single pair of dinosaurs. Perhaps they're communal nests, representing the combined output of two or more females. In birds today, communal nesting is practised by ostriches, the South American rheas, and by various rails, cuckoos and perching birds.

This fabulous oviraptorosaur from Mongolia – nicknamed 'Big momma' – is preserved on top of an egg-filled nest, its arms wrapped around the eggs. Much of the dinosaur's skeleton has been lost to erosion. It now seems that 'Big momma' was a male, not a female.

PARENTAL CARE AFTER HATCHING, OR LACK OF IT

What happened after a baby non-bird dinosaur emerged from its egg? Did it leave the nest as quickly as possible to live a life on its own, or did it receive care from its parents? Again, bracketing gives us clues on the sorts of behaviours we might expect. Crocodylians and birds both practise parental care, and bonds between babies and their parents are also seen in several lizard groups. Even turtles of one species (the giant South American river turtle) use noises to guide their newly hatched babies on migration journeys. Further afield in the tree of life, care of babies is known in various amphibians and fish. Although lizards, turtles, amphibians and fish are not close relatives of dinosaurs, it's clear that complex parental behaviours are widespread among those animals where parents invest time and energy in the care of their eggs.

Fossil evidence suggests that several non-bird dinosaurs did indeed practise post-hatching parental care. The greatest amount of information comes from hadrosaurs, and in particular from Late Cretaceous members of the group from the USA, *Maiasaura* especially. Babies that seem to have been several weeks old have been discovered inside their crater-like nests where they had presumably been fed and protected by one or both parents. Fragmented eggshell discovered inside these nests has been taken as showing that it was trampled by the babies, although eggshell can get broken to pieces in other ways too. Fossil plant fragments found in *Maiasaura* nests might be the remains of meals brought to the nest by a parent.

For hadrosaurs at least, the idea that juveniles stayed in the nest after hatching and that they were fed and defended by one or both of the parents remains a reasonable interpretation of the evidence we have. How widespread was post-hatching care like this across non-bird dinosaurs?

Work by Robert Reisz and colleagues provides possible indications of post-hatching parental care in the sauropodomorph *Massospondylus* from the Early Jurassic of South Africa. The babies are unusual little animals, very different in appearance from adults. They have large heads, short necks, and limb proportions suggesting that they walked on all fours. They're also toothless, unlike adults and older juveniles. Reisz and

Living crocodylians like this Nile crocodile practise what's called post-hatching parental care. The mother guards her babies from predators and even transports them to the water, sometimes carrying them in her mouth. She might even help them find food too.

This incredible Chinese fossil preserves 34 baby specimens of *Psittacosaurus* and a single large one. The large individual is almost certainly not there by coincidence since all of these animals were buried at the same time. Was it a parent or even a baby-sitter?

colleagues suggest that these clumsy, strangely proportioned, toothless babies must have needed parental care. Perhaps their parents brought chewed up mush to the nest for them to eat, and perhaps they were unable to forage for themselves. For now, this idea remains speculative and more evidence is needed.

One of the most remarkable insights into post-hatching parental care concerns a single specimen of the ceratopsian *Psittacosaurus*, preserved together with 34 babies. These animals all died when they were drowned in a mudflow, and the large individual was presumably guarding or caring for the babies before death. The number of babies is so high relative to what we expect for a normal clutch that this may well represent a crèche – a collection of babies that originated from different clutches. The large individual is not fully adult but was itself a large juvenile. Was it a parent? After all, we already know that non-bird dinosaurs of many sorts could breed before reaching full adulthood. Or was it a baby-sitter, perhaps related to some or all of the babies it died with? Humans aren't the only animals where friends and relatives look after babies – helping of this sort is widespread in birds and could have been present in non-bird dinosaurs too.

Another assemblage of ornithischians concerns the North American *Oryctodromeus*. Three specimens were discovered together, one of which is an adult while the other two are juveniles. All died in close contact, presumably from drowning when their large, coiled burrow flooded. Not only were some small ornithiscians social animals that denned in family groups, they were also burrow-frequenting dinosaurs. Were they burrow-digging dinosaurs? This looks plausible given that *Oryctodromeus* has several features which suggest adaptation to a digging way of life.

What happened as young non-bird dinosaurs matured and left the nesting environment? Did the parents continue to care for them until they were larger, or did the babies and parents go their separate ways? Fossils relevant to this question are rare, but the information we have indicates that different dinosaurs did different things. There are some dinosaurs – examples include non-bird coelurosaurian theropods – where young juveniles are found on their own, and seem to have been capable of feeding and caring for themselves. An example is provided by *Scipionyx*, which we met earlier (see pp. 112–113). This small juvenile has especially big teeth and hand claws for its size, and its stomach and gut contents suggest that it was hunting and feeding independently. Maybe there was no post-hatching parental care at all in this dinosaur.

In contrast, we also have cases where juveniles were found in direct association with adults. An example is provided by the four juveniles of the North American iguanodontian *Tenontosaurus* found beneath the skeleton of an adult. These juveniles had reached lengths of 2 m (6½ft) or so, so were some months old. The fact that they were discovered right next to an adult cannot be used as proof of parental care, but it is suggestive.

Finally, there are several dinosaurs where juveniles seem to have lived together in groups, separately from adults. Such groups are known for the theropods *Falcarius* and *Sinornithomimus*, the ankylosaur *Pinacosaurus*, the ceratopsians *Psittacosaurus* and *Protoceratops*, and others too. Trackways provide support for the idea that such groups of juveniles – sometimes called pods – were commonplace in some non-bird dinosaur species. We also know of living reptiles and birds where the juveniles live together for a time, including iguanas, caimans, ostriches, rheas and ravens. In iguanas, the juveniles sleep together in a pile, groom one another, and the larger males protect the smaller females from hawks and other predators.

Large coiled burrows like this one discovered in Montana, USA were used, and presumably manufactured, by the bipedal North American ornithischian *Oryctodromeus*. It seems that these burrows were used for shelter and also for the raising of babies. Maybe burrow-dwelling was common in small ornithischians.

Maybe – and we stress the word maybe – similar kinds of behaviours were present in these non-bird dinosaurs too.

The existence of juvenile-only groups that lived separately from adults seems to have been widespread in non-bird dinosaurs, and it seems that juveniles only joined groups of adults once they had grown to near-adult size. We normally imagine the Mesozoic world as being filled with herds of adults that seasonally formed breeding colonies. But roving gangs of juveniles, generally too young to breed and without the fully formed physical features of the adults of their species, were a major part of the dinosaur-occupied landscapes of the Mesozoic too.

SEX AND THE EVOLUTION OF DINOSAURS

Some modern animals like this cassowary possess extravagant structures – in this case a horn-covered casque – that strongly resemble similar features seen in some non-bird dinosaurs.

One final subject area relevant to dinosaur reproduction deserves discussion. This is the idea that the evolutionary pressures related to mating success – a phenomenon termed sexual selection (see p.67) – may have had a major impact on what dinosaurs looked like and how they evolved. In other words, maybe dinosaurs of certain groups evolved crests, frills, spines, plates, showy feathers and other extravagant structures to improve their ability to woo mates and pass on their genes. A competing idea is that dinosaurs evolved these structures so that members of the various species could tell each other apart. Indeed, it's interesting that these extravagant structures are most prevalent in dinosaur communities where several ornamented species occur together.

If we look at living animals with similar extravagant structures – animals like deer, antelope, rhinoceros beetles or chameleons – we see them using these structures in sexual display, not as 'species identification badges'. A structure used in sexual display typically only reaches full size when its owner reaches sexual maturity, and usually grows at a rate much faster than the rest of the body. These sorts of structures also tend to be expensive when it comes to the energy involved in growing them – they're costly to their owners, since the whole reason for their evolution is that they provide a way for potential mates to judge the genetic quality of the animal that bears them. By applying all of this information to what we know

about the extravagant structures in non-bird dinosaurs and archaic birds, it does seem that they evolved as sexual display structures.

Modern birds are often showy, colourful animals that use mating displays and even dances to advertise their genetic quality. It looks likely that extinct dinosaurs of many sorts used these same tricks, and perhaps we should imagine the frills of ceratopsians, the crests of hadrosaurs, the sails of spinosaurids and so on as flashy, colourful features used by these animals in attention-grabbing ways.

It has also been suggested that one of the most important structures that dinosaurs ever evolved – complex feathers – were among these sexual display structures. Fossils show that complex feathers appeared on the forelimbs and tails of theropods at a time when the rest of the body was covered in simpler, hair-like filaments. The oldest complex feathers we see in the fossil record lack the details of shape and structure expected for a role in flight and first appear in animals that have short arms and were definitely not engaging in flying or even gliding behaviour, like the oviraptorosaur *Caudipteryx*.

Feathers are also excellent display structures, being made of materials ideal for the flaunting of colour and even iridescence, plus they can be shed outside the breeding season. We know from one

Large, Late Cretaceous ceratopsians like the *Triceratops*, *Pachyrhinosaurus* and *Styracosaurus* shown here, are famous for possessing a spectacular array of horns, frills and spines. There is little doubt that these structures were used as visual display devices.

Cretaceous maniraptoran – the Chinese oviraptorosaur *Similicaudipteryx* – that juveniles lacked the large, complex wing and tail feathers of adults, a fact which further supports a sexual display role. All in all, the possibility that a role in display might have contributed to the evolution of complex feathers appears plausible. But given that feathers also have roles in locomotion and insulation, the precise story of feather origins remains hard to pin down.

If the extravagant horns, frills, elaborate feathers and so on present in non-bird dinosaurs did evolve under sexual selection pressure, shouldn't we expect males and females to look different – in other words, to express what we call sexual dimorphism? Convincing cases of sexual dimorphism have yet to be reported from any non-bird dinosaur, and females and males both possess the same elaborate structures (the situation is somewhat different for some Cretaceous birds, a subject we'll return to in Chapter 5).

In the modern world, there are many animals where extremely similar or identical display structures are present in members of both sexes. In these animals – examples include various seabirds, swans, starlings and pipefishes – females are decorated creatures that show off to potential mates and competitors, just as the very similar males do as well. This phenomenon is termed mutual sexual selection and the possibility that it was at play in extinct dinosaurs of several lineages has to be considered as a serious possibility.

The Chinese oviraptorosaur *Caudipteryx* was covered in feathers and had a large, fan-like array of feathers at the end of its tail. Indeed its name means 'tail feather'. Its long, slender legs show that it was a fast runner, and not a climber, percher or glider.

Caudipteryx has especially long feathers on its hands and tail (right). These couldn't have been used in flight of any sort. Were they instead waved about in mating displays?

It isn't always just the males alone who are showy and extravagant. The females of many species – these birds are Crested auklets (far right) – have crests and bright colours that make them look just like the males.

WHAT IS SEXUAL SELECTION?

One of the main driving forces of evolution is natural selection. This is the process, famously identified by Charles Darwin, in which those organisms best able to survive in their environment are the ones that produce the greatest number of surviving offspring. Natural selection is not the only process driving evolutionary change. Another is sexual selection, the process in which those living things best able to pass on their genes are more successful in the long term. In other words, sexual selection describes the process that makes living things better at successful mating. In living animals, sexually selected features include head crests, antlers, bright colours, elaborate feathers and those other structures that make animals attractive as mates. These features often carry significant handicaps – they make it harder for their owners to escape predators, hide from the weather, or keep clean and tidy – and are therefore sometimes at odds with the forces of natural selection.

DINOSAUR GROWTH AND ONTOGENY

It was once assumed that non-bird dinosaurs – especially the very large species – grew at rates similar to those of tortoises and crocodiles, and had lifespans on par with, or exceeding, those of modern reptiles. As recently as the late 1970s, some palaeontologists proposed that giant sauropods might have lived for over 200 years, and that mid-sized sauropods didn't reach adulthood until 60 years of age. Bigger sauropods, like *Brachiosaurus*, were suggested to reach maturity at ages in excess of 100 years. This idea of super-slow-growing dinosaurs is incredibly unlikely given work which shows that large animals have to breed within the first few decades of life if they are to successfully reproduce at all. After this age, the odds are high that the animal will die (through disease, predation, accident or starvation) before ever breeding.

Not only is the slow-growing dinosaur idea inconsistent with theory, it's also inconsistent with work on dinosaur bone anatomy. Studies of various mid-sized dinosaurs (including the theropod *Troodon*, the sauropodomorph *Massospondylus*, and the ornithischian *Psittacosaurus*) show that these dinosaurs reached full size somewhere between 2 and 15 years of age. Among bigger dinosaurs, *Maiasaura* seems to

Big living reptiles, like this Galapagos tortoise, take decades to mature and can live for over 100 years. For a long time, dinosaur growth and lifespan was assumed to be similar in pattern.

This is 'Sue', the famous giant *Tyrannosaurus* specimen on display at the Field Museum in Chicago, USA. Perhaps surprisingly, this animal seems to have been less than 30 years old when it died. So far as we can tell, this was typical for *Tyrannosaurus*.

have reached adult size at just 8 or so years of age, and a 2004 study that looked at seven *Tyrannosaurus* specimens found that all had reached full size before 20 years of age. These animals hadn't lived much beyond the age at which they'd reached full size. The very oldest *Tyrannosaurus* specimen yet studied had died at just 28 or 29 years of age. Three of the other *Tyrannosaurus* looked at in this study had also died only a few years after growth had stopped, suggesting that *Tyrannosaurus* didn't continue living for decades after reaching full adult size. Similar results have been discovered for other non-bird dinosaurs: even the very biggest sauropods were adult in two or three decades.

Non-bird dinosaurs changed in proportions and appearance as they grew. The process by which animals grow is termed ontogeny, and it's typical when describing growth to refer to the ontogenetic changes that occur. We predict that non-bird dinosaurs underwent an ontogenetic process similar to that of living animals, and this is confirmed by what we know of dinosaur embryos, hatchlings and older juveniles. Bodies, heads

and limbs changed shape and proportion relative to one another. The skulls of juveniles are shorter-snouted and with bigger eyes, for example, than those of adults. We also know that the juveniles of horned, frilled and crested species possessed small, prototype versions of the structures present in adults. And juvenile sauropods had proportionally shorter necks than adults. Again, these kinds of changes aren't surprising since they're typical of living animals.

One of the most interesting ideas about non-bird dinosaur biology is that several species didn't change in the ways that we might expect, but instead underwent rather unusual patterns of ontogenetic change. During the 1980s, a new, Late Cretaceous tyrannosaurid was described from Montana and named *Nanotyrannus*. This dinosaur was described on the basis of a skull suggestive of a total length of just 5 m (16½ ft), yet it was claimed to be an adult, an interpretation that would make it a dwarf

Dinosaurs grew quickly, even giant species reaching full size in a couple of decades. This graph shows how the giant theropod *Tyrannosaurus* grew at an elevated rate during its teenage years and stopped growing in its third decade.

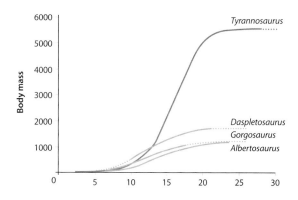

member of the tyrannosaurid family. In contrast to giant tyrannosaurids like *Tyrannosaurus*, *Nanotyrannus* has a shallow, daintily built snout, and teeth that are compressed from side to side rather than thick and rounded in cross-section.

The idea that *Nanotyrannus* might be an unusual dwarf tyrannosaurid came under fire in 1999 when tyrannosaurid expert Thomas Carr showed that the single skull known at the time is obviously not that of a fully mature animal but, instead, that of a juvenile – a juvenile that almost certainly belongs to *Tyrannosaurus rex*. The *Nanotyrannus* skull has the characteristic fibrous bone texture of juveniles, and the junctions between most of its skull bones are still open and not fused as they are in adults.

Arguably, the interpretation of 'Nanotyrannus' as a *T. rex* juvenile is even more interesting than the idea that it represents a distinct species, since here is good evidence that *T. rex* juveniles were very different from adults. Adults were broad-headed, massively powerful super-predators with thick, crushing teeth, but youngsters were slim, lightweight, shallow-snouted, dagger-toothed animals that followed a very different lifestyle and hunted very different prey. In other words, juveniles and adults were so different that they effectively looked, and behaved, like different species.

Some experts argue that this phenomenon was widespread in non-bird dinosaurs, and that dinosaurs originally interpreted as distinct species are actually the growth stages of others. A classic case concerns the dome-skulled dinosaurs of Late Cretaceous North America: big, round-skulled *Pachycephalosaurus*, smaller, spiky-domed *Stygimoloch*, and the smaller, spikier, long-snouted *Dracorex*. All three were originally thought to belong to different branches of the pachycephalosaur family tree.

Jack Horner – best known for his discovery of those *Maiasaura* nesting sites – noted how all three share features suggesting that they might be growth phases of the same animal. By looking at growth patterns within the domes and horns of these dinosaurs, Horner and colleague Mark Goodwin concluded that pachycephalosaurs resorbed their horns and spikes as they matured, at the same time growing a larger, more domed skull. If this is correct, pachycephalosaurs started life as spiky-headed dinosaurs, and became smoother-skulled as they matured. This model of growth is unusual compared to what we see in living animals, but maybe these dinosaurs were just really, really weird.

Three ornithischian dinosaurs from the Late Cretaceous of North America may be growth stages of the same one species. *Dracorex* is smallest and spikiest. *Stygimoloch* is medium-sized and has the longest horns. *Pachycephalosaurus* is the biggest and also the least spikiest, but it has the largest, thickest dome.

The idea that pachycephalosaurs underwent major growth changes may affect members of the group outside this proposed *Dracorex* to *Stygimoloch* to *Pachycephalosaurus* growth series. As we saw in Chapter 2, pachycephalosaurs were long thought to consist of distinct flat-skulled and dome-skulled groups. But the more we've learnt, the more similar these two groups have become. Flat-skulled *Homalocephale*, for example, has the same pattern of knobs and lumps on its skull as does the dome-skulled *Prenocephale* from the same time and place. The two are enough alike that, if we imagine *Homalocephale* growing a rounded dome, we end up with *Prenocephale*. Maybe *Prenocephale* is the adult of *Homalocephale*, and maybe all flat-skulled pachycephalosaurs are juveniles.

It's also been argued – again by Horner and his colleagues – that similar changes occurred within ceratopsians. Three gigantic horned dinosaurs – *Triceratops*, *Nedoceratops* and *Torosaurus* – were more or less contemporaries, and all inhabited the same region of western North America. Differences in the shapes of their faces, horns and frills mean that all three have been regarded as distinct but related species.

Good evidence shows that the small '*Nanotyrannus*' skull from Montana is a juvenile specimen of *Tyrannosaurus rex*, a species first discovered in Montana but later discovered in rocks that come from New Mexico and Texas in the south of the USA to Alberta in the north.

There is little doubt that the giant North American ceratopsian *Triceratops* changed in skull anatomy as it matured. But is the giant, long-frilled ceratopsian *Torosaurus* – represented by the large skull at the bottom right – part of this growth sequences too?

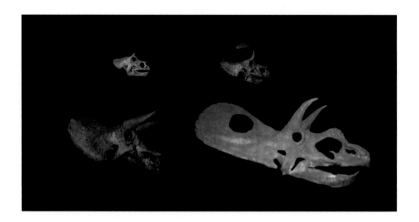

Again, growth changes observed in the microscopic structure of their bones has led Horner and colleagues to argue that these dinosaurs represent a growth series. They propose that *Torosaurus* – which has an enormously long frill, perforated by two oval openings – actually represents old adult specimens of *Triceratops* (which has a shorter, solid frill), whereas *Nedoceratops* – which is *Triceratops*-like but has small openings in the frill – is interpreted as an intermediate growth stage between these two.

The claim that *Triceratops*-type animals turn into *Torosaurus*-type ones via a *Nedoceratops*-type stage is controversial, and other experts argue that it's contradicted by the snout and frill shapes of these dinosaurs, and by the existence of young animals that seem to have *Torosaurus*-like features and old animals that seem to have *Triceratops*-like features. Opinion remains divided, and many experts are unconvinced by this particular proposal. Nevertheless it serves as a reminder that non-bird dinosaurs of some species may well have undergone radical changes as they matured.

If *Nanotyrannus* really is a juvenile *Tyrannosaurus*, and if *Dracorex* really is a juvenile *Pachycephalosaurus*, then here's evidence that dinosaurs of some species produced growth stages that probably acted as different 'species' from their parents. Maybe an ability to occupy several different lifestyles and habitats and exploit different resources gave these species an evolutionary advantage over others. Or maybe this was a dinosaur-wide phenomenon and it helps explain why they were so successful for so long. The idea that juveniles (in at least some species) lived different lives from adults receives support from the fact that the fossils of juveniles are often found apart from adults.

Non-bird dinosaurs were similar to living animals in a great many ways, but here are indications that they might also, sometimes, have been quite different.

DINOSAUR COMMUNITIES

Non-bird dinosaurs and archaic birds inhabited a world that was diverse and alive with plants and animals, including other dinosaur species. And while some dinosaur species that inhabited the same habitat may have had virtually nothing to do with one another, others would have interacted regularly, or had an impact on the environment so significant that it influenced the evolution, distribution and lifestyle of their contemporaries. Interactions of this sort are common in modern animal communities and are so important that a whole branch of biology is devoted to their study. It's termed community ecology.

We cannot, of course, directly observe non-bird dinosaurs and archaic bird species interacting with their contemporaries or environments, so we have to build up our understanding of these communities by looking at numerous different pieces of evidence.

While some of our ideas about the structure of ancient animal communities are speculative, we can at least be sure that certain dinosaurs were contemporaries. The diplodocids *Apatosaurus* and *Diplodocus* really did live alongside one another, for example, and their fossils are found in the same quarries as those of *Stegosaurus*, the ornithopod *Camptosaurus*, the big theropods *Allosaurus*, *Ceratosaurus* and *Torvosaurus*, and the small theropods *Ornitholestes* and *Tanycolagreus*. It's tempting to imagine these animals forming a complex community much like that present today in, say, modern tropical Africa: giraffes and elephants feed on trees, rhinos and antelopes browse from shrubs, lions sleep nearby, and ostriches, guineafowl and hornbills pick up food items from the ground.

During Late Jurassic times, western North America was inhabited by numerous dinosaurs known from excellent, well preserved skeletons – *Stegosaurus*, *Allosaurus* and *Diplodocus*, all shown here, are among them. Thanks to rich fossil-bearing localities in Colorado, Wyoming and elsewhere, we know that these particular dinosaurs really did live alongside one another.

But, can we go further? Can we learn how an extinct dinosaur species fitted into its environment, and how it interacted with its neighbours? For starters, we need to develop hypotheses about the feeding and foraging behaviour of the species concerned. As discussed elsewhere in this book, the substantial amount of work done on topics such as jaw mechanics and tooth wear allows us to devise detailed views of what and how these animals ate, and where they ate it from.

Sticking with the comparatively well-studied Late Jurassic sauropods of North America, different skull shapes, tooth forms, neck lengths and body shapes indicate that *Camarasaurus*, *Apatosaurus*, *Diplodocus* and others avoided direct competition by exploiting different kinds of food. Support for this idea comes from tooth microwear and FEA studies of the sort we looked at in Chapter 4. A study in 2014 led by sauropod specialist David Button showed how the deep-skulled *Camarasaurus* had a stronger bite than the shallow-snouted *Diplodocus*, and that both sauropods were feeding on different kinds of plants. In other words, these contemporaries were practising niche partitioning – the phenomenon whereby animals make use of different parts of a habitat, or different resources, and therefore share a habitat without competing.

Additional evidence for niche partitioning in sauropods comes from the different neck lengths we see in these animals, with some being adapted for feeding at greater heights than others. This need to avoid competition and even to take advantage of resources unavailable to other animals may well have been one of the main driving forces of sauropod neck evolution.

Evidence for community structure is seen among other herbivorous dinosaurs. During the Campanian age of the Late Cretaceous, western

Digital reconstructions of the skulls of the Jurassic sauropods *Camarasaurus* (left) and *Diplodocus* (right) show that they differed considerably in the size and shape of their jaw muscles, and therefore in bite strength. Some of the more important muscles used in opening and closing the jaws are shown in the two reconstructions.

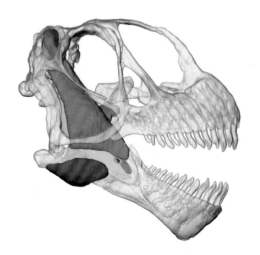
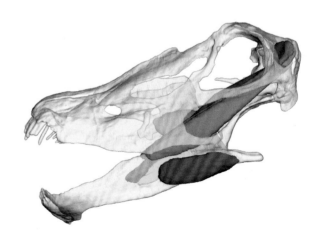

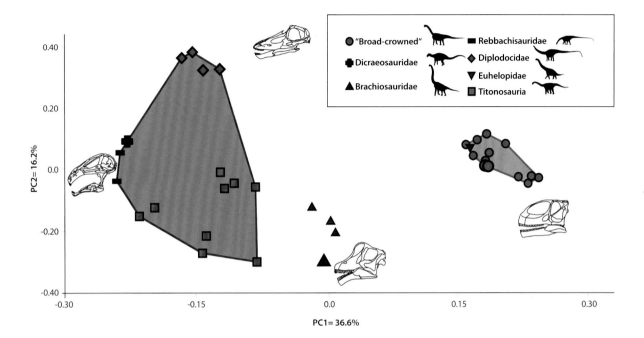

North America was home to numerous ceratopsians and hadrosaurs, species famous for their frills, horns and head crests. Narrow-snouted ceratopsians and broad-mouthed ankylosaurs, both with little ability to feed higher than 2 m (6½ ft) above the ground, lived alongside hadrosaurs that were able to feed from plants 5 m (16 ft) or more above ground level. Again, studies that have looked at bite strength, tooth wear, mouth shape and feeding height indicate that these different dinosaurs were practising niche partitioning, with the different groups avoiding competition by specializing on different plant foods.

The sheer number of species involved in these Campanian communities is surprising, as is the way they were distributed across ancient North America. In the modern world, big animals tend to have large, continent-wide ranges. Yet many Campanian dinosaurs seem to have been more restricted. Perhaps this is because the North America of the time was especially lush and complicated with regard to the shape of its environments and the diversity of its plants, and perhaps these dinosaurs were more specialized for particular habitats or regions than is typical for big animals today, or indeed for big dinosaurs at other times of the Mesozoic. These 'crowded' communities of localized species were not at all typical of the Late Cretaceous. Just a few million years later, they were gone entirely, replaced by blander, simpler communities where a smaller number of dinosaurs – including *Triceratops*, *Edmontosaurus* and *Tyrannosaurus* – occurred continuously across the same region and beyond it.

When measurements from their skulls and teeth are compared, sauropods fall into two major clusters. Narrow-toothed sauropods are on the left, and broad-toothed sauropods are on the right. Members of these distinct clusters surely differed in feeding style and dietary preferences. Several sauropod species possess a tooth form intermediate between these two clusters.

Especially rich dinosaur faunas are known from the Upper Cretaceous rock of western North America. This scene shows several of the dinosaurs that lived together in what is now Montana during the Campanian age. The tyrannosaurid *Gorgosaurus* (far left) watches the ankylosaur *Edmontonia*, the hadrosaur *Brachylophosaurus*, the small pachycephalosaur *Stegoceras*, and the ceratopsians *Chasmosaurus* and *Styracosaurus*.

A final point is that nobody doubts the fact that we're missing a huge part of the picture when it comes to the shape of Mesozoic dinosaur communities. In other words, we're almost certainly unaware of many of the small, surprising relationships that must have existed. Many modern species have special or unusual relationships that would be unknown to us if these animals were extinct. Consider the birds, for example,

that climb on the bodies of large herbivorous mammals, the hateful interactions between big predators like lions and hyenas, and the co-operative, mutually beneficial systems of communication present within mixed groups of hornbills, duiker antelopes and monkeys that have been documented in African forests. Unfortunately, the fossil record is unlikely to reveal the existence of many of these subtle, specialized interactions.

THE ORIGIN OF BIRDS

EVER SINCE CHARLES DARWIN proposed his theory of evolution by natural selection in 1859 it has been agreed that birds are close relatives of reptiles. Some scientists have gone as far as saying that birds are feathered, flying, big-brained, 'glorified reptiles'. Birds share many features of their anatomy and behaviour with crocodylians, and as a result there has never been reasonable doubt that birds are archosaurs, part of the great group of reptiles that includes crocodylians, dinosaurs and kin. A poor fossil record meant, alas, that close extinct relatives of birds were long missing from the geological record, and hence there was doubt about where in the archosaur family tree birds belonged.

Today, this is no longer true. We now have scores of fossil archosaurs that are closely related to birds and which possess all manner of features previously expected or predicted for bird ancestors. In many cases, the animals concerned look like ideal bird ancestors or, at least, close relatives of those ancestors. All are theropod dinosaurs.

When John Ostrom proposed his hypothesis that birds evolved from among theropods (see Chapter 1), a large amount of anatomical data supported his view. Put as simply as possible, he proposed that *Deinonychus*-like maniraptorans evolved into smaller, *Archaeopteryx*-like animals, and that these eventually gave rise to modern birds. At the time, only a handful of non-bird maniraptorans were known, and it was

Archaeopteryx – alone among non-bird dinosaurs and archaic birds – that preserved direct evidence for a feathery covering.

Since then, the state of our knowledge has increased enormously. A substantial number of bird-like maniraptorans are now known, all of which share anatomical features with early birds that are not present in other animal groups. Among the more obvious of these features are long, slender, three-fingered hands, a semi-circular bone in the wrist that allows the hand to be rotated against the bones of the lower arm, and a series of air-filled openings at the back of the big-brained skull. Birds and non-bird maniraptorans also share features of their hips, shoulder girdles and backbones not seen in other animals.

This classic illustration from the 1980s depicts John Ostrom's idea that ground-running theropods somehow evolved feathers and a flight ability, and eventually gave rise to birds. The idea that birds might actually have evolved in this way is no longer considered likely.

Fossils also show that non-bird maniraptorans were fully feathered, with large, complex feathers growing from their arms and hands, their tails, and sometimes their legs and feet. Simpler filament-like structures and thin, small complex feathers covered the rest of their bodies. This extensive covering was typical of oviraptorosaurs, troodontids, dromaeosaurids and a few other maniraptoran groups (all of which were discussed in Chapter 2). It means that these dinosaurs looked incredibly bird-like overall.

Today we know that the skeletons of early members of the bird lineage – like *Archaeopteryx*, shown at the top – are extremely similar to those of bird-like maniraptorans like *Deinonychus*, shown below. *Archaeopteryx* is, in fact, little more than a small, lightly built, version of *Deinonychus*.

THE ORIGIN OF AVIAN FEATURES

A great number of fossils now shed light on the evolutionary transitions that occurred within birds and their close relatives – a real contrast to the state of our knowledge prior to the 1990s. We now have fossils that show how a deep, toothy snout became a shallow, toothless, beaked one; how the arms and hands became longer and turned into wings; how a hand with three separate clawed fingers evolved into the fused-up, feather-supporting hand of modern birds; how a foot suited for running turned into one suited for perching and grasping; and how the tail became shortened and used in the support of a broad fan of feathers.

Before the 1990s, it was thought that many of the anatomical features associated with birds – including feathers, a wishbone, an extensive pneumatic system and a perching foot – originated at the same time as birds did. Fossils actually show that birds inherited some of these features – feathers and the wishbone among them – from earlier dinosaurs. Meanwhile, other features regarded as typical of birds, like toothless jaws and an enlarged breastbone, evolved late in bird history and were not typical of birds during the early part of their history. In fact, the very earliest birds – animals like *Archaeopteryx* from the Late Jurassic of Germany, and *Anchiornis* and *Xiaotingia* from the Late Jurassic of China – were highly similar to dromaeosaurids and other non-bird maniraptorans and almost certainly had very similar lifestyles.

The skulls of many of the oldest birds are similar to those of oviraptorosaurs, troodontids and dromaeosaurids. They have a blunt, toothy snout, and peg-like teeth suggestive of an omnivorous diet. Larger, more blade-like teeth, suited for grabbing small animals, are present in other early birds. Only in more advanced, later birds – a group called the ornithurines – did the snout become shallower, more lightweight, and more similar to what we see in birds today.

For most of their evolutionary history, birds had teeth. Bottom left is the long-jawed skull of the Cretaceous diving bird *Hesperornis*. Pointed, conical teeth line the edges of its lower jaw and parts of its upper jaw.

The skull of a modern bird – this one below belongs to a bittern – is completely toothless, and also bigger-brained than that of a Mesozoic bird. Modern birds also tend to have flexible zones between the base of the bill and the rest of the skull.

It looks likely that beak tissue covered the edges of the upper and lower jaws in all birds, but not until the rise of ornithurines can we say that a beak evolved. Early ornithurines – examples include *Ichthyornis* from the Late Cretaceous of the USA – have recurved, blade-like, unserrated teeth that look suited for fish-grabbing, but the teeth later declined in size and number as horny beak tissue came to cover more of the snout and jaws. It has often been suggested that birds lost their teeth as a weight-saving adaptation, but this is unlikely given calculations that show that the teeth represented a tiny, unimportant fraction of total weight. Perhaps beak tissue took over the role of teeth because it's more versatile: beak tissue grows throughout life, it rapidly changes shape according to how it's used, and beaks might be more adaptable and quicker to respond to change than teeth are. Beaks are made of a tough protein called keratin, which is very similar to the protein that makes up claws, scales and feathers, and it is an easier, cheaper tissue to make than the enamel and dentine that form teeth.

Another feature typical of modern birds is an especially big sternum, or breastbone. In many modern birds that fly, the sternum is boat-shaped with a deep crest, called the keel, running along its lower surface. It's the main attachment site for the large muscles that pull the wing downwards

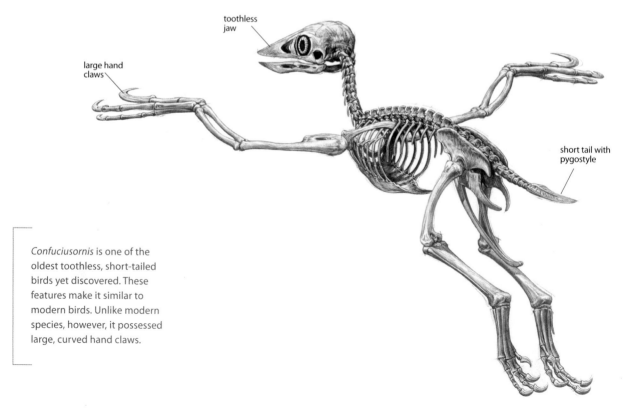

large hand claws

toothless jaw

short tail with pygostyle

Confuciusornis is one of the oldest toothless, short-tailed birds yet discovered. These features make it similar to modern birds. Unlike modern species, however, it possessed large, curved hand claws.

during the flight stroke, so it's often been thought that a giant bony sternum is an essential piece of bird anatomy. And a large, plate-like sternum is present in dromaeosaurids and in such early birds as long-tailed *Jeholornis* and toothless *Confuciusornis*. This all supports the idea that the sternum was present in birds throughout their history. But if there's anything that the fossil record has taught us, it's that evolutionary events are often complicated, sometimes involving twists and turns that we might not predict.

Surprisingly, a bony sternum is lacking from all the *Archaeopteryx* specimens discovered so far, and it's also missing from the early birds *Anchiornis* and *Sapeornis*. Both of these animals are known from over 100 specimens each, so we can be confident that the absence of the sternum in these animals is a genuine feature of their anatomy. We have to conclude that a bony sternum was absent at the start of bird history. This is important because it suggests that a powerful flapping stroke, and maybe flight altogether, was impossible in the earliest birds. Perhaps this also shows that the bony sternum of ornithurines and related bird groups is a new structure, not one that evolved directly from the sternum present in dromaeosaurids and other non-bird maniraptorans.

Another feature once thought to be present in birds right at the start of their history is an enlarged inner toe, or hallux. In modern birds, the hallux is large, positioned low down on the foot, and points backwards. It therefore operates in similar fashion to the human thumb, giving the bird foot an opposable grip. An enlarged, opposable hallux is great for a lifestyle that involves perching, and it's also used by birds that grab prey with their feet, or clutch fruits or flowers. Incidentally, the hallux is not present in all living birds – those specialized for a running lifestyle, like ostriches, have lost it during their evolution.

The idea that birds possessed a large, reversed hallux throughout history has gone hand-in-hand with the concept that birds were always tree-dwelling animals, and that their special features evolved as adaptations to life in the trees. But detailed studies and well-preserved fossils disprove this view. In *Archaeopteryx* and other early birds, the hallux points forwards and is not positioned low enough on the foot to be used in grasping. The feet of early birds were very similar to those of other theropods – a fact that has implications for how flight originated, as we'll see in a moment. In later Mesozoic bird groups, like enantiornithines (the so-called opposite birds, see p.195), the hallux was directed inwards more than it was forwards, but a large, back-turned hallux doesn't seem to have evolved until the origin of modern birds.

Modern birds differ from other theropods in that the hallux – the toe on the inner side of the foot – is enlarged and directed backwards. It was long assumed that this configuration was true of ancient Mesozoic birds as well. It wasn't.

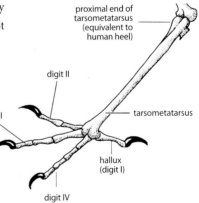

proximal end of tarsometatarsus (equivalent to human heel)

digit II

digit III

tarsometatarsus

hallux (digit I)

digit IV

Fossils also give us insights into how and when birds evolved some of their unusual internal features. We saw in Chapter 3 that certain Cretaceous birds, including *Sapeornis*, possess crops and gizzards and hence were similar to modern birds in the anatomy of their digestive tract. Another feature that makes modern birds unusual, relative to other reptiles, is that females only use one of their oviducts, not both of these normally paired structures. (In many bird species the right oviduct becomes reduced as the bird matures.) The fact that the eggs produced by non-bird maniraptorans were produced two at a time confirms the existence of paired oviducts in these dinosaurs. But can we gain any indication from the fossil record when dinosaurs switched from paired oviducts to a single one?

The answer is – probably – yes. Several Cretaceous bird fossils, including *Jeholornis* and two Chinese enantiornithines, have structures that look like developing egg cells preserved in their bodies, and these structures are only present on their left sides. *Jeholornis* belongs to one of the oldest branches of the bird family tree, so here's evidence that the single oviduct system evolved early in bird history, close to the origin of the group. Why birds made this change is not entirely clear, but the explanation favoured most often is that birds lost the right oviduct for weight-saving reasons to help with flight.

Birds also have to be seen as part of several long-term trends present across the whole evolutionary history of theropods. Over the course of about 50 million years, those theropods belonging to the line that ultimately led to birds became smaller and smaller, and evolved slimmer, longer, more lightweight bones. The theropods close to birds also evolved longer forelimbs and larger arm and chest muscles over time. One way of looking at birds, therefore, is as the inevitable 'end products' of long, continuous trends in theropod history – they are the smallest, most lightly built, most long-armed theropods of them all. And we saw in Chapter 3 how coelurosaurian theropods gradually reduced the size of their tail-based caudofemoral muscles, a change that allowed the tail to become slimmer, shorter and more lightweight. The extremely shortened tails of enantiornithines, ornithurines and some other bird groups are the ultimate development of that trend. In modern birds, the caudofemoral muscles play virtually no role in walking, and the tail's main roles concern control during flight (it functions as a rudder and provides lift), and display.

The way in which modern birds acquired the features we associate with them today is therefore quite complicated. Birds should be imagined as maniraptorans that possess most of the features typical for this group, including large and complex feathers, a big-brained skull and long forelimbs. Fossils show that all of these features originated about 170 million years ago, during the middle part of the Jurassic Period. And birds also possess features typical of theropods as a whole, like the furcula and pneumatic system – features that evolved 200 million years ago or so, at the dawn of the Jurassic.

But superimposed on top of this set of common features are unusual structures unique to the bird lineage. Some of these – like the possession of a single oviduct – evolved early in bird history, perhaps 130 million years ago or so during the Early Cretaceous. Others – like the toothless, beaked snout, reversed hallux, large sternum and shortened tail – evolved later and were not present in early birds at all. However this set of features was assembled, it proved a winning combination. Birds went on to become the most successful dinosaur group of them all. They are the only dinosaurs to survive the end-Cretaceous mass extinction, and they're represented by over 10,000 living species today.

Birds can be seen as the 'end' products of about 50 million years of gradual size reduction across the course of theropod history. Giant size did evolve on many separate occasions within certain theropod lineages, but the group that led to birds continually decreased in size.

THE VEXING ISSUE OF FEATHER ORIGINS

Feathers have been described as the most complex structures to grow from any animal's skin. Feathers initially grow as tubular buds that form inside pockets in the skin called follicles. As they emerge, they uncurl to form flattened plates formed of a central stiffening rib called the rachis or shaft, and two flexible sheets on either side termed the vanes. Each vane is formed of fine, hair-like structures called barbs. Growing from the sides of the barbs are smaller structures known as barbules, and growing from the sides of the barbules are hook-like structures, the tiny barbicels. The

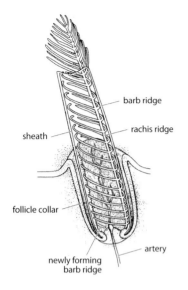

barb ridge

rachis ridge

sheath

follicle collar

artery

newly forming
barb ridge

Feathers are weird and
complicated compared to the
other structures that grow from
skin. A growing feather starts life as
a tubular object encased within a
tough sheath, called the pin. Once
the pin is lost, the feather unfurls.

Numerous small, feathered
maniraptorans are known from
Jurassic and Cretaceous rocks.
Anchiornis and *Xiaotingia*,
shown here, are both crow-sized
animals from the Jurassic of
China. They seem to be early
members of the bird lineage.

barbicels and barbules interlock and help the vanes remain tidy and sheet-like. It should be said that this description applies to a typical feather – many birds have feathers different from those described here.

The oldest complex feathers are preserved on the Late Jurassic Chinese maniraptorans *Anchiornis* and *Xiaotingia*, both of which are regarded by many (though not all) experts as early members of the bird lineage. But, as we've seen, complex feathers are not unique to birds – they were also present in maniraptoran groups only distantly related to birds, like oviraptorosaurs. Feathers are therefore older than birds are, and were inherited by birds from earlier maniraptorans.

How and why feathers originated is one of the greatest mysteries in vertebrate biology. An old idea is that they're modified scales that became frayed and split, the split segments evolving into barbs. But this is inconsistent with the fact that feathers and scales are not made of exactly the same kind of material. Furthermore, the theropod fossil record shows that filaments evolved first, and that feathers evolved from increasingly complex, ever more branched versions of these filaments. So, why did theropods evolve filaments? Perhaps they first functioned as sensory, whisker-like structures, or perhaps they proved advantageous because they helped their owners retain body heat, or were useful in display.

The fact that complex feathers are part of a continuum that also involves filaments poses a problem regarding the words we use for these structures. If the filaments of non-bird theropods really were ancestral to complex feathers, should they be called feathers too? Some experts think so. Others use the term 'proto-feathers' for the filaments instead. Another solution is to restrict the term 'feather' to complex feathers, and to refer to those filament-like feather ancestors simply as filaments, which is what we do here.

What we think happened within the history of coelurosaurian theropods is that their filaments evolved a branching structure, that these

branches then evolved their own tiny hooks and side branches, and that those hooks and branches eventually allowed the development of sheet-like vanes. This sequence is supported by the anatomy of the filaments we see in theropods when we map them onto the dinosaur family tree. It's not quite clear why this increasing complexity evolved. The most 'traditional' idea concerning feather origins is that they evolved within an aerial context – that is, that early birds (or direct ancestors of birds) developed them because they gave them an advantage in leaping and gliding. As we discuss further below, this is not supported by what we know of theropod diversity and biology.

Another possibility is that filaments and feathers became more complicated because this complexity proved advantageous at trapping body heat. Maybe this is part of the story. It fits with the idea that small theropods (including early birds) were endothermic (see Chapter 4), and it receives support from the exceptional insulatory quality that feathers have. Finally, some experts suggest that the evolution of complex feathers was driven by a role in sexual selection, an idea we covered in Chapter 4.

As feathers have roles in protection, locomotion, insulation and sexual display, it shouldn't be surprising that experts have yet to settle on a single answer to the question of why feathers evolved. Maybe this is because there is no one answer – maybe the evolution of feathers was driven by the fact that, with each evolutionary step, they were becoming more useful for all of these functions at the same time.

HOW FLIGHT AROSE

At some point during the Mesozoic Era, probably during the middle part of the Jurassic about 160 million years ago, small, feathered theropods evolved a set of anatomical features that enabled them to make initial forays into the air. Fast forward some tens of millions of years, and we know of birds that were capable of true, flapping flight, and seemingly relied on flight as their main means of getting around and finding food and shelter.

Scientists have argued for decades over how bird flight arose. Even now, with so many fossils to go on, this debate shows little sign of going away. Did bird ancestors take to leaping or launching from among the branches of trees (the 'trees down' scenario), or did they learn to glide, flutter or launch directly from the ground (the 'ground up' scenario)? Or did some kind of combined version of these two things happen? Or was there something else altogether behind those very earliest forays into flight?

This *Sinosauropteryx* specimen, announced in 1996, was the very first non-bird dinosaur to be discovered with feather-like structures on its body. Hair-like filaments are obvious as a dark mane along its neck, back and tail. They're preserved elsewhere on its body too.

The ability to glide has evolved on numerous occasions during the history of life. Gliders like this flying squirrel typically have huge skin flaps growing from the sides of the body and limbs.

There are even gliding frogs. Large webs between their fingers and toes and skin flaps on their bodies help them to parachute away from danger. These sorts of animals are very different from maniraptorans, making it seem unlikely that bird ancestors went through a dedicated gliding stage in their evolution.

One of the most popular ideas for the evolution of flight is that those animals ancestral to birds were gliders that leapt with outstretched arms. Gliders can't get into the air simply by leaping from the ground since gravity and acceleration are both key to the ability to glide – in other words, an animal needs to fall from height for gliding to occur. For as long as gliding has been imagined a part of flight evolution, climbing and even tree-living or cliff-living has been part of the scenario.

The immediate problem with this idea is that it's inconsistent with what we know about the anatomy of early birds and related maniraptorans. All of these animals have hindlimbs and feet suited for walking and running. Like the majority of Mesozoic theropods, they look like animals specialized for terrestrial activity, and there's no definite indication from their anatomy that they were specialized for climbing, perching, or doing anything in trees or on cliffs. We saw previously that small dromaeosaurids like *Microraptor* might have been capable of climbing and gliding, but the shapes of their legs and bodies, and the fact that a *Microraptor* specimen preserves a fish in its belly, indicate that they were also spending time on the ground.

Archaeopteryx lived on arid islands where the plant life was formed of low shrubs. This means that all those classic reconstructions which show it living among tall trees and dense forests may well be wrong, and it seems likely that it, also, was a mostly ground-dwelling animal.

If these animals were runners and walkers, could it be that birds and bird flight originated in a terrestrial setting? The idea that birds started their history as ground-bound animals, and that the earliest birds to fly did so while running on the ground, is popular among some palaeontologists. This is the 'ground up' hypothesis of flight origins.

Some experts have argued that a running, *Archaeopteryx*-like maniraptoran could increase its running speed by flapping its wings during a run, the thrust provided by the flapping enabling the animal to build up enough speed to leave the ground. But this seems unlikely, because an animal that launches into the air from a run slows down as soon as it leaves the ground. It therefore loses whatever advantage it gained from launching in the first place.

Maybe an explanation somewhere between the 'trees down' and 'ground up' ideas is what's needed. None of the early birds or bird-like maniraptorans were specialized climbers, but it looks as if they were able to hop about among branches, or leap up into shrubby vegetation. After all, many living animals less specialized for climbing than Mesozoic

Archaeopteryx seems to have been something of a generalist, able to run on the ground and perhaps climb and jump around among branches. There are no clear indications that it was a dedicated tree-dweller as often shown in artwork. This modern reconstruction shows how extensively feathered *Archaeopteryx* was in life.

Modern birds belonging to several groups – this is a gamebird called a chukar – are able to run up steep surfaces while vigorously flapping their wings. Experts argue over whether this strategy was used by early birds and bird-like maniraptorans.

maniraptorans are able to do likewise. There are foxes and goats that climb trees, for example. Could it be that feathered maniraptorans, already equipped with large feathered surfaces on their limbs and tails and able to leap among the branches of trees and shrubs, took to using their feathers for short glides, pouncing jumps, or flapping excursions? Could this be how flight originated?

Or, could it be that those feathered surfaces simply provided an advantage in getting up into high places? The chicks of some modern bird species, including certain partridges and doves, are capable of running up steep slopes such as hillsides and tree trunks when escaping danger. They scramble with their claws and flap their wings at the same time, enabling speedy escape. This behaviour is known as wing-assisted incline running, or WAIR for short. WAIR is of special interest when it comes to the study of flight origins, since the baby birds that practise it have short wings that are proportioned like those of Mesozoic non-bird maniraptorans.

Perhaps non-bird maniraptorans – lacking the especially large, long wings of birds – were using their feathered forelimbs in the same way. The dinosaurs concerned were small, chicken-sized or crow-sized, and could well have been in danger from larger predators that lacked an ability to run up slopes or ascend trees. If non-bird maniraptorans were capable of WAIR, it's conceivable that it provided enough of an advantage that these animals became better adapted for it over time, evolving larger feathers, longer forelimbs, and more powerful chest and arm muscles. Eventually, these features would have been so well developed that true flight would have been possible. Feathers would also have provided an advantage if these animals needed to jump around between branches, or back down to the ground.

As with all ideas about flight origins, the hypothesis that WAIR was practised by bird ancestors and that it led to the origin of flight has its detractors. Modern birds that practise WAIR have large, well-muscled chest bones, and wings that can be elevated well above the horizontal. It seems that these things were not true of early birds or their close relatives. We've already seen how early birds lacked a large bony sternum, a fact which suggests that they lacked the big chest muscles needed for powerful flapping. For these reasons, some experts on bird flight argue that WAIR was not possible in these animals at all.

With all of these competing ideas on the evolution of flight, it's difficult to work out what might really have happened. The idea that bird flight evolved from specialized gliding looks unlikely, and there are problems too with the idea that vigorous flapping, or a ground-based take-off, might explain how birds first got into the air. Many bird-like maniraptorans and early birds were generalized predators. They were mostly ground-bound but could also have leapt and climbed among the branches of shrubs and trees, and the large feathered surfaces on their limbs might have made them especially good at controlling their position and direction during their leaps. The fact that many non-bird maniraptorans were predatory animals, which seem to have pounced on prey with their feet, may well have enhanced their balancing and fluttering abilities when standing on top of objects.

Was it a combination of leaping onto prey, of hopping and fluttering from branches, and of using their feathered limbs and tails for manoeuvrability that actually explains how birds evolved their ability to fly? It's difficult to say, and it might be that we can never really say for sure.

BIRDS TAKE OFF

Today, around 10,000 bird species live worldwide in almost all of the different habitats found on Earth. Consider the diversity of living birds. There are giant, flightless runners and walkers like ostriches and emus, many different seabirds, and all those birds that wade, swim, dive and forage and feed at the water's edge, like ducks, swans, pelicans, cormorants, grebes, sandpipers and herons. Then there are the predatory hawks, eagles, falcons and owls, the scavenging vultures and condors, the climbing fruit-eaters like parrots, mousebirds and turacos, the myriad small perching birds, like crows, wrens, warblers, finches and sparrows, and so on. We know from the fossil record that the majority of these groups had originated by about 40 million years ago – that is, by the part of the Cenozoic known as the Eocene. But what of bird history before the time when modern birds evolved?

We've known of truly archaic birds since the 1860s when *Archaeopteryx* – the famous toothed, long-tailed 'Urvogel' (a German term meaning 'original bird') – was discovered in the Upper Jurassic Solnhofen Limestone of Bavaria in Germany. *Archaeopteryx* is extremely similar to its close relatives among the non-bird maniraptorans, so much so that

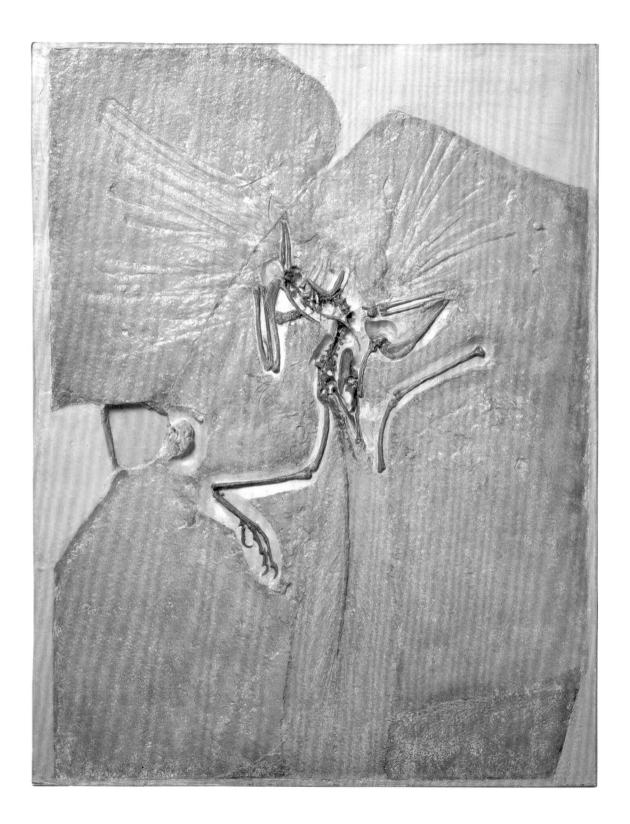

experts have sometimes argued that *Archaeopteryx* is more likely to be a member of one of those other groups than it is a 'true' bird. *Archaeopteryx* is bird-like, but it isn't obviously more bird-like than other small, fully feathered, Jurassic maniraptorans. Indeed, the main reason for its crucial role in our view of bird evolution is that it was discovered so early on in palaeontological history. The point remains, however, that birds had their origins in *Archaeopteryx*-like maniraptorans.

At least eleven *Archaeopteryx* specimens are known. Several are beautifully preserved, near-complete and articulated, meaning that we know a lot about its anatomy. *Archaeopteryx* has a shallow, triangular snout and shallow lower jaw, and the claws on its three fingers are strongly curved with sharp tips. The claw on the second toe of its foot is slightly larger and more strongly curved than the others, with the joint at the base of the toe suggesting that it could be raised upwards above the foot surface – an unusual feature not typical for birds but present in some other maniraptoran groups.

The thing that most people know about *Archaeopteryx* is that several of the specimens are preserved with their feathers (or impressions of them) in place. Long feathers on its arms and hands give it a winged appearance, and paired feathers sprout from either side of its long, bony tail. Short, slim, vaned feathers cover its body and neck, and long feathers emerge from its shins.

Until recently, *Archaeopteryx* was the only fossil bird known that was in possession of a long bony tail. This is no longer the case – several long-tailed fossil birds are known today, most of which are from the Early Cretaceous of China. These are the jeholornithids, a toothed group with robust jawbones and feet which show that they were ground-living, non-perching birds. One jeholornithid specimen has a large number of seeds preserved in its stomach region. Another has a fan-like arrangement of feathers at the tail-tip as well as a second, shorter fan that sticks upwards from the tail's base. A fan at the tail-tip is a typical and expected feature for a maniraptoran, but a second fan certainly is not.

One of the best understood of Cretaceous birds is *Confuciusornis* from the Early Cretaceous of China, a member of a small group called the confuciusornithids (a name that means 'Confucius birds', after the

The specimen of *Archaeopteryx* at the Natural History Museum, London opposite was discovered in 1861 and clearly preserves the impressions of its large wing feathers around the bones of its forelimbs. Long, paired feathers also grow from both sides of the long tail skeleton.

Small, pointed teeth are present in both the upper and lower jaws of *Archaeopteryx*. These teeth are in keeping with the idea that *Archaeopteryx* was a generalist – a small predator able to exploit many different food items, from plant parts to insects, crustaceans and perhaps fish.

famous Chinese philosopher). These are among the oldest birds to possess a shortened tail skeleton, and we think that they evolved from long-tailed, jeholornithid-type ancestors. *Confuciusornis* is known from many hundreds of specimens, most of which died following volcanic eruptions and then became preserved in the mud at the bottom of lakes and ponds. It has especially big claws on its first and third fingers and – in contrast to older birds – its jaws are toothless.

Confuciusornis is close to the base of the bird family tree, as it lacks a set of anatomical features that unite the enantiornithines and ornithurines. It therefore does not belong to the great group that gave rise to modern birds. Yet many of those more advanced birds possessed teeth. This means that *Confuciusornis* must have evolved its toothlessness independently of the toothlessness present in those other groups. Some experts have suggested that these toothless, beaked jaws were suited for a diet of leaves or seeds but stomach contents show that *Confuciusornis* ate fish, at least on occasion.

Confuciusornis is peculiar in several other respects. Despite having a shortened tail and the fused mass of vertebrae at the tail-tip typical of modern birds (termed the pygostyle), it lacks a tail fan. Its tail is made further interesting by the fact that some specimens possess a pair of long, ribbon-like structures. Because these look similar to the tail streamers present in the males of several living bird species, it's always seemed likely that they're a display feature, presumably one that evolved under sexual selection pressure (see Chapter 4). Direct support for this view comes from the discovery of medullary bone (the special bone type associated with egg-laying, discussed earlier) in a specimen that lacks these tail streamers, indicating that it was a female.

Birds similar to *Confuciusornis,* though without its specific peculiarities, gave rise to the two groups that would dominate bird diversity in the Cretaceous. The first of these are the enantiornithines, or 'opposite birds'. The first enantiornithines to be discovered were isolated bones from Argentina, described in 1981 by fossil bird expert Cyril Walker. The anatomy of this bird group is unusual. Some of their bones fit together in ways that seem almost like mirror images of the anatomy of modern birds, and it's this feature which explains the name that Walker gave to the group.

Today, over 100 enantiornithine species have been identified, many of which are represented by articulated skeletons. The first enantiornithines known from well-preserved remains of this sort

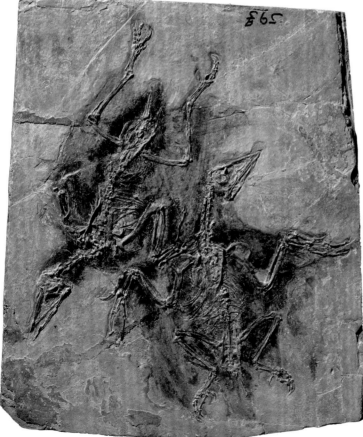

Confuciusornis is a toothless, long-winged, short-tailed Cretaceous bird. Its feet show that it was a capable percher. Debate continues over its flight abilities. Some experts argue that it was restricted to gliding, but this is hard to reconcile with a lifestyle that apparently involved swooping over lakes and catching fish. It is one of the world's best known fossil birds. Hundreds of specimens have been discovered, sometimes found in twos or threes (left). They appear to have been highly social, perhaps living and foraging in flocks.

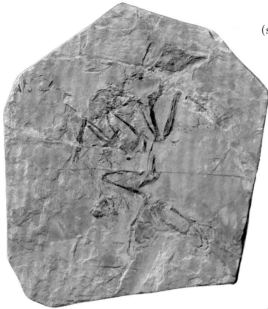

(such as *Iberomesornis* and *Concornis* from Spain, and *Sinornis* from China) were omnivores or predators that foraged in waterside habitats, eating crustaceans, worms and small fish. As more enantiornithine fossils have been discovered, it's become obvious that they underwent an explosion of diversity, evolving sizes and lifestyles paralleling those evolved in ornithurines. There were long-skulled, predatory species, tree-climbing enantiornithines with unusual feet built for bark-clinging, and long-jawed small-toothed species that probably ate aquatic prey. Most were similar in size to sparrows or starlings, but the largest had wingspans in excess of 1 m (3¼ ft).

Finally, we come to the ornithurines, the group that includes modern birds and a number of toothed and toothless groups from the Cretaceous. Among these are the vaguely gull-like *Ichthyornis* from the Late Cretaceous of the USA and a group of flightless diving birds called the hesperornithiforms.

Many Cretaceous enantiornithines – this example is from China – are similar in size to modern finches and sparrows. Their tiny, delicate skeletons could only ever be preserved in places where fine-grained muds allow such small animals to be quickly entombed.

Birds have evolved flightlessness on a huge number of occasions. *Hesperornis* is a large, toothed, flightless Cretaceous seabird. Its wings were tiny stumps that must have been almost invisible in the live animal. Large lobes grew from its toes and were used to provide thrust during swimming.

Early hesperornithiforms were small and might have been capable of flight but later ones were highly modified for a diving, marine lifestyle. Their wings were reduced to stumps (the hand and lower arm bones were absent), they possessed enormous, powerful legs and feet attached to a long, narrow pelvis, and they had long, slender, toothed jaws. These advanced hesperornithiforms were also enormous – as much as 2 m (6½ ft) long. These big hesperornithiforms – the best known is *Hesperornis* from the Late Cretaceous of the USA, Canada and Russia – were so specialized for swimming that they almost certainly had a restricted range of movement when on land.

THE RISE OF MODERN BIRDS

Ornithurines like *Ichthyornis* and the hesperornithiforms must have been close relatives of those species that gave rise to modern birds. We know of several small birds from the Cretaceous (including swimmers, shorebird-type birds and land-living, ground-dwelling birds) close to the ancestry of modern birds, the one dinosaur group that made it through the extinction event at the end of the Cretaceous. Several features make modern birds unusual compared to other bird groups. They're toothless, their skulls have more complicated flexible (kinetic) zones, and the two halves of their lower jaw are firmly fused together in the chin region (the joint between the jaws remains flexible in most other dinosaurs). Data from bone microstructure also shows that modern birds grow faster, and mature faster, than did members of the other bird groups.

Exactly when modern birds evolved is controversial. Genetic studies have led some experts to argue that modern birds evolved way back in the early part of the Cretaceous, about 130 million years ago. At the other extreme, some experts argue that modern birds didn't arise until after the end-Cretaceous extinction, in which case the whole group is 'only' 66 or so million years old. The fossil record seems to contradict that latter idea. Fossils identified as early ducks, gamebirds and divers or loons have been identified in Upper Cretaceous rocks, and there are even Cretaceous fossils that have been suggested to be early parrots or relatives of cormorants or pelicans. Even if these fossils have been misidentified, the many fossil birds we know from the following Paleocene show that modern birds had most likely started to diversify before the Cretaceous was over.

6

THE GREAT EXTINCTION AND BEYOND

DINOSAURS WERE THE DOMINANT group of land-living animals for approximately 160 million years, and giant species were by far the biggest, most important animals in habitats and ecosystems worldwide throughout the whole of the later Mesozoic. But this changed 66 million years ago when a major extinction event occurred. This event killed off all non-bird dinosaurs and also resulted in the disappearance of pterosaurs, most marine reptile groups, several bird, lizard and mammal groups, and numerous groups of plankton and sea-going invertebrates. The event brought a close to the Cretaceous, and indeed to the entire Mesozoic. A new age, the Cenozoic, was to begin, the first geological sub-division of which is called the Paleogene. We term this extinction event the 'K–Pg event': 'K' stands for Cretaceous ('C' can't be used as it's already the official symbol for the Cambrian age of 541–485 million years ago) and 'Pg' stands for Paleogene. What happened, and why were dinosaurs affected so severely?

Extinction is as much a part of the history of life as is evolution. Species evolve, but they also go extinct, and the geological record shows us that whole groups of hundreds and even thousands of species have disappeared entirely from existence over time. The geological record shows that several major extinction events have occurred during the history of life, some of greater magnitude than others. Some are also more

mysterious than others – for some of these events, little data exists and experts are still trying to establish which climatic or ecological events can be linked to the extinctions themselves. A mass extinction at the end of the Devonian, about 360 million years ago, remains a significant mystery, its main cause perhaps being a combination of climate change, sea-level fluctuation and atmospheric change. And an even greater mass extinction event – the one that ended the Permian, about 252 million years ago – has also eluded simple explanation.

For all their significance, the end-Devonian and end-Permian extinctions are not well known outside the palaeontological research community. Contrast this with the K–Pg event. Nearly everybody has heard of this, and is aware of the fact that it's an area of uncertainty and debate among scientists.

In a way, the familiarity of the K–Pg event is a bad thing – the idea has long been out there that it's such a mystery that virtually any possible cause might be worth suggesting. A result of this attitude is that over 60 explanations have been put forward for the K–Pg event. The extinction has been blamed on disease, on sex changes brought about by changing temperatures, on evil fungi, on a spread of parasites or sexual diseases, on ravenous caterpillars, on the spread of new poisonous plant species, on a tendency of dinosaurs to evolve into poorly adapted species doomed to

Long before the K-Pg event of 66 million years ago, an even larger extinction event occurred about 252 million years ago. Whole groups of animal species – among them the many synapsids shown in this reconstruction – were killed off entirely.

extinction, on the climate becoming too cold, or too hot, or too dry, or too wet, and so on.

Virtually all of these suggestions fail as explanations for the evidence we have on the K–Pg event, and many are simply throwaway ideas that lack support. It wasn't until the 1980s that our understanding of the K–Pg event changed from an area of speculation to one where geological evidence gave us precise clues on what had happened.

AN EXTRATERRESTRIAL IMPACT

Of the many ideas proposed over the years to explain the K–Pg extinction event, one of the most plausible has always been that an object from outer space – a comet or asteroid – collided with the planet and caused global devastation. After all, we've long known that impact events of this sort have happened throughout history. The moon is covered in prehistoric craters, the biggest of which are more than 50 km (30 miles) wide, and several craters are obvious on the surface of the Earth, including, in North America, Meteor Crater in Arizona and Manicouagan Crater in Québec. This hypothesis of an end-Cretaceous impact event remained nothing more than an interesting speculation until the 1980s.

In 1980, the physicist Luis Alvarez and his colleagues announced their discovery of the metal iridium in end-Cretaceous rock layers in Italy and Denmark. Iridium is rare on Earth, but one way it arrives here is via the impact of rocks from space. Research showed how the iridium present in those end-Cretaceous rock layers has a chemical signature typical of rocky extraterrestrial objects, not of sediments on Earth. Based on this data, Alvarez and his team proposed that a giant object from space had slammed into the Earth at the close of the Cretaceous, and that this event was responsible for the extinction. They described how the impact would have thrown a huge quantity of rock dust into the atmosphere, and that this would have darkened the sky for years and prevented plants from growing. The death of plants would lead to the shutting down of most ecosystems, and eventually to extinctions across whole groups of living things. This idea immediately caught the attention of other scientists as well as the public. It became known as the Alvarez Hypothesis.

Many independent lines of evidence demonstrate that an asteroid impact occurred 66 million years ago. Fragments of quartz marked with numerous fracture marks are preserved in numerous rocks dating to the end of the Cretaceous. They must have been blasted far and wide by the power of the impact.

200

Several other pieces of geological evidence were soon discovered which provided additional support for the impact hypothesis. Cooled blobs of molten glass that had been blasted far away from the impact site – termed tektites – were discovered in end-Cretaceous sediments, and fragments of the mineral quartz possessing microscopic fracture marks, characteristic of massive explosions or impacts, were reported too.

Finally, the most compelling piece of evidence of all – a gigantic crater, preserved in rock layers of exactly the right age – was discovered in the sediments of the Yucatán Peninsula in Mexico. This feature, termed the Chicxulub Crater, had been discovered in 1978 by oil geologists looking for promising new sites, but not until 1990 was it properly linked with the impact data collected by Alvarez and his team. The Chicxulub Crater is the right age to be linked to the impact of the time, and the right size, being more than 180 km (110 miles) wide and suggestive of an initial object about 10 km (more than 6 miles) wide. It's also in the right place, since those geological pieces of evidence that seem linked to an impact (the tektites, shocked quartz and so on) mostly come from the Caribbean region and the adjacent parts of the North American continent.

At the end of the Cretaceous, the Yucatán Peninsula was covered by sea. The Chicxulub impact would therefore have been a 'splashdown', not an impact on dry land. Huge tidal waves, 100 to 300 m (about 325 to nearly 1,000 ft) high, would have washed across the nearby coasts of North and South America. Geological evidence for these events comes from jumbled and ripped up rock layers present in the Caribbean and Texas. Evidence that massive earthquakes were triggered by the impact comes from slumped rock layers in Mexico.

The impact debris blasted across nearby landmasses might have been hot enough to start forest fires, and some experts suggest that ancient charcoal is evidence for raging fires that spread across parts of the world. It's also been suggested that the heat pulse created by the impact would have been hot enough to literally cook animals to death. Both of these ideas – that of devastating wildfires and a 'global heat pulse' – are controversial and neither are well supported by geological evidence or by computer models of the effects of an impact. Charcoal is present in end-Cretaceous sediments (it preserves evidence of ancient forest fires caused by lightning strikes), but it's also present throughout the whole of

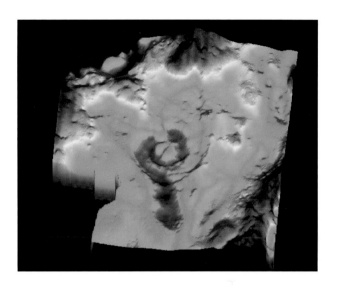

This computer-generated image depicts the shape of the seafloor around the Yucatán Peninsula in Mexico. A great rounded depression in the middle marks the impact site of the giant asteroid that struck the region 66 million years ago.

the Mesozoic rock record and is actually less abundant in end-Cretaceous sediments than in older ones.

Some scientists have suggested that other collisions elsewhere occurred at the same time. A structure in the North Sea called the Silverpit Crater and another from Ukraine called the Boltysh Crater might have been formed by the impact of much smaller objects. A larger feature in India, called the Shiva Crater, has also been identified as an end-Cretaceous impact site. The geological evidence used to support the identification of these structures as impact craters is not as convincing as that for Chicxulub. The idea that several collisions might have occurred at about the same time is not unreasonable though. In 1994, the comet Shoemaker-Levy 9 broke up into over 20 separate chunks before colliding with Jupiter.

Regardless of the controversies about wildfires, heat pulses and multiple impacts, evidence for an impact in Mexico is compelling. Doubts over the precise age of the Chicxulub Crater also mean that the sediments in the region have been checked and checked again using several different methods. So far as we can tell, the impact really did occur at the same time as the K–Pg extinction.

BAD TIMES FOR DINOSAURS

The idea that a catastrophic extraterrestrial collision event occurred at the end of the Cretaceous is not in serious doubt, and the idea that this event had a serious impact on life of the time is supported by good data. But there are also good reasons for thinking that this was not the sole factor contributing to the K–Pg event and that other, more long-term events also contributed to the extinction of non-bird dinosaurs.

It has long seemed that the dinosaur assemblages of the very latest part of the Cretaceous were unusual relative to those of earlier times. Approximately 76 million years ago, during what's known as the Campanian age of the Late Cretaceous, dinosaurs of several groups were thriving at high diversity. Western North America – one of the regions with the best fossil dinosaur assemblage of the time – was home to five ankylosaur species, as many as ten different ceratopsians, seven or more different hadrosaurs, and three or more tyrannosaurids.

There's no indication that this assemblage of dinosaur species was in decline or in trouble. If we now compare this Campanian assemblage with that present in the same region during the latest part of the Cretaceous – an age known as the late Maastrichtian, around 68 million years ago – we see a very different picture. Large ceratopsians were now represented by

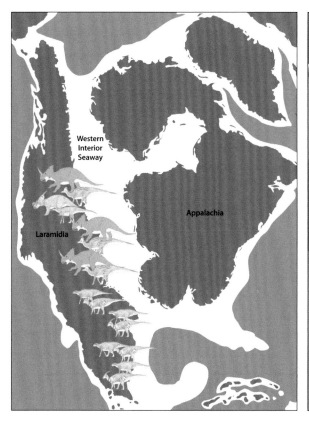

Triceratops and *Torosaurus* alone. The only late Maastrichtian duckbill was *Edmontosaurus*: all those elaborate species with bony head crests were long gone, and so were the several hook-nosed and solid-crested lineages that had lived alongside edmontosaur-type duckbills during the Campanian. And, among the big predators, just a single species – the infamous *Tyrannosaurus rex* – represented what had previously been an entire set of similar animals.

Whatever was happening at the very end of the Cretaceous, ceratopsians, hadrosaurs, tyrannosaurids and other groups were all existing at a level of diversity far lower than that present just a few million years beforehand.

One reason for this decline might be habitat change, and habitat loss. The final part of the Maastrichtian age saw sea levels decline as the seas retreated from the edges of the continents. Such events are called marine regressions, and the Maastrichtian marine regression resulted in the exposure of something like 29 million square kilometres (11 million square miles) of land worldwide. It might seem that the appearance of huge new tracts of dry land would be a good thing for land-living animals

During Campanian times, about 76 million years ago, western North America was home to a diverse assemblage of dinosaur species, including numerous elaborately crested hadrosaurs and ceratopsians (above left). By the end of Maastrichtian times, about 68 million years ago, dinosaur diversity had declined substantially and only a few rather plain species occurred across the same region (above right).

like dinosaurs. Actually, the changes made to coastal environments by this regression are of the sort predicted to cause decline in the diversity of large animals. They would have meant the loss of fertile coastal habitats, the creation of new landbridges, and a cooling of global temperatures.

It stands to reason that animal groups are more vulnerable to extinction when they exist at low diversity – a group reduced to just a single species is more at risk of dying out than one where several species are alive at the same time. The set of dinosaur species present during the late Maastrichtian in western North America therefore looks like an 'extinction-prone' community.

But are we sure that this situation was true across the dinosaur communities of the time? And what about the other animal groups that became extinct at the K–Pg event? Actually, the picture is somewhat complicated. Dinosaur assemblages in Europe and Asia seem to have been healthy, with there being no clear indication of decline in diversity in the run-up to the extinction event. Some marine reptile groups, like the long-necked plesiosaurs, also seem to have been healthy and not in decline. But several groups of fossil organisms – including the sea-going mosasaurs and certain important plankton and mollusc groups – do seem to have been in gradual decline across the same timeframe.

THE IMPACT OF VOLCANISM

Animal communities in at least some parts of the world were changing during late Maastrichtian times, quite probably because sea-level changes were changing the way habitats and ecosystems were distributed. But another factor might have been having an impact on animal and plant communities, too.

The Maastrichtian was a highly volcanic time. Active volcanoes were present around the fringes of the Pacific, around Greenland, and on islands in the South Atlantic. This sustained volcanic activity caused global carbon dioxide (CO_2) levels to rise and the amount of microscopic dust in the atmosphere to increase as well – two processes known to contribute to climate change. All of these volcanic events were significantly out-classed by an enormous, long-term phase of activity that occurred in central India. Over a timespan of several hundred thousand years, an enormous out-pouring of liquid rock resulted in the creation of a feature known as the Deccan Traps. This formed as 2 million cubic kilometres or so (about 0.5 million cubic miles) of lava spewed from volcanic fissures and vents, eventually covering an area greater than that of France, Germany and Spain combined, or similar in size to Mexico. Some of the lava flows that

formed the Deccan Traps were 50 m (about 165 ft) thick, and some were an unbelievable 150 m (nearly 500 ft) thick.

The Deccan Traps don't represent a sudden single event, a real contrast to the instantaneous effects of the Chicxulub impact. This continuous volcanic activity must have resulted in the release of vast quantities of CO_2 and sulphur dioxide (SO_2) gas. It's likely that these gases contributed to the phases of global warming that happened during the Late Cretaceous. Both trap heat in the atmosphere, and both contribute to global warming today. These gases might also have contributed to the production of acid rain. Acid rain is damaging to ecosystems both on land and at sea. It causes plants to die and it kills marine animals by

Parts of Late Cretaceous India were dominated by an amazing amount of volcanic activity. Great fissures, kilometres long, would have been alive with eruptions of magma and the venting of hot gases.

Atmospheric pollution caused by Late Cretaceous volcanic activity seems to have caused climate change, and also damaging acidic rain. Modern acid rain can kill entire forests.

changing the chemistry of the water and weakening or dissolving their skeletons.

Volcanic events also cause global cooling as suspended dust particles reflect sunlight and result in a cooler atmosphere. The fact that major volcanic events can cause both warming and cooling may explain why the global temperatures of the late Maastrichian fluctuated so much – gradual cooling, rapid warming and rapid cooling all happened in the last 1.5 million years of the Cretaceous. These sorts of changes would have thrown ecosystems into chaos by disrupting the breeding and migration cycles of animals, and by making plant growth unpredictable and unreliable in some regions.

What seems likely is that the volcanic events of the Maastrichtian – the creation of the Deccan Traps in particular – caused global climate change, resulted in acid rain, and contributed overall to environmental deterioration across parts of the world. Living things in many environments would therefore have been stressed, and forced into decline. Direct evidence for this view comes from the fossil plankton discovered in Maastrichtian sediments of the Indian Ocean. We see Maastrichtian plankton as a whole decreasing massively in diversity, species suited for low-oxygen conditions becoming more abundant, and, eventually, those species uniquely able to thrive in nutrient-poor water and stressed communities becoming incredibly abundant. Incidentally, while most of the focus on the K–Pg event has centred on dinosaurs, it's probably true to say that tiny, super-abundant fossils like plankton provide far more information on the trends and changes of the time.

THE 'INTEGRATED SCENARIO'

During the 1980s and 1990s, the idea of volcanic activity as the cause of the K–Pg event was seen as a direct competitor to the Alvarez Hypothesis of extraterrestrial impact. At the time, scientists interested in the K–Pg event argued that one or the other of these events had caused the extinction, and some researchers who favoured the volcanism hypothesis even denied that an impact occurred at all. Today, it's widely accepted that the Chicxulub impact occurred and that major volcanic events were happening at the same time. Could it be that these events combined caused the extinction event?

The event at Chicxulub would have killed huge numbers of animals instantly, it would have had an enormous immediate effect on the habitats within those hundreds of kilometres closest to the impact, and it would have had a long-term influence on habitats and animal communities over

The sediments of latest Cretaceous times show how plankton groups underwent major changes in abundance and diversity. This selection of Maastrichtian plankton shows some of the species typical of the time.

the next few centuries or more. Palaeontologists have never doubted the idea that an impact of this sort would have been a bad thing for the animals alive at the time. The problem is the evidence showing that certain dinosaur and other animal groups were declining before the impact happened. What has often been thought likely, then, is that the impact event was 'the last straw', the one terrible event that wreaked havoc for living things already stressed and in decline.

Even before we add in the significance of an extraterrestrial impact, we have to imagine a world where dinosaur diversity was dangerously low in some parts of the world, and where sustained volcanic activity, and long-term environmental change, was having an impact on climate and the health of ecosystems. Many of those dinosaurs far away from the volcanic events of southern Asia would have survived and gone on to give rise to new species, and maybe those far from the Chicxulub impact would, likewise, have pulled through these difficult times. But that's not what happened. Conditions deteriorated worldwide, enough to spell the end for most dinosaur species and for numerous other groups of living things.

This might be termed the 'integrated scenario'. It combines our understanding of the catastrophic extraterrestrial and volcanic events that occurred at the end of the Cretaceous with a more long-term picture of declining dinosaur diversity.

DINOSAURS SURVIVED

The extinction event at the end of the Cretaceous is, quite understandably, always described as a catastrophically bad event for dinosaurs. For the dinosaur lineages that ended at this time, it clearly was. But, as we've seen throughout this book, dinosaurs didn't become extinct. Birds of several lineages survived, meaning that dinosaurs as a whole did not become extinct. And the birds that survived didn't belong to a single lineage – species belonging to four or more groups all made it through. Early members of the palaeognath lineage survived (the group that includes ostriches and emus), as did members of the wildfowl and gamebird lineage, as did members of the lineage that led to seabirds, hawks, perching birds, and so on.

Why these bird groups survived when other dinosaur groups didn't is a good question, and one that hasn't been answered satisfactorily. Several suggestions have been made. Birds are mostly small and highly mobile, so it seems likely that they could have taken shelter more easily than their giant, ground-bound relatives. They could also have flown to new

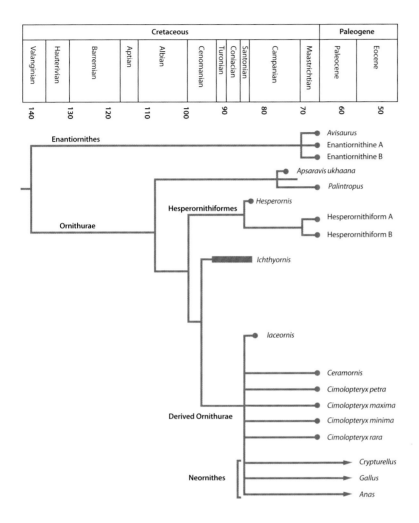

Of all the dinosaur groups present at the very end of the Cretaceous, birds alone survived. However, birds hardly sailed through the extinction event. As this diagram shows, many bird lineages became extinct and only those belonging to the group Neornithes survived.

areas when it became hard to survive in a given region. As small animals, birds would also have the advantage of lower dietary demands than their larger cousins. It's also been argued that many of the bird groups that survived mostly inhabited the southern hemisphere, where the effects of the extinction might have been less severe.

The issue of bird survival is made more complicated by the fact that other bird groups alive during the Late Cretaceous didn't survive. Enantiornithines didn't, nor did any of those toothed seabirds. It seems that these groups didn't survive right up to the boundary and die during the mass extinction event. Instead, they apparently petered out beforehand, and so they might have been victims of gradual environmental change.

It also has to be remembered that extinct bird groups like enantiornithines were not exactly the same as modern birds in biology or behaviour. Bone microstructure shows that modern birds grow faster and mature earlier than groups like enantiornithines. Modern birds also have anatomical features – most notably the adaptable, toothless beak – that could have made them more able to switch quickly from one food type to another. The adaptability of the modern bird beak is no trivial matter. Some birds, like oystercatchers, are able to change the shape of their bills in a matter of weeks. Even in groups where super-rapid changes like this are not possible, it often only takes two or three generations for members of a species to evolve a new beak shape. This adaptability was probably not present in other bird groups, most of which still had teeth and lacked the extensive horny beak covering characteristic of modern birds.

DINOSAURS BEYOND THE CRETACEOUS

In a world where large non-bird dinosaurs were absent, the animal groups that had survived the K–Pg event quickly began to evolve larger body size. Ecological niches previously occupied by hadrosaurs, ceratopsians and other groups were now there for the taking and several bird lineages evolved to take advantage. Palaeognaths evolved large species weighing a

One of the first birds to evolve into a giant was *Gastornis*, a flightless bird known from Europe, Asia and North America. *Gastornis* was conventionally imagined as a predator, but was more likely an omnivore or herbivore. *Gastornis* is also often referred to as *Diatryma*.

few hundred kilograms by the Eocene (about 55 million years ago) and an entirely extinct group called the gastornithids had also evolved similar giant size by the same time. Members of this flightless group inhabited North America, Europe and Asia. Their deep, massively robust skulls and jaws have been regarded by some experts as proof of a predatory, bone-cracking lifestyle, and by others as evidence for a lifestyle that involved cracking nuts, and snipping twigs and branches.

These animals were all large compared to the majority of other birds, and indeed to many of the mammals and other animals of the time. Even so, they didn't approach the size of the large non-bird dinosaurs of the Jurassic and Cretaceous, among which even mid-sized species were more than 5 m (16½ ft) long and several hundred kilograms in weight. Why have birds not populated the 'giant' niche occupied so successfully by other dinosaur groups? It may be that the bird body plan is just too specialized for a lifestyle dedicated to flight to ever become gigantic and heavy-bodied – all birds are two-legged, with forelimbs specialized for use in flight, and cannot easily give rise to body shapes suited for gigantic size. Another reason may be that birds might not ever have been under the same evolutionary pressures as other dinosaur groups to evolve giant size.

Big-bodied flightless birds have been a constant part of bird diversity ever since those giant species evolved during the Eocene, and even today giant flightless birds inhabit South America (rheas), Africa (ostriches) and Australasia (emus and cassowaries). Giant flightless palaeognaths also evolved on Madagascar (elephant birds) and New Zealand (moas) where, devoid of predators, they evolved lifestyles where slow growth and a low rate of reproduction became normal. Unfortunately, these attributes made them vulnerable to the activities of newly arriving predators like humans. Elephant birds and moas were hunted to extinction within the last few hundred years.

Palaeognaths are vastly outnumbered by the members of the second group of modern birds, the neognaths. The thousands of species that belong here are usually classified into about 30 distinct groups, and ornithologists have spent decades trying to understand and unravel the complex history of their evolution. Thanks to major efforts to collect and analyse DNA samples from hundreds of bird species, experts have recently been able to piece together a new evolutionary tree for neognaths.

Several of the relationships supported by these studies are remarkably odd compared to what was previously

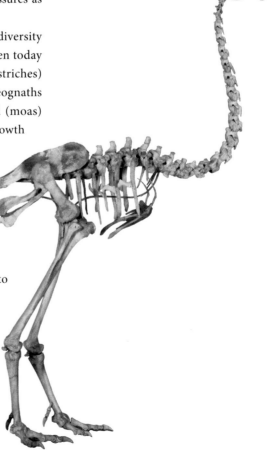

Moas were herbivorous flightless birds unique to New Zealand, so specialized for flightlessness that their skeletons lack all trace of a wing. This is the largest of them, *Dinornis*. Moas were hunted to extinction by humans within the last 1,000 years.

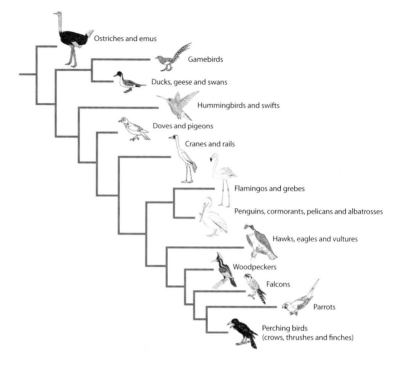

An enormous amount of work on anatomy and behaviour but especially genetics has allowed ornithologists to piece together the neornithine family tree. Many traditional ideas about how birds might be related to one another have proved incorrect.

Some time around 60 million years ago, a group of swimming seabirds related to albatrosses lost the power of flight and became better able to dive deep and forage and breed in cold, polar environments. They are the penguins, and they persist today as about 18 species.

predicted on the basis of anatomical and behavioural data. Long-legged, filter-feeding flamingos and foot-propelled, diving grebes, for example, appear to be each other's closest relatives. Parrots, falcons and songbirds also seem to be close relatives, meaning that falcons are not close kin of hawks, eagles and vultures as had long been thought. These discoveries are wonderful revelations, but they're somewhat worrying to those who reconstruct the evolutionary affinities of animals based on anatomy alone – they indicate that various apparently strong, reasonable hypotheses might be completely wrong.

Despite this, it would be misleading to be completely pessimistic, since many other relationships supported by these DNA-based studies were previously predicted on the basis of other lines of evidence. Wildfowl and gamebirds belong together in one major branch of the neognath tree, another branch contains the majority of seabirds and waterbirds, and another branch includes eagles, hawks, vultures and condors, woodpeckers and kin, and the parrot, falcon and songbird group. Many of these bird groups are adapted for lifestyles that were never exploited by the non-bird dinosaurs of the Mesozoic.

As we saw earlier in this book, some non-bird dinosaurs might have been swimmers, waders or fish-catchers, but none evolved into animals as specialized for waterside life as gannets, penguins, petrels or albatrosses. Densely insulated, feathery bodies, small size and a flight ability has allowed birds to evolve species that cross vast tracts of oceans in search of fish and squid, to become divers, plungers and underwater fliers that can pursue prey beneath the ocean surface, and to hunt and breed in freezing polar conditions that did not exist during the Mesozoic. You can imagine the many birds that are part of this story as an entire new chapter in the dinosaur story, as an amazingly successful branch of the theropod family tree that couldn't possibly have been predicted based on those ground-running, small, feathery maniraptorans of the Jurassic and Cretaceous.

Small size and an ability to fly also means that birds have been able to take on lifestyles that involve grabbing flying insects, or visiting plant parts that hang from well above the ground and can only be exploited by small animals. Among the most specialized and unusual of birds are the swifts – dedicated sky-hunting insectivores with wide mouths, scythe-shaped wings and tiny legs and feet – and the nectar-sipping, long-tongued hummingbirds. Anatomy, genetics and fossils show that both groups are close relatives, and part of a larger group that includes the mostly nocturnal, highly secretive nightjars, potoos, oilbirds and owlet-nightjars. This whole group, the Strisores, has to be regarded as one of the weirdest dinosaur groups of all.

Then there are the birds that use flight, excellent eyesight and hearing and powerful, grasping feet to capture other animals. The biggest eagles are capable of killing prey as large as deer; owls are consummate, often nocturnal predators of all manner of other creatures; and hawks, hawk-eagles, kites and harriers prey on everything from insects and snails to

Albatrosses (above left) are oceanic soaring specialists with elongate, narrow wings that allow them to take advantage of thermals, updrafts and gusts over the waves. Albatrosses are tubenosed seabirds – part of the same group as petrels, storm petrels and diving petrels.

Other seabirds exploit fish and other marine prey by diving at speed into the water. Gannets and boobies (above right) are consummate experts at this and are specialised plunge-divers. Gannets like this northern gannet hit the water at 24 m/s (86 km/h or 53 mph).

Several bird groups include specialized aerial insectivores. Among the most modified are the swifts (above). Swifts have a rich fossil record and species alive 40 million years ago were essentially similar to modern ones.

Hummingbirds are close relatives of swifts and are among the most specialized of all birds. Modern hummingbirds (above right) are exclusively American but fossils show that they originated in Europe more than 40 million years ago. This is a Rufous crested coquette.

lizards, mammals and other birds. In some respects, modern predatory birds carry on a way of life initiated 200 million years earlier, deep in the Mesozoic. Certainly those that hunt on the ground – the African secretary bird is one of the best examples – somewhat resemble non-bird theropods in behaviour and general appearance. But the ability to fly – to cross enormous distances with relative ease, to nest and hunt in treetops, and among mountains and cliffs – has again allowed these birds to take advantage of habitats and prey not available to their Mesozoic ancestors. Yes, they are predatory theropods, but they are theropods of a wholly new sort, performing feats and pursuing lifestyles impossible for their forebears.

Finally, we come to the great branch of the neognath family tree that includes woodpeckers and kin, parrots, falcons, and the passerines, or perching birds. Included among this assemblage are hundreds of species that climb on tree trunks, forage at the slender tips of branches, exploit fruits, nuts and seeds, and hunt invertebrate prey in leaf litter, beneath bark, in the soil, and even in streams. One of the most remarkable things about birds from this part of the family tree is how big and complicated their brains are. Crows are members of the passerine group, and both they and parrots have brains that (compared to the overall size of the animal) are similar in size to those of primates. These are 'smart dinosaurs', equipped with excellent memories, able to learn and master complex tasks, with an innate ability (in some species) to build and use tools, and with complex social lives on par with those of monkeys and apes. Some studies indicate that certain parrot species, most notably the African grey parrot, are as intelligent as four-year-old human children.

One surprise from DNA-based work on bird evolution is that a group of long-legged, predatory, mostly South American birds belong to this

section of the family tree too. The only living members of this group are the seriemas, but extinct members include the phorusrhacids, a group of hook-billed, flightless predators that hunted in grasslands and forests between about 50 and 2 million years ago. The biggest phorusrhacids, like *Kelenken* from the 15-million-year-old rocks of Argentina, were over 2 m (6½ ft) tall and had heads over 70 cm (27½ in) long. These are among the most spectacular birds to have ever evolved and, had they survived to the present, we would be living in a world where some of the most powerful, spectacular and dangerous predators were still theropod dinosaurs.

Today, the niche once occupied by ground-dwelling maniraptoran predators like *Velociraptor* is mostly taken by mammals. But maniraptorans do dominate the skies. Large eagles (above left) use massively powerful feet and huge curved talons to grab and kill prey including mammals, other birds and fish.

Curved foot claws, dextrous feet and roughened, spiky foot skin are used by ospreys (above) to grab fish from the water's surface. Several other predatory birds, including certain owls and eagles, have also become specialized fish-grabbers.

Parrots share an ancestor with falcons – a discovery which shows that falcons are not especially close relatives of hawks and eagles. The majority of the world's more than 370 parrot species are forest-dwelling birds that break open fruits and seeds with their powerful, curved bills.

These South American seriemas belong to a group of terrestrial birds that were once far more widespread and diverse. Most were predatory but the earliest species may have been omnivorous or even herbivorous.

Among the most spectacular of fossil birds are the phorusrhacids. The enormous hooked bills, giant size and long, powerful legs of these birds show that they were predators of large mammals and other prey. This replica skull (below right) belongs to *Phoruschacos*, an Argentinean phorusrhacid that lived about 15 million years ago. *Kelenken* (below) had a longer, shallower skull. It was over 2 m (6½ ft) tall.

In real contrast to phorusrhacids, the vast majority of birds belonging to this particular branch of the family tree are tiny – less than 20 cm (8 in) long and weighing just a few tens of grammes. The majority of birds are of this sort – about 60% of all living species are members of the mostly small-bodied passerine group alone. Small size, an ability to fly, and a physiology and anatomy that allows them to live in environments from the tropics to the polar regions have combined to make passerines the most successful bird group, and hence most successful dinosaur group, of them all. Ovenbirds, lyrebirds, bowerbirds, birds-of-paradise, orioles, shrikes, crows, tits, waxwings, wrens, swallows, dippers, thrushes, chats, warblers, flycatchers, grackles, starlings, larks, pipits, wagtails, sparrows, weavers, cardinals, finches and others all belong to the passerine group.

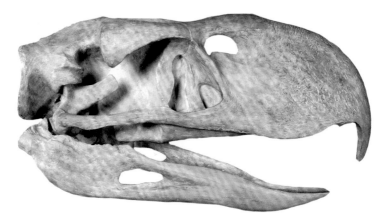

There are currently over 20 billion domestic chickens in the world. Chickens have become a crucial component of human economy and diet. All descend from the forest-dwelling junglefowl of tropical Asia.

We've seen throughout this book that dinosaurs had a rich, varied and complex past. We've also seen that our knowledge of that past improves constantly as new fossils are found, as we learn or discover new scientific techniques, and as technological advances allow us to better study or understand those fossils. But today we know that dinosaurs are also animals of the present, and one of the key revelations of dinosaur research over the past few decades is that dinosaurs did not die out 66 million years ago. They live alongside us, they are important in the environments that surround us, and some species – those we keep as pets or eat – are an important part of our daily lives.

Dinosaurs today – birds – are so abundant, so widely distributed, and so rich in terms of diversity that it seems inevitable that species belonging to many groups will persist into the future, and that dinosaurs will continue to be an important group of animals for many millions of years yet to come. We also know that climate change, the destruction of wild places, and human hunting, greed and ineptitude will force hundreds of species into extinction. Consequently, many bird groups – some of which consist of small numbers of species that preserve unusual combinations of anatomical and genetic features – will disappear altogether in the coming decades. Dinosaurs have a future, but it is a great irony that part of this future is very much in our hands.

GLOSSARY

Anatomy Anything pertaining to the way animals and plants are put together and how their parts and structures function. The term anatomy can refer both to the structure and function of these parts, and to the science of studying them.

Appalachia An irregularly shaped continent that existed between the Cretaceous and the Paleogene, and which corresponds to the eastern part of the USA and Canada.

Archosaurs The major group of diapsid reptiles that includes crocodylians and all of their relatives, and birds and all of their relatives (including non-bird dinosaurs).

Cenozoic The great section of time – the so-called 'Age of Mammals' or 'age of new life' – that began 66 million years ago and continues today. Birds have outnumbered mammals throughout the Cenozoic, so it might be better named the 'Age of Birds'.

Clade A group of organisms where all the included species descend from the same common ancestor.

Cretaceous The section of the Mesozoic Era that lasted between 145 and 66 million years ago. Laurasia and Gondwana began to break apart to form the modern continents during the Cretaceous. Many environments would have looked somewhat modern, but temperatures were higher than they are today.

Crocodylians The archosaur group that includes living crocodiles, alligators and gharials and their fossil relatives. Crocodylians are the only living representatives of the crocodile-line archosaur clade.

CT-scanning Properly called computed tomography, CT-scanning uses x-rays from many different angles to examine the interior of an object and then uses this information to build a digital model as a computer file. The technique has proved hugely important in helping palaeontologists understand the internal anatomy of fossils.

Diapsids The major group of reptiles that includes lizards and snakes and all of their relatives as well as archosaurs and all of their relatives. Diapsid means 'two openings' and refers to the two skull openings present behind the eye socket in these animals.

Dinosauromorphs The archosaur group that contains dinosaurs and several closely related, dinosaur-like groups. Together with pterosaurs, dinosauromorphs form an archosaur group termed Ornithodira.

Evolution The process in which organisms change across the generations, the changes being heritable and passed from parent to offspring, and with the persistence of the changes varying according to the process of natural selection.

FEA (or finite element analysis) A technique, invented for use in engineering, in which mathematical principles are used to work out how structures perform when subjected to stress, vibration or movement.

Fenestra In anatomy, a large opening in the skeleton, surrounded by bone. The plural term is fenestrae.

Gondwana The great southern supercontinent that existed during the Jurassic and Cretaceous. During the Cretaceous, Gondwana split into Antarctica, Australasia, Africa, India, Madagascar and South America. The alternative name Gondwanaland is sometimes used.

Hypothesis An idea put forward as an explanation for an observation with some information being available that might allow other people to test the success of the explanation.

Juvenile An individual that has not reached the full adult condition for its species.

Jurassic The section of the Mesozoic that lasted between 201 and 145 million years ago. Dinosaurs large and small dominated Jurassic life. Climates were seasonal but mostly tropical. Pangaea split into distinct northern and southern continents termed Laurasia and Gondwana.

Laramidia A long, narrow continent that existed during the Late Cretaceous and that corresponds to what is now the western part of the USA and Canada. Familiar Cretaceous dinosaurs, including tyrannosaurs, ceratopsians and hadrosaurs, inhabited Laramidia.

Laurasia The great northern supercontinent that existed during the Jurassic and Cretaceous. It was separated from Gondwana by the Tethys Sea. During the Cretaceous, the opening of the Atlantic Ocean caused Laurasia to split into North America and Eurasia (Europe + Asia).

Liaoning A province in northeastern China that borders the Yellow Sea, famous among palaeontologists for its numerous dinosaur-bearing Cretaceous rock localities. An enormous number of well-preserved Cretaceous dinosaurs (and other fossil organisms) come from Liaoning, including virtually all of the world's feathered non-bird dinosaurs.

Marginocephalians The ornithischian group that includes pachycephalosaurs and ceratopsians. Members of this group tend to possess a bony shelf at the back of the skull. Elaborate skulls with horns, frills and bony domes are typical.

Mesozoic Era The great section of time – the so-called 'Age of Reptiles' or 'age of middle life' – that lasted between 252 and 66 million years ago. The Mesozoic is divided into three subdivisions: the Triassic, Jurassic and Cretaceous periods.

Microwear Tiny (typically microscopic) marks made on teeth during an animal's life, and relating to the way teeth meet, or to the way teeth interact with food items.

Ornithischians The great group of dinosaurs that includes thyreophorans, ornithopods and marginocephalians. They were predominantly herbivorous and possess a unique bone – the predentary – at the front of the lower jaw. They are often called 'bird-hipped dinosaurs' because their hip bones are arranged in a configuration otherwise typical of birds. However, birds are not part of this group.

Palaeontology The science of studying the life of the past, practised by scientists termed palaeontologists. Palaeontology encompasses the study of ancient microfossils, plants, animals, traces left by organisms, and ancient environments and communities.

Pangaea The ancient supercontinent present during the Late Palaeozoic and Triassic. It broke apart into northern and southern sections (termed Laurasia and

Gondwana) during the Jurassic.

Photogrammetry
A technique used in visualising and studying landscapes or objects that involves taking images from different angles, and then combining the measurements between given points on those landscapes or objects to replicate their size and shape.

Phylogeny The history of a given organism's evolution. The term phylogeny is also used for the diagrammatic trees we use when depicting a hypothesis of evolutionary relationships.

Physiology Everything pertaining to the way an organism functions – how it regulates and maintains its internal workings, including temperature control, water balance and salt balance, how energy is used, how it grows, and so on. The term is used both for the biological processes themselves, and for the science devoted to their study.

Pterosaurs An extinct archosaur group, present throughout the Mesozoic, which contains the famous membranous-winged reptiles formerly called 'pterodactyls'. Pterosaurs were close relatives of dinosauromorphs within the archosaur group Ornithodira.

Reptiles The major group of vertebrate animals that includes turtles, lizards, snakes, archosaurs and all of their relatives. The scientific meaning of the term is somewhat different from common usage, since 'reptiles' in the scientific sense includes birds.

Saurischians The great group of dinosaurs that includes theropods and sauropodomorphs. Unlike ornithischians, saurischians often have pneumatic bones. They are often called 'lizard-hipped dinosaurs' because their hip bones are arranged in a manner typical for reptiles. However, some saurischian groups evolved a different configuration, birds among them.

Sauropodomorphs
The major group of saurischians that includes the familiar sauropods as well as a number of bipedal, omnivorous species of the Triassic and Early Jurassic, often informally called 'prosauropods'.

Sauropods The quadrupedal long-necked sauropodomorphs of the Late Triassic, Jurassic and Cretaceous. Sauropods were mostly gigantic and include the largest land-living animals of all time. Familiar sauropods include *Diplodocus*, *Brontosaurus* and *Brachiosaurus*.

Species A population of organisms where all individuals share features not present in other populations, and which generally all look alike and are all capable of breeding with one another.

Theropods The major group of saurischians, often called predatory dinosaurs or meat-eating dinosaurs, that includes all the bipedal, predatory dinosaurs as well as birds. Familiar Mesozoic theropods include *Megalosaurus*, *Allosaurus* and *Tyrannosaurus*.

Trackway A series of tracks (also called footprints) formed by an individual animal as it moved across the substrate. Fossil trackways tend to be short but the longest dinosaur trackways are as much as 130 m (426 ft) long.

Triassic The section of the Mesozoic that lasted between 252 and 201 million years ago. Dinosaurs originated during the Triassic. The world was hot and huge deserts covered much of Pangaea, the lone supercontinent of the time.

Trochanter In anatomy, the name given to a raised lump, bump or projection on a bone that served in life as a muscle- or ligament-attachment site.

FURTHER INFORMATION

Brett-Surman, Michael, Holtz Jr., Thomas R. and Farlow, James. *The Complete Dinosaur, Second Edition*. Indiana University Press, 2012.

Brusatte, Stephen. *Dinosaur Paleobiology*. Wiley-Blackwell, 2012.

Currie, Philip J. and Padian, Kevin (Eds). *Encyclopedia of Dinosaurs*. Academic Press, 1997.

Dodson, Peter. *The Horned Dinosaurs*. Princeton University Press, 1996.

Holtz Jr., Thomas R. *Dinosaurs: the Most Complete, Up-to-Date Encyclopedia for Dinosaur Lovers of all Ages*. Random House, 2007.

Martill, Dave and Naish, Darren. *Walking With Dinosaurs: The Evidence*. BBC Worldwide, 2000.

Naish, Darren. *The Great Dinosaur Discoveries*. A & C Black, 2009.

Norman, David. *Dinosaurs: A Very Short Introduction*. Oxford University Press, 2005.

Weishampel, David and White, Nadine. *The Dinosaur Papers 1676-1906*. Smithsonian Books, 2003.

INDEX

PICTURE CREDITS

Pg. 5 top, 12/13, 29, 46, 92, 125, 146, 159, 165, 166 top, 180, 182, 194, 210, 216 bottom left ©John Sibbick/The Trustees of the Natural History Museum, London; pg. 5 bottom, 52, 54, 135, 140 ©Emily Willoughby; p g. 7 ©Kirby Seiber/Sauriermuseum Aathal; pg. 8, 10, 16, 17, 18 top, 45, 48, 49, 50, 57 bottom, 62 bottom, 63, 65, 66, 67, 70, 71, 72, 73, 74, 76 top, 77, 81, 84, 86 top, 87, 88, 89, 90 , 91, 97, 99, 101, 103, 104, 116, 123, 124, 126, 127, 128 bottom, 129 top, 131, 138, 141 bottom, 148, 156 bottom, 157, 158, 166 middle, 171 top, 192, 193, 211, 216 bottom right ©The Trustees of the Natural History Museum, London; pg. 9, 19, 41, 51, 56, 57 top, 68, 93, 105, 107 © Darren Naish; pg. 18 bottom ©Smithsonian Institution Archives; pg. 21 ©Citadel Press; pg. 22/23, 31 © Robert Nicholls/ The Trustees of the Natural History Museum, London; pg. 24, 30, 37, 39, 42, 43 ©Bobby Birchall/NHM; pg. 25, 26 ©Ron Blakey, Colorado Plateau Geosystems Inc.; pg. 27 ©Lara Wilson/NHM; pg. 28 ©Joschua Knuppe; pg. 32 left ©Steveoc 86/Wikipedia; pg. 34, 69 ©Mark Witton; pg. 35 ©De Agostini / The Trustees of the Natural History Museum, London; pg. 36©John Sibbick; pg. 38 ©Mark Witton/The Trustees of the Natural History Museum, London; pg. 44 ©Robert Nicholls; pg. 48/49 ©Davide Bonadonna/National Geographic Creative; pg. 53, 82 ©Scott Hartman; pg. 55 ©Andrey Atuchin/The Trustees of the Natural History Museum, London; pg. 59, 96 bottom ©Heinrich Mallisson; pg. 60 ©Adam Yates; pg. 61, 78, 79 ©Berislav Krzic/The Trustees of the Natural History Museum, London; pg. 62 top ©Mike Taylor; pg. 64 ©Bob Nicholls/Leicester Museum; pg. 76 bottom, 132, 133 ©Paul Barrett; pg. 85 ©Institut Royal des Sciences Naturelles de Belgique; pg. 86 bottom ©Erik van den Brulle/gettyimages; pg. 95 ©Czerkas & Czerkas; pg. 96 top and middle ©Michael P. Taylor; pg. 106 top ©Victoria Harbor; pg. 106 bottom left ©AMNH; pg. 106 bottom right ©Victoria Arbor & AMNH; pg. 109 ©Mathew Wedel, Research Associate at the Sam Noble Oklahoma Museum of Natural History; pg. 102, 110, 147 ©Image courtesy of Donald Henderson, Royal Tyrrell Museum of Palaeontology, Drumheller, Alberta, Canada; pg. 112, 113 Reprinted with permission from Dal Sasso C. & Maganuco S., 2011 - Scipionyx samniticus (Theropoda: Compsognathidae) from the Lower Cretaceous of Italy. Mem. Soc. It. Sci. Nat. Mus. Civ. St. Nat. Milano, XXXVII (I), 282 pgs. Photo: Roberto Appiani & Leonardo Vitola, © Soprintendenza per i Beni Archeologici di Salerno, Av., Bn. e Cs. / Museo di Storia Naturale di Milano; pg. 115 ©Bill Parsons; pg. 117, 196 bottom ©John Conway; pg. 118 ©Alan Turner; pg.

119 ©Gerald Mayer; pg. 120 ©Stuart Kearns; pg. 121 ©Museum für Naturkunde Berlin, Antje Dittmann; pg. 129 bottom ©Jordan C. Mallon; pg. 130 ©Bruce Rubidge from the Evolutionary Studies Institute, University of the Witwatersrand, Johannesburg; pg. 136, 137 ©Emily Rayfield; pg. 141 top ©Queensland Museum, Brisbane; pg. 142 ©John Hutchinson; pg. 143 ©Gareth Monger/The Trustees of the Natural History Museum, London; pg. 144 ©Patrick Dumas/ Look at Sciences/Science Photo Library; pg. 145 ©Falkingham & Gatesy 2014; pg. 149 ©Colin Palmer; pg. 150 ©Aflo/naturepl.com; pg. 151 ©Doc White/naturepl.com; pg. 154 top ©Adrian Warren/ ardea.com;pg. 154 bottom ©Brandon Cole/naturepl.com; pg. 155 ©Pierre Vernay/Biosphoto/ardea.com; pg. 156 top ©Dave Watts/ naturepl.com; pg.160 top left & top middle ©Jeffrey A. Wilson; pg. 160 top right, 173, 175/176 ©Julius T. Csotonyi; pg. 160 bottom ©AMNH; pg. 161 ©Anup Shah/naturepl.com; pg. 162 ©John Cancalos/gettyimages.com; pg. 163 ©David Varricchio; pg. 164, 212 bottom, 213, 214, 215 ©David Tipling; pg. 166 bottom, Wikipedia Public Domain; pg. 167 ©Mark Harding/The Trustees of the Natural History Museum, London; pg. 168/169 ©Dallas Krentzel/Flickr; pg. 170 ©Holly Woodward Ballard; pg. 171 bottom ©Thomas Carr; pg. 172 ©Courtesy of Andrew A. Farke, Ph.D. Augustyn Family Curator and Director of Research & Collections Raymond M. Alf Museum of Paleontology at The Webb Schools; pg. 174 top ©David Button; pg. 179 ©Mark Hallett; pg. 181 right ©Laurent Geslin/naturepl.com; pg. 184/185 ©Davide Bonadonna; pg. 186 bottom left ©Piotr Gryz; pg. 186 bottom right ©Leandro Sanches; pg. 187, 195, 196 top ©The Geological Museum of China/The Trustees of the Natural History Museum, London; pg. 188 left ©Kim Taylor/naturepl.com; pg. 188 right ©Stephen Dalton/naturepl.com; pg. 189 ©Bob Nichols/The Trustees of the Natural History Museum, London; pg. 190 ©Robert Clark; pg. 198 ©Peter Barrett/Mitchell Beazley/Octopus Publishing; pg. 200 ©David A. Kring/Science Photo Library; pg. 201 ©Mark Pilkington/Geological Survey of Canada/Science Photo Library; pg. 205 ©Juan-Carlos Munoz/The Trustees of the Natural History Museum, London; pg. 206 ©David Woodfall/gettyimages.com; pg. 207©Norman McLeod; pg. 216 top ©Luiz Claudio Marigo/naturepl. com; pg. 217 ©Nigel Cattlin/FLPA.

Every effort has been made to contact and accurately credit all copyright holders. If we have been unsuccessful, we apologise and welcome corrections for future editions.

ACKNOWLEDGEMENTS

For allowing use of their artwork, we thank Davide Bonadonna, John Conway, Julius Csotonyi, Joschua Knüppe, Robert Nicholls, John Sibbick, Emily Willoughby and Mark Witton. We also thank Heinrich Mallison for allowing use of his CG *Plateosaurus* and *Kentrosaurus* models and Norman MacLeod for his assistance with images of Cretaceous plankton. We are grateful to the many colleagues and associates who allowed use of the other images used throughout this book, and those with whom we have discussed the various ideas covered herein. Finally, we thank the staff in NHM Publishing and NHM Image Resources for their help and support throughout the production of this book.